ACCA

PAPER F6

TAXATION (UK)

FA 2016

BPP Learning Media is an **ACCA Approved Content Provider** for the ACCA qualification. This means we work closely with ACCA to ensure our products fully prepare you for your ACCA exams.

In this Practice and Revision Kit, which has been reviewed by the **ACCA examination team,** we:

- Discuss the **best strategies** for revising and taking your ACCA exams

- Ensure you are well **prepared** for your exam

- Provide you with **lots of great guidance** on tackling questions

- Provide you with **three** mock exams

Our **Passcards** also supports this paper.

P.RACTICE & REVISION KIT

FOR EXAMS IN JUNE 2017, SEPTEMBER 2017, DECEMBER 2017 AND MARCH 2018

BPP
LEARNING MEDIA

First edition 2008
Eleventh edition October 2016

ISBN 9781 5097 0838 3
(previous ISBN 9781 4727 4438 8)

e-ISBN 9781 5097 0840 6

British Library Cataloguing-in-Publication Data
A catalogue record for this book
is available from the British Library

Published by

BPP Learning Media Ltd
BPP House, Aldine Place
London W12 8AA

www.bpp.com/learningmedia

Printed in the United Kingdom by Wheatons Exeter Ltd
Hennock Road
Marsh Barton
Exeter
EX2 8RP

Your learning materials, published by BPP Learning Media Ltd, are printed on paper obtained from traceable sustainable sources.

We are grateful to the Association of Chartered Certified Accountants for permission to reproduce past examination questions. The suggested solutions in the Practice & Revision Kit have been prepared by BPP Learning Media Ltd, except where otherwise stated.

BPP LEARNING MEDIA

About this Practice & Revision Kit

ACCA have commenced the transition of F5–F9 to computer based examination (CBE), beginning with a pilot in limited markets in September 2016. Students will initially have the choice of CBE or paper exams and as a result, changes will be made to BPP's learning materials to ensure that we fully support students through this transition.

This Practice & Revision Kit is valid for exams from the June 2017 sitting through to the March 2018 sitting and in this Practice & Revision Kit you will find questions in both multiple choice question (MCQ) and objective testing question (OTQ) format. OTQs include a wider variety of questions types including MCQ as well as number entry, multiple response and drag and drop. More information on these question types will be available on the ACCA website.

OTQ's will only appear in computer based exams but these questions will still provide valuable practice for all students whichever version of the exam is taken. These are clearly marked on the contents page as either CBE style OTQ bank or CBE style OTQ case.

More information on the exam formats can be found on page xvi.

All timings given throughout this Practice & Revision Kit are based on the paper-based exam which is 3 hours and 15 minutes long. Time management is a key skill for success in this exam and so we recommend you use these indicative timings when attempting questions to time on paper.

ACCA are recommending that all students consult the ACCA website on a regular basis for updates on the launch of the new CBEs.

Contents

Question index

The headings in this checklist/index indicate the main topics of questions, but questions may cover several different topics.

Questions set under the old F6 (UK) exam format are included in this Kit because their style and content are similar to those that may appear in the F6 (UK) exams from 1 September 2016. Some of these questions have been amended to reflect new exam format and this is shown by (amended) in the title of the question.

	Marks	Time allocation Mins	Page number Question	Answer
Part A: The UK tax system and its administration				
Section A Questions				
1 – 5 MCQ bank – The UK tax system and its administration 1	10	20	3	101
6 – 10 CBE style OTQ bank – The UK tax system and its administration 2	10	20	4	101
Section B Questions				
11 – 15 Domingo and Fargo (06/09) (amended)	10	20	5	102
16 – 20 CBE style OT case – Joe (A) (12/10) (amended)	10	20	6	102
21 – 25 CBE style OT case – Ernest (06/10) (amended)	10	20	8	103
26 – 30 Thai Curry Ltd	10	20	9	104
Section C Questions				
31 John	10	20	10	104
32 Sugar plc	10	20	11	105
Part B: Income tax and NIC liabilities				
Section A Questions				
33 – 42 MCQ bank – Income tax and NIC liabilities 1	20	39	12	107
43 – 52 MCQ bank – Income tax and NIC liabilities 2	20	39	14	108
53 – 62 CBE style OTQ bank – Income tax and NIC liabilities 3	20	39	16	110
Section B Questions				
63 – 67 CBE style OT case – Ann, Basil and Chloe (12/08) (amended)	10	20	19	112
68 – 72 Ae, Bee, Cae, and Eu (12/08) (amended)	10	20	20	113
73 – 77 Fang and Hong (12/13) (amended)	10	20	22	114
78 – 82 CBE style OT case – Chi (06/14) (amended)	10	20	23	115
Section C Questions				
83 Michael and Sean (06/12) (amended)	10	20	25	116
84 Samantha (12/07)	10	20	26	117
85 Martin	10	20	26	118

BPP
LEARNING MEDIA

		Time allocation Mins	Page number	
	Marks		Question	Answer
Part F: Value added tax				
Section A Questions				
191 – 195 MCQ bank – Value added tax 1	10	20	79	198
196 – 205 CBE style OTQ bank – Value added tax 2	20	39	80	198
Section B Questions				
206 – 210 CBE style OT case – Anne (06/09) (amended)	10	20	82	199
211 – 215 Auy and Bim (06/10) (amended)	10	20	84	200
216 – 220 Aston (06/11) (amended)	10	20	86	201
221 – 225 Starfish Ltd (B) (12/11) (amended)	10	20	88	202
226 – 230 CBE style OT case – Long Ltd group (B) (06/14) (amended)	10	20	89	203
231 – 235 CBE style OT case – Smart Ltd (Sep/Dec 15) (amended)	10	20	91	204
Section C Questions				
236 Jogger Ltd (B) (12/08) (amended)	10	20	94	205
237 Flick (B) (06/12) (amended)	10	20	94	206
238 Richard (B) (12/13) (amended)	10	20	95	207
239 Clueless Ltd (A) (12/12) (amended)	10	20	95	208
240 Garfield (Mar/Jun 16)	10	20	96	209

Topic index

Listed below are the key Paper F6 (UK) syllabus topics and the numbers of the questions of this Kit (excluding the Mock exams) covering those topics.

If you need to concentrate your practice and revision on certain topics or if you want to attempt all available questions that refer to a particular subject, you will find this index useful.

BPP
LEARNING MEDIA

Helping you with your revision

BPP Learning Media – Approved Content Provider

As an ACCA **Approved Content Provider**, BPP Learning Media gives you the **opportunity** to use revision materials reviewed by the ACCA examination team. By incorporating the ACCA examination team's comments and suggestions regarding the depth and breadth of syllabus coverage, the BPP Learning Media Practice & Revision Kit provides excellent **ACCA approved** support for your revision.

Tackling revision and the exam

Using feedback obtained from the ACCA examination team review:

- We look at the dos and don'ts of revising for, and taking, ACCA exams
- We focus on Paper F6 (UK); we discuss revising the syllabus, what to do (and what not to do) in the exam, how to approach different types of question and ways of obtaining easy marks

Selecting questions

We provide signposts to help you plan your revision.

- A full **question index**
- A **topic index** listing all the questions that cover key topics, so that you can locate the questions that provide practice on these topics, and see the different ways in which they might be examined

Making the most of question practice

At BPP Learning Media we realise that you need more than just questions and model answers to get the most from your question practice.

- Our **Top tips** included for certain questions provide essential advice on tackling questions, presenting answers and the key points that answers need to include.
- We show you how you can pick up **easy marks** on some questions, as we know that picking up all readily available marks often can make the difference between passing and failing.
- We include **marking guides** to show you what the examination team rewards.
- We include **comments from the** examination team to show you where students struggled or performed well in the actual exam.
- We refer to the **FA 2016 Study Text** (for exams in June 2017, September 2017, December 2017 and March 2018) for detailed coverage of the topics covered in questions.

Attempting mock exams

There are three mock exams that provide practice at coping with the pressures of the exam day. We strongly recommend that you attempt them under exam conditions. **Mock exams 1 and 2** reflect the question styles and syllabus coverage of the paper-based and computer-based exams respectively; **Mock exam 3** is the Specimen exam paper.

Revising F6 (UK)

Topics to revise

All questions are compulsory so you must revise the **whole** syllabus. Since the exam includes 15 objective test questions in Section A and 15 objective test questions in Section B, you should expect questions to cover a large part of the syllabus. Selective revision **will limit** the number of questions you can answer and hence reduce your chances of passing. It is better to go into the exam knowing a reasonable amount about most of the syllabus rather than concentrating on a few topics to the exclusion of the rest.

Question practice

Practising as many exam-style questions as possible will be the key to passing this exam. You must do questions under **timed conditions** and ensure you write full answers to the discussion parts as well as doing the calculations.

Also ensure that you attempt all three mock exams under exam conditions.

Passing the F6 (UK) exam

Displaying the right qualities

- You will be required to identify the requirements of objective test questions quickly, so that you can make your answers confidently within the available time.

- In constructed response questions you will be required to carry out calculations, with clear workings and a logical structure. If your numbers are not perfect you will not necessarily lose too many marks so long as your method is correct and you have stated any assumptions you have made.

- You will also be expected to apply your tax knowledge to the facts of each particular question and also to identify the compliance issues for your client.

- You may also be required to describe rules and conditions, so take care to practise the descriptive elements of the answers.

Avoiding weaknesses

- There is no choice in this paper, all questions have to be answered. You must therefore study the entire syllabus, there are no short-cuts.

- Ability to answer objective test questions and cases improves with practice. Try to get as much practice with these questions as you can.

- The constructed response questions will be based on simple scenarios and answers must be focused and specific to the requirement of the question.

- Answer all parts of the constructed response questions. Even if you cannot do all the calculation elements, you will still be able to gain marks in the descriptive parts.

Gaining the easy marks

Easy marks in this paper tend to fall into three categories.

Objective test questions (OTQs)

Some OTQs are easier than others. Answer those that you feel fairly confident about as quickly as you can. Come back later to those you find more difficult. This could be a way of making use of the time in the examination most efficiently and effectively. Some OTQs will not involve calculations. Make sure that you understand the wording of 'written' OTQs before selecting your answer.

Calculations in Section C questions

There will always be basic marks available for straightforward tasks such as putting easy figures into proformas, for example putting the cost figure for an addition into a capital allowances proforma. Do not miss out on these easy marks by not learning your proformas properly.

Discussions in Section C questions

A constructed response question may separate descriptive requirements from calculations, so that you do not need to do the calculations first in order to answer the descriptive parts. This means that you should be able to gain marks from the descriptive parts without having to complete the calculations.

Descriptive requirements may focus on administrative, or compliance, details such as filing deadlines and tax payment dates. Make your points concisely, bearing in mind that one mark usually equates to one point to be made.

Read the question carefully and more than once, to ensure you are actually answering the specific requirements. Don't write about matters which are not specifically required – even if these are technically correct, you will not gain any marks and will waste valuable time.

Tackling Objective Test Case Questions

First, read the whole case scenario. Make a note of any specific instructions or assumptions, such as 'Ignore the annual exempt amount' in a capital gains tax question. Then skim through the requirements of the five questions. The questions are independent of each other and can be answered in any order.

Some of the OTQs will be easier than others. For example, you may be asked to identify the filing date for a tax return and the penalty for late filing. Answer these OTQs quickly.

Other OTQs will be more difficult and/or complex. There are two types of OTQ that may take you longer to answer.

The first more time-consuming OTQ will involve doing a computation. For example, you may be asked to calculate the personal allowance available to a taxpayer whose adjusted net income exceeds £100,000. You will probably need to jot down a quick pro-forma to answer a computational question like this.

If the OTQ is a multiple choice question, remember that the wrong answers will usually involve common errors, so don't assume that because you have the same answer as one of the options that your answer is necessarily correct! Double check to make sure you haven't made any silly mistakes, such as deducting the whole of excess of adjusted net income over the £100,000 threshold (instead of half of it) when working out the restriction for the personal allowance. If you haven't got the same answer as any of the options, rework your computation, thinking carefully about what errors you could have made. If you still haven't got one of the options, choose the one which is nearest to your answer.

The second more time-consuming OTQ is one where you are asked to consider a number of statements and identify which one (or more) of them is correct. Make sure that you read each statement at least twice before making your selection. Be careful to follow the requirements of the OTQ exactly, for example if you are asked to identify **TWO** correct statements.

Exam information

Computer based exams

ACCA have commenced the launch of computer based exams (CBE's) for F5-F9. They have been piloting computer based exams in limited markets since September 2016 with the aim of rolling out into all markets internationally over a five year period. Paper based examinations will be run in parallel while the CBE's are phased in and BPP materials have been designed to support you, whichever exam option you choose.

Exam duration

The Skills module examinations F5-F9 contain a mix of objective and longer type questions with a duration of three hours for 100 marks. For paper-based exams there is an extra 15 minutes to reflect the manual effort required.

As ACCA increase their offering of F5-F9 session CBEs, they will be introducing seeded content to guarantee all exams are equivalent and fair. When the seeded content is introduced, students will be given more time to complete the exams – increasing to 3 hours and 20 minutes to take into account the inclusion of additional seeded content.

For more information on these changes and when they will be implemented, please visit the ACCA website. http://www.accaglobal.com/uk/en/student/changes-to-exams/f5-f9-session-cbe.html

Format of the exam

The exam format is the same irrespective of the mode of delivery and will comprise three exam sections.

Section	Style of question type	Description	Proportion of exam, %
A	Objective test (OT)	15 questions × 2 marks	30
B	Objective test (OT) case	3 questions × 10 marks Each question will contain 5 subparts each worth 2 marks	30
C	Constructed Response (Long questions)	1 question × 10 marks 2 questions × 15 marks	40
Total			100

Section A and B questions will be selected from the entire syllabus. The paper version of these objective test questions contains multiple choice only and the computer-based version will contain a variety. The responses to each question or subpart in the case of OT cases are marked automatically as either correct or incorrect by computer.

The 10 mark Section C question can come from any part of the syllabus. The 15 mark Section C questions will mainly focus on the following syllabus areas but a minority of marks can be drawn from any other area of the syllabus:

- Income tax (syllabus area B)
- Corporation tax (syllabus area E)

The responses to these questions are human marked.

Additional information

The Study Guide provides more detailed guidance on the syllabus.

Useful websites

The websites below provide additional sources of information of relevance to your studies for F6 (UK) *Taxation*.

- www.accaglobal.com

  ACCA's website. The students' section of the website is invaluable for detailed information about the qualification, past issues of *Student Accountant* (including technical articles) and a free downloadable Student Planner App.

- www.bpp.com

  Our website provides information about BPP products and services, with a link to the ACCA website.

Questions

PART A THE UK TAX SYSTEM AND ITS ADMINISTRATION

Questions 1 to 32 cover the UK tax system and its administration, the subject of Chapters 1, 17 and 23 of the BPP Study Text for Paper F6.

MCQ bank – The UK tax system and its administration 1

20 mins

1   Which **TWO** of the following statements are true about inheritance tax?

    (1)   It is an indirect tax.
    (2)   It is a progressive tax.
    (3)   It is an environmental tax.
    (4)   It is a redistributive tax.

    A   1 and 3
    B   1 and 4
    C   2 and 3
    D   2 and 4   **(2 marks)**

2   Which **TWO** of the following have legal force?

    (1)   Revenue and Customs Brief
    (2)   A Statutory Instrument
    (3)   An Act of Parliament
    (4)   An Extra Statutory Concession

    A   1 and 2
    B   2 and 3
    C   1 and 3
    D   2 and 4   **(2 marks)**

3   F plc wishes to appeal against the assessment of £10,000,000 of corporation tax by HM Revenue and Customs.

    By whom is F plc's appeal most likely to be heard?

    A   By the First Tier Tribunal
    B   By the Upper Tribunal
    C   By the Supreme Court
    D   By the Court of Appeal   **(2 marks)**

4   Daren made a chargeable gain of £50,000 on 30 June 2016. This was Daren's only disposal in the tax year 2016/17. He had previously paid his income tax through deduction at source so has not had to submit a self-assessment tax return.

    By what date must Daren notify HM Revenue and Customs (HMRC) of his chargeability to capital gains tax in relation to the gain made on 30 June 2016 and by what date must he pay the capital gains tax liability?

	Notification	*Payment*
A	31 January 2018	31 January 2018
B	5 October 2017	31 January 2018
C	5 October 2017	31 July 2018
D	31 January 2018	31 July 2018

    (2 marks)

5   Sarah received NS&I investment account interest of £5,300 in the tax year 2016/17 which she deliberately omitted from her self-assessment tax return for that tax year. She did not attempt to conceal the omission. HM Revenue and Customs (HMRC) discovered the error from records collected from NS&I and Sarah then made a prompted disclosure of the error. Sarah is a higher rate taxpayer and she had already used her savings income nil rate band on other income.

What is the minimum penalty that HMRC may impose on Sarah in respect of this error?

A   £742
B   £1,484
C   £424
D   £1,855

(2 marks)

(Total = 10 marks)

CBE style OTQ bank – The UK tax system and its administration 2   20 mins

6   HM Revenue and Customs (HMRC) issued Lenny with a notice to file his tax return for the tax year 2016/17 on 30 April 2017. Lenny submitted the return online on 15 March 2018.

Match the due date for submission of the online return and the date by which HMRC will have to notify Lenny of a compliance check into this return.

31 October 2017		31 January 2018

15 March 2019		30 April 2019

Submission	

Notification	

(2 marks)

7   Gareth's tax payable for 2015/16 and 2016/17 is as follows:

	2015/16 £	2016/17 £
Income tax	10,000	12,500
Class 2 NIC	146	146
Class 4 NIC	2,000	2,500
Capital gains tax	1,000	2,000

Gareth always pays the correct amount of tax on each due date.

What is the amount payable by Gareth to HM Revenue and Customs (HMRC) on 31 January 2018 in respect of the tax year 2016/17?

Select... ▼
£5,000
£5,146
£4,500
£4,146

(2 marks)

8   For the year to 31 March 2017 K Ltd, which is not a large company, had a corporation tax liability of £22,400. It paid £10,000 of this liability on 1 December 2017 and the remaining £12,400 on 1 February 2018.

What is the interest payable by K Ltd on late paid tax?

£	

(2 marks)

9   J plc is required to pay corporation tax by instalments. It had prepared accounts to 31 March each year but decided to prepare accounts for the 10 month period to 31 January 2017. J plc's corporation tax liability for the period to 31 January 2017 was £500,000.

What is the amount of the final instalment of corporation tax for the period ended 31 January 2017 and when is it due?

○ £125,000 due on 1 November 2017

○ £166,667 due on 14 January 2017

○ £50,000 due on 14 May 2017

○ £150,000 due on 14 May 2017

(2 marks)

10   M Ltd prepares accounts to 30 September each year. It was given notice by HM Revenue and Customs (HMRC) to submit its corporation tax return for the year to 30 September 2016 on 30 November 2016. The return was submitted on 1 December 2017. This was the first late return for the company.

What is the maximum penalty payable by M Ltd as a result of its late submission?

£	

(2 marks)

(Total = 10 marks)

Domingo and Fargo (06/09) (amended)   20 mins

The following scenario relates to questions 11 to 15.

Domingo and Fargo are brothers. In the tax year 2016/17 Domingo is employed and Fargo is self-employed. Fargo is required to make a balancing payment of £1,800 in respect of his income tax liability for the tax year 2016/17 and payments on account for the tax year 2017/18.

For the tax year 2016/17 Domingo wants to file a paper self-assessment tax return. Fargo wants to file his tax return online. Both notices to file returns were issued by HMRC to Domingo and Fargo on 1 July 2017.

11   What are the latest dates for Domingo and Fargo to submit their respective self-assessment tax returns for the tax year 2016/17 given their stated filing preferences?

	Domingo	Fargo
A	31 October 2017	31 October 2017
B	31 October 2017	31 January 2018
C	31 January 2018	31 October 2017
D	31 January 2018	31 January 2018

(2 marks)

12   How long must Domingo and Fargo retain the records used in preparing their respective tax returns for the tax year 2016/17?

	Domingo	Fargo
A	31 January 2023	31 January 2019
B	31 January 2023	31 January 2023
C	31 January 2019	31 January 2019
D	31 January 2019	31 January 2023

(2 marks)

13   What is the maximum penalty that may be imposed on Domingo and Fargo for not retaining their records for the required period?

A	£100
B	£500
C	£1,500
D	£3,000

(2 marks)

14   What are the dates by which Fargo should make the balancing payment for the tax year 2016/17 and the first payment on account for the tax year 2017/18, and the second payment on account for the tax year 2017/18?

	Balancing payment 2016/17 and first POA 2017/18	Second POA 2017/18
A	31 July 2017	31 July 2018
B	31 July 2017	31 January 2019
C	31 January 2018	31 July 2018
D	31 January 2018	31 January 2019

(2 marks)

15   What are the interest payable and maximum penalty payable if Fargo makes the balancing payment for the tax year 2016/17 exactly four months late?

A	Interest £18, penalty £90
B	Interest £54, penalty £90
C	Interest £18, penalty £180
D	Interest £54, penalty £180

(2 marks)

(Total = 10 marks)

CBE style OT case – Joe (A)(12/10) amended   20 mins

This objective test question contains question types which will only appear in a computer-based exam, but this question provides valuable practice for all students whichever version of the exam they are taking.

The following scenario relates to questions 16 to 20.

On 31 December 2016 Joe resigned as an employee of Firstly plc, and on 1 January 2017 commenced employment with Secondly plc. He received a salary and taxable benefits from both Firstly plc and Secondly plc. He is paid monthly by both Firstly plc and Secondly plc.

Secondly plc has 700 employees. It filed its PAYE return due on 31 January 2017 on 4 April 2017. This was the second return that it had submitted late in the tax year 2016/17.

16   Which **TWO** of the following statements about Joe's PAYE tax code are correct?

☐ The code number for Joe, if he was only entitled to a personal allowance, would be 1100L.

☐ Joe's tax code cannot be adjusted for unpaid tax on income from earlier years.

☐ Joe's tax code will be applied to his salary when calculating the amount of income tax that has to be paid each month under the PAYE system.

☐ Joe's employer will be issued with the tax code at the start of the tax year and must use the same code throughout the tax year.

(2 marks)

17   By what date and by whom must Joe be provided with PAYE form P45?

Date	By whom
⦿ 31 May 2017	Firstly plc
⦿ 31 May 2017	Secondly plc
⦿ 31 December 2016	Firstly plc
⦿ 31 December 2016	Secondly plc

(2 marks)

18   By what date and by whom must Joe be provided with PAYE form P60?

Date	By whom
⦿ 31 May 2017	Firstly plc
⦿ 31 May 2017	Secondly plc
⦿ 6 July 2017	Firstly plc
⦿ 6 July 2017	Secondly plc

(2 marks)

19   By what date must Joe be provided with PAYE form P11D and what information will it contain?

Date	Information
⦿ 31 May 2017	Cash equivalents of the benefits
⦿ 31 May 2017	Total taxable earnings
⦿ 6 July 2017	Cash equivalents of the benefits
⦿ 6 July 2017	Total taxable earnings

(2 marks)

20   What is the penalty that may be imposed by HMRC on Secondly plc for the late filing of its PAYE return due on 31 January 2017?

£ _____

(2 marks)

(Total = 10 marks)

CBE style OT case – Ernest (06/10) (amended)　20 mins

This objective test question contains question types which will only appear in a computer-based exam, but this question provides valuable practice for all students whichever version of the exam they are taking.

The following scenario relates to questions 21 to 25.

You should assume that today's date is 30 June 2017.

You are a trainee Chartered Certified Accountant and your firm is dealing with the tax affairs of Ernest.

Ernest's self-assessment tax return for the tax year 2015/16 was submitted to HM Revenue & Customs (HMRC) on 15 May 2016 and Ernest paid the resulting income tax liability by the due date. However, you have just discovered that during the tax year 2015/16 Ernest disposed of a freehold property, the details of which were omitted from his self-assessment tax return. The capital gains tax liability in respect of this disposal is £18,000 and this amount has not been paid.

Ernest has suggested that since HMRC's right to make a compliance check enquiry into his self-assessment tax return for the tax year 2015/16 expired on 15 May 2017, no disclosure should be made to HMRC of the capital gain.

21　Identify, by clicking on the relevant boxes in the table below, whether each of the following statements concerning tax evasion and tax avoidance is true or false.

Tax evasion is illegal	TRUE	FALSE
Both tax evasion and tax avoidance are illegal	TRUE	FALSE
Tax avoidance involves any legal method of reducing the taxpayer's tax burden	TRUE	FALSE
Tax evasion always involves providing HM Revenue and Customs with false information	TRUE	FALSE

(2 marks)

22　Which **TWO** of the following statements are correct about how your firm should deal with the suggestion from Ernest that no disclosure is made to HMRC of his capital gain?

☐　Ernest should be advised to disclose details of the capital gain to HMRC.

☐　If Ernest does not disclose the gain to HMRC, your firm can definitely still continue to act for him.

☐　If your firm ceases to act for Ernest, it must disclose this to HMRC and provide detailed reasons why it has ceased to act.

☐　If Ernest does not disclose the gain to HMRC, your firm would be obliged to report under the money laundering regulations.

(2 marks)

23　What is the maximum penalty that could be imposed on Ernest for the error by omission in his tax return in relation to the capital gain, assuming that it is considered to be deliberate but not concealed?

○　£18,000

○　£12,600

○　£9,000

○　£5,400

(2 marks)

24 Assuming that HMRC discover the capital gain and Ernest then makes a disclosure of it, what is the minimum penalty that could be imposed on Ernest for the error if it is considered to be deliberate but not concealed?

○ £0

○ £2,700

○ £3,600

○ £9,000

(2 marks)

25 If Ernest pays the capital gains tax liability on 31 July 2017, what is the interest that will be charged on this late payment?

○ £540

○ £405

○ £270

○ £135

(2 marks)

(Total = 10 marks)

Thai Curry Ltd

20 mins

The following scenario relates to questions 26 to 30.

Thai Curry Ltd prepares accounts for the year ended 31 March 2017 and has taxable total profits of £163,120, resulting in a corporation tax liability of £32,624.

Thai Curry Ltd has previously always submitted its corporation tax returns on time and had a corporation tax liability for the year to 31 March 2016 of £22,000.

The company is in dispute with HM Revenue and Customs (HMRC) in relation to its corporation tax return for the year ended 31 March 2016 and has been offered an internal review of the case. The case is likely to be allocated to either the complex track or the standard track if it instead chooses to go to a formal appeal.

26 What is the date by which Thai Curry Ltd's self-assessment corporation tax return for the year ended 31 March 2017 should be submitted?

A 31 December 2017
B 31 January 2018
C 31 March 2018
D 31 July 2018

(2 marks)

27 What is the total amount of late filing penalties that will be charged on Thai Curry Ltd if it submits its return for the year ended 31 March 2017 and pays the corporation tax due eight months late?

A £3,262
B £6,525
C £6,725
D £3,462

(2 marks)

28 How should Thai Curry Ltd's corporation tax liability for the year ended 31 March 2017 be paid?

A £32,624 on 1 January 2018
B £11,000 on 31 January 2017 and 31 July 2017, £10,624 on 31 January 2018
C £8,156 on 14 October 2016, 14 January 2017, 14 April 2017 and 14 July 2017
D £5,500 on 14 October 2016, 14 January 2017 and 14 April 2017, £16,124 on 14 July 2017

(2 marks)

29 Which **TWO** of the following statements are correct about the internal review procedure?

(1) An internal review is a less costly and more effective way to resolve disputes informally than a formal appeal.

(2) The review is carried out by the HMRC officer who has previously dealt with the case.

(3) HMRC must usually carry out the review within 45 days.

(4) After the review conclusion is notified, the company cannot make a further appeal.

A 1 and 2
B 2 and 3
C 1 and 3
D 2 and 4

(2 marks)

30 If Thai Curry Ltd does not take up the offer of the internal review, what body is initially likely to hear its appeal?

	Complex track	Standard track
A	First tier	First tier
B	Upper tier	Upper tier
C	First tier	Upper tier
D	Upper tier	First tier

(2 marks)

(Total = 10 marks)

31 John
20 mins

(a) **You should assume today's date is 30 November 2016.**

John is a new client whom you met today. On 6 April 2015, he commenced in self-employment and prepared his first set of accounts to 5 April 2016. John had not previously filed a self-assessment tax return and has not received any communication from HM Revenue and Customs (HMRC) about his tax affairs.

As this will be his first self-assessment tax return, John is also concerned that HMRC might carry out a compliance check.

Required

(i) Advise John of the latest date by which he should have notified HMRC of his chargeability to income tax for the tax year 2015/16 and the maximum and minimum penalties for late notification if he immediately notifies HMRC of his chargeability and is deemed to have been careless. **(3 marks)**

(ii) State the period during which HMRC will have to notify John if they intend to carry out a compliance check in respect of his self-assessment tax return for the tax year 2015/16, and the possible reasons why such a check would be made.

Note. You should assume for part (ii) that John will file his tax return by the due filing date. **(3 marks)**

(b)   The UK Government uses tax policies to encourage certain types of activity.

Required

Briefly explain how the UK Government's tax policies encourage:

(i)   Individuals to save   **(1 mark)**
(ii)   Individuals to support charities   **(1 mark)**
(iii)   Entrepreneurs to build their own businesses and to invest in plant and machinery.   **(2 marks)**

(Total = 10 marks)

32 Sugar plc   20 mins

Sugar plc has been in business for many years. It owns 45% of the ordinary shares of Honey plc and 75% of the ordinary shares of Molasses plc. Molasses plc owns 70% of the ordinary shares of Treacle plc. This structure has existed for many years.

In the year to 31 March 2017, Sugar plc had taxable total profits of £470,000. It also received dividends of £50,000 from Honey plc. In the year to 31 March 2018, Sugar plc will have taxable total profits of £600,000. It will not receive any dividends in that year.

Required

(a)   Define what is meant by a related 51% group company and explain which companies are related 51% group companies of Sugar plc.   **(3 marks)**

(b)   Explain whether or not Sugar plc is a large company for the purposes of payment of corporation tax for the years ended 31 March 2017 and 31 March 2018.   **(3 marks)**

(c)   Assuming that Sugar plc is a large company in both years but was not a large company for any previous year, calculate Sugar plc's corporation tax liabilities for the years ended 31 March 2017 and 31 March 2018 and explain when these will be paid. Assume the rate of corporation tax in financial year 2017 is the same as in financial year 2016.

(4 marks)

(Total = 10 marks)

PART B INCOME TAX AND NIC LIABILITIES

Questions 33 to 99 cover income tax and NIC liabilities, the subject of Chapters 2 to 12 of the BPP Study Text for Paper F6.

MCQ bank – Income tax and NIC liabilities 1

39 mins

33   Which of the following taxpayers is UK resident for the tax year 2016/17 on the basis of the information given?

(1)   Suzy, previously UK resident, present in UK between 6 April 2016 and 5 December 2016.

(2)   Miles, not previously UK resident, present in UK between 6 April 2016 and 5 May 2016.

A   1 and 2
B   1 only
C   2 only
D   Neither 1 nor 2   **(2 marks)**

34   In the tax year 2016/17 Claudio has taxable income (after deduction of his personal allowance) consisting of £3,000 of non-savings income and £12,500 of savings income.

What is Claudio's income tax liability for the tax year 2016/17?

A   £2,500
B   £2,900
C   £2,700
D   £3,100   **(2 marks)**

35   Which **TWO** of the following types of income are exempt from income tax?

(1)   Interest on an NS&I Investment account
(2)   Premium bond prizes
(3)   Interest on UK Government stocks ('gilts')
(4)   Dividends on shares held in an Individual Savings Account

A   1 and 2
B   1 and 4
C   2 and 3
D   2 and 4   **(2 marks)**

36   Mike and Delia are a married couple. In the tax year 2016/17, Mike has taxable non-savings income (after deducting his personal allowance) of £12,400. Delia has no income in the tax year 2016/17. Delia has made an election in relation to her personal allowance for the tax year 2016/17.

What is Mike's income tax liability for the tax year 2016/17?

A   £280
B   £2,260
C   £1,380
D   £2,480   **(2 marks)**

37 Marion bought £20,000 (nominal value) 5% UK Government Loan Stock on 1 July 2016. Interest is payable on 30 June and 31 December each year. Marion sold the loan stock to Gerald on 31 October 2016 including interest.

What is the amount of savings income taxable on Marion and Gerald in respect of the loan stock for the tax year 2016/17?

	Marion	Gerald
A	£nil	£500
B	£333	£500
C	£333	£167
D	£nil	£167

(2 marks)

38 In the tax year 2016/17 Susie receives employment income of £170,000. She made a gross gift aid donation of £10,000 in January 2017.

What is Susie's income tax liability for the tax year 2016/17?

A   £60,600
B   £62,600
C   £60,100
D   £55,200

(2 marks)

39 Petunia is a single parent with a two year old son. She receives child benefit of £1,076 in the tax year 2016/17. Petunia has net income of £57,000 in 2016/17 and she made gross personal pension contributions of £2,000 during 2016/17.

What is Petunia's child benefit income tax charge for the tax year 2016/17?

A   £1,076
B   £430
C   £538
D   £753

(2 marks)

40 Judith works for S Ltd for an annual salary of £18,000. On 30 September 2016, she received a bonus of £4,000 in respect of S Ltd's trading results for the year ended 31 March 2016. She expects to receive a bonus of £4,800 on 30 September 2017 in respect of S Ltd's results for the year ended 31 March 2017. Judith also received £500 from a customer on 1 December 2016 as a gratuity for good service.

What is Judith's employment income for the tax year 2016/17?

A   £22,000
B   £22,800
C   £22,500
D   £23,300

(2 marks)

41 Which **TWO** of the following are not qualifying travel expenses?

(1)   Travel from employer's office to visit a client.

(2)   Travel from home to a workplace to which an employee has been seconded for 36 months.

(3)   Travel from home to a permanent place of work.

(4)   Travel from home to visit a trade fair relevant to the employer's business 100 miles away from permanent place of work.

A   1 and 2
B   2 and 3
C   1 and 3
D   2 and 4

(2 marks)

42   Trevor is employed by C plc at a salary of £25,000 a year. He is provided with a car available for private use for the tax year 2016/17. The car has CO_2 emissions of 118 g/km and a list price of £20,000 although C plc actually paid £18,000 for the car as the result of a dealer discount. The car has a diesel engine. No private fuel is provided.

What is Trevor's taxable car benefit for the tax year 2016/17?

A   £3,600
B   £4,140
C   £4,000
D   £4,600   (2 marks)

                                                                                                (Total = 20 marks)

MCQ bank – Income tax and NIC liabilities 2   39 mins

43   John is employed by Z plc. He was provided with a computer for private use on 6 November 2015. The market value of the computer when first provided to an employee for private use was £3,600 and the computer had a market value of £2,000 when first provided to John for private use. Z plc gave the computer to John on 5 April 2017 when it had a market value of £1,000.

What are the total taxable benefits for John in respect of the computer for the tax year 2016/17?

A   £2,880
B   £3,300
C   £1,720
D   £1,833   (2 marks)

44   Jonas is an employee of the LP partnership. His employer provided Jonas with the use of free accommodation from 6 April 2016 to 5 April 2017. It was not deemed to be job related. The accommodation cost the LP partnership £93,000 in February 2014 and has an annual value of £8,000. The accommodation was valued at £109,000 on 6 April 2016.

What are the total taxable benefits for Jonas in respect of the accommodation for the tax year 2016/17?

A   £9,020
B   £10,790
C   £8,540
D   £8,000   (2 marks)

45   Troy is a sole trader who had trading income of £60,000 in the tax year 2015/16 and £80,000 in the tax year 2016/17. He joined a personal pension scheme on 6 April 2015 and made gross contributions of £25,000 in 2015/16. This was the first pension provision that Troy had made.

What gross amount can Troy contribute to his personal pension scheme in March 2017 without incurring an annual allowance charge?

A   £55,000
B   £40,000
C   £145,000
D   £65,000   (2 marks)

46 Luke rents out a room in his own residence throughout 2016/17. The rent is £150 a week. Luke's expenses of the letting are £20 per week.

What is the amount of property business income taxable on Luke for 2016/17 if he makes any relevant election?

A   £6,760

B   £0

C   £7,800

D   £300   **(2 marks)**

47 Susie rents out a furnished house. The house does not qualify as a furnished holiday letting. The furnishings include a new sofa which was bought in the tax year 2016/17 to replace an old one which was disposed of at the same time. The old sofa cost £3,000 in 2007 and was disposed of in January 2017 for proceeds of £200. The new sofa was bought in January 2017 for £5,500 and was larger than the old one. If Susie had bought a newer sofa of the same model as the old one it would have cost £4,000.

What deduction against property business income can Susie claim for the cost of the sofa bought in 2016/17?

A   £5,500

B   £3,800

C   £5,300

D   £4,000   **(2 marks)**

48 Greg is a sole trader. His accounts for the year to 5 April 2017 included a deduction in the statement of profit or loss for legal expenses of £7,240. These comprised:

	£
Grant of a new short lease on retail premises	2,400
Preparation of employment contract	720
Purchase of freehold retail premises	3,200
Debt collection for trade debts	920
	7,240

What are the legal fees deductible for the year to 5 April 2017?

A   £4,040

B   £1,640

C   £920

D   £7,240   **(2 marks)**

49 Harry is a sole trader. He prepares accounts for the year ended 5 April 2017 and has deducted the following items of expenditure in the statement of profit or loss:

		£
Depreciation		3,000
Accountancy fees for preparing accounts		1,000
Entertainment of:	staff (party at £300 per person for 6 employees)	1,800
	customers	2,400

How much should be added back to Harry's net profit to arrive at his adjusted taxable profit?

A   £8,200

B   £6,300

C   £7,200

D   £5,400   **(2 marks)**

50 Rose is a sole trader who prepares accounts to 5 April each year using the cash basis of accounting. Her results for the period of account to 5 April 2017 show the following:

	£
Cash sales	41,000
Invoice sales	4,000
Cash expenses	20,200

The figure for invoice sales includes an invoice for £1,500 which was paid on 10 April 2017. In addition to the cash expenses of £20,200, Rose incurred motoring expenses of £2,800 for driving 8,000 miles of which 6,500 miles were for business purposes. Rose wishes to use the flat rate allowance for motoring.

What is Rose's taxable trading income for the tax year 2016/17?

- A £17,575
- B £20,500
- C £20,375
- D £24,800

(2 marks)

51 Philip is a sole trader who prepares accounts to 5 April each year. He purchased a motor car for both business and private purposes on 6 April 2016. The motor car has CO_2 emissions of 160 grams per kilometre and cost £22,000. In the year to 5 April 2017, Philip drove a total of 9,000 miles of which 4,950 miles were for business journeys.

What is the maximum capital allowance that Philip can claim in respect of the motor car for the period of account to 5 April 2017?

- A £968
- B £2,178
- C £1,760
- D £792

(2 marks)

52 Ella started in business as a sole trader on 6 November 2016 and prepared her first set of accounts to 5 April 2017. On 6 December 2016 she acquired plant at a cost of £95,000.

What are the maximum capital allowances that Ella can claim for the period of account to 5 April 207?

- A £68,367
- B £85,433
- C £84,208
- D £95,000

(2 marks)

(Total = 20 marks)

CBE style OTQ bank – Income tax and NIC liabilities 3   39 mins

53 Joe has been in business for many years preparing accounts to 5 April each year. The tax written down value of his main pool at 6 April 2016 was £12,000. Joe sold machinery on 10 June 2016 for £11,900 which had originally cost £11,600. He made no acquisitions during the year ended 5 April 2017.

What is the maximum capital allowance that Joe can claim for the period of account to 5 April 2017?

- ○ £1,000
- ○ £400
- ○ £100
- ○ £72

(2 marks)

54 Alexandra started in business as a sole trader on 1 August 2015 and prepared her first set of accounts to 30 April 2017.

What is Alexandra's basis period for the tax year 2016/17, her second tax year of trading?

○ 6 April 2016 to 5 April 2017

○ 1 August 2015 to 31 July 2016

○ 1 May 2016 to 30 April 2017

○ 1 August 2015 to 30 April 2017

(2 marks)

---

55 Timothy started in business as a sole trader on 1 February 2015. He prepared his first set of accounts to 30 November 2015 and his second set of accounts to 30 November 2016. His taxable trading profits were as follows:

p/e 30 November 2015	£30,000
y/e 30 November 2016	£42,000

What are Timothy's overlap profits?

£ _____

(2 marks)

---

56 Walter had been in business as a sole trader for many years preparing accounts to 31 December each year. He ceased trading on 31 March 2017. Walter had overlap profits of £2,000 on commencement. His taxable trading profits were as follows:

y/e 31 December 2016	£18,000
p/e 31 March 2017	£3,000

What is Walter's taxable trading income for the final year of trading?

£ _____

(2 marks)

---

57 Joyce started in business as a sole trader on 1 January 2016 and prepared her first set of accounts to 30 September 2016 and her second set of accounts to 30 September 2017. She made the following losses in her first two periods of trading:

	£
p/e 30 September 2016	(9,000)
y/e 30 September 2017	(14,400)

Match the amounts of the trading losses with the tax years.

£3,000	£9,000	£9,600

£11,400	£12,600	£14,400

2015/16	

2016/17	

(2 marks)

58 Francis is a sole trader who has been in business for many years preparing accounts to 5 April each year. His recent results have been as follows:

	£
y/e 5 April 2016 Profit	16,000
y/e 5 April 2017 Loss	(25,000)

Francis has gross investment income of £3,000 each year. He is expected to make trading profits of around £12,000 per annum over the next few years.

What is the trading loss to carry forward to the tax year 2017/18 if Francis makes the most advantageous claim for loss relief?

£ [   ]

(2 marks)

59 Peter and Jane have been in partnership for many years preparing accounts to 31 July each year and sharing profits equally. On 1 September 2015, they changed their profit sharing agreement so that Peter was entitled to a salary of £9,000 each year and the remaining profits were then split 2 parts to Peter and 3 parts to Jane. The partnership made a trading profit of £96,000 in the year to 31 July 2016.

What is Peter's taxable trading profit for the tax year 2016/17?

£ [   ]

(2 marks)

60 Robin and Stuart had been in partnership for many years preparing accounts to 31 December each year and sharing profits equally. On 1 January 2017, Tania joined the partnership and profits were then split 2:2:1. The partnership made a profit of £96,000 in the year to 31 December 2016 and £112,000 in the year to 31 December 2017.

What the taxable trading profits of the partners for 2016/17?

	Robin and Stuart each	Tania
O	£47,200	£5,600
O	£48,000	£5,600
O	£11,200	£5,600
O	£48,000	£22,400

(2 marks)

61 Shona started in business on 1 January 2017 as a sole trader and prepared her first set of accounts for the 14 weeks to 5 April 2017. Her taxable trading profit for that period was £9,400.

What are Shona's total national insurance contributions for the tax year 2016/17?

£ [   ]

(2 marks)

62 Mark has been in business as a sole trader for many years preparing accounts to 5 April. He made a trading loss of £(2,000) in the year to 5 April 2016 and has not made any claim in respect of this loss. In the year to 5 April 2017, he made a trading profit of £13,500.

What are Mark's class 4 national insurance contributions for the tax year 2016/17?

£ [   ]

(2 marks)

(Total = 20 marks)

CBE style OT case – Ann, Basil and Chloe (12/08) (amended)

20 mins

This objective test question contains question types which will only appear in a computer-based exam, but this question provides valuable practice for all students whichever version of the exam they are taking.

The following scenario relates to questions 63 to 67.

Ann

Ann is self-employed. Her taxable income for the tax year 2016/17 was £76,000 which was all trading income. Ann made contributions of £49,000 (gross) into a personal pension scheme between September 2016 and March 2017. This was the second year that she had been a member of a pension scheme and she had an unused annual allowance of £20,000 brought forward from 2015/16.

Basil

Basil is employed. During the tax year 2016/17 Basil had taxable income of £160,000 which was all employment income. Basil made contributions of £50,000 (gross) into a personal pension scheme during the tax year 2016/17. This was the first year that he had been a member of a pension scheme. In future, his employer may contribute to Basil's personal pension scheme.

Chloe

Chloe lets out an unfurnished property. For the tax year 2016/17 her taxable income was £16,630 which was all property business income. Chloe made contributions of £8,200 (gross) into a personal pension scheme during the tax year 2016/17. This was the first year that she had been a member of a pension scheme.

63 Which **TWO** of the following statements about relevant earnings are correct?

(1) Individuals can always make gross pension contributions of £3,600 in 2016/17 even if they do not have any relevant earnings in that tax year.

(2) Relevant earnings relate both to contributions to personal pension schemes and to occupational pension schemes.

(3) If an individual makes pension contributions less than relevant earnings in a tax year, the excess can be carried forward for three years and used to cover pension contributions.

(4) Relevant earnings do not include income from furnished holiday lettings.

O 1 and 2

O 2 and 3

O 1 and 4

O 2 and 4

(2 marks)

64   Identify, by clicking on the relevant boxes in the table below, whether each of following statements about the annual allowance is true or false.

Employer contributions do not count towards the annual allowance	TRUE	FALSE
The annual allowance can be carried forward for three years to the extent that it is unused in the tax year	TRUE	FALSE
The annual allowance is available even if the individual is not a member of a pension scheme in a tax year and so can be carried forward	TRUE	FALSE
If tax-relievable pension contributions exceed the annual allowance, there is a charge to income tax	TRUE	FALSE

(2 marks)

65   What is Ann's income tax liability for the tax year 2016/17?

£ [   ]

(2 marks)

66   What is Basil's annual allowance charge for the tax year 2016/17?

£ [   ]

(2 marks)

67   What is Chloe's tax relief on her pension contribution for the tax year 2016/17?

O Nil

O £1,640

O £900

O £720

(2 marks)

(Total = 10 marks)

Ae, Bee, Cae, and Eu (12/08) (amended)   20 mins

The following scenario relates to questions 68 to 72.

Ae, Bee and Cae

Ae and Bee commenced in partnership on 1 July 2014 preparing accounts to 30 April. Cae joined as a partner on 1 July 2016. Profits were always shared equally. The partnership's trading profits since the commencement of trading have been as follows:

	£
Period ended 30 April 2015	54,000
Year ended 30 April 2016	66,000
Year ended 30 April 2017	87,000

Eu

Eu ceased trading on 30 September 2018, having been self-employed since 1 July 2008.

(1)   Eu's trading profits for the final three periods of trading were as follows:

	£
Year ended 30 June 2017	62,775
Year ended 30 June 2018	57,600
Three-month period ended 30 September 2018	14,400

These figures are before taking account of capital allowances.

(2)   Eu's capital allowances in the year to 30 June 2017 were £1,575 and in the year to 30 June 2018 were £1,292.

(3)   The tax written-down value of the capital allowances main pool at 1 July 2018 was £5,883. On 15 September 2018 Eu purchased office furniture for £2,400. All of the items included in the main pool were sold for £5,175 (all for more than cost) on 30 September 2018.

(4)   Until the final period of trading Eu had always prepared accounts to 30 June. Her overlap profits for the period 1 July 2008 to 5 April 2009 were £9,800.

68   What is Ae's trading income assessment for the tax year 2015/16?

A   £27,000
B   £24,300
C   £32,500
D   £33,000

(2 marks)

---

69   What is Cae's trading income assessment for the tax year 2016/17?

A   £26,583
B   £24,167
C   £29,000
D   £21,750

(2 marks)

---

70   What is Eu's trading income assessment for the tax year 2017/18?

A   £56,025
B   £62,775
C   £57,600
D   £61,200

(2 marks)

---

71   What are Eu's capital allowances for the three-month period ended 30 September 2018?

A   £3,108
B   £1,491
C   £2,775
D   £559

(2 marks)

---

72   Assuming that the capital allowances for three-month period ended 30 September 2018 were £3,000, what is Eu's trading income assessment for the tax year 2018/19?

A   £1,600
B   £57,908
C   £62,200
D   £67,708

(2 marks)

(Total = 10 marks)

Fang and Hong (12/13) (amended)

20 mins

The following scenario relates to questions 73 to 77.

Fang

Fang commenced self-employment on 1 August 2014. She has a trading profit of £45,960 for the year ended 31 July 2015, and a trading profit of £39,360 for the year ended 31 July 2016. Fang has overlap profits on commencement.

Hong

Hong has been in self-employment since 2005, preparing accounts to 5 April. For the year ended 5 April 2017 she made a trading loss of £45,800, and has claimed this against her total income for the tax year 2015/16.

For the year ended 5 April 2016 Hong made a trading profit of £29,700. She also has a property business profit of £3,900 for the tax year 2015/16. Hong has an unused trading loss of £2,600 brought forward from the tax year 2014/15.

During the tax year 2015/16 Hong disposed of an investment property and this resulted in a chargeable gain. As Hong has claimed relief against total income of this tax year, she may include a further claim to set the trading loss against her chargeable gain for the year.

73   What is the amount of trading profit which will have been assessed on Fang for each of the tax years 2014/15 and 2015/16?

    A   2014/15 £45,960, 2015/16 £39,360
    B   2014/15 £45,960, 2015/16 £45,960
    C   2014/15 £30,640, 2015/16 £45,960
    D   2014/15 £30,640, 2015/16 £39,360   **(2 marks)**

---

74   In which one of the following ways can overlap profits be relieved?

    A   Against first available current year basis profits
    B   Against trading income on cessation
    C   Against general income of the tax year of commencement and/or the preceding tax year
    D   Against general income in the three tax years preceding the year of commencement   **(2 marks)**

---

75   How could Fang have obtained relief for trading expenditure incurred prior to 1 August 2014 and for computer equipment which Fang already owned which was brought into business use on 1 August 2014?

	Trading expenditure	Computer equipment
A	Added to overlap profit and relieved on cessation	Addition for capital allowances purposes based on its original cost
B	Treated as incurred on 1 August 2014	Addition for capital allowances purposes based on its original cost
C	Added to overlap profit and relieved on cessation	Addition for capital allowances purposes based on its market value at 1 August 2014
D	Treated as incurred on 1 August 2014	Addition for capital allowances purposes based on its market value at 1 August 2014

    (2 marks)

76   What was the amount of loss for the year ended 5 April 2017 which was relieved against Hong's income for the tax year 2015/16?

      A   £2,600
      B   £31,000
      C   £33,600
      D   £23,000   **(2 marks)**

77   Which **TWO** of the following statements about the further claim to set Hong's trading loss against her chargeable gain for the tax year 2015/16 are correct?

      (1)   The trading loss is first set against general income of the tax year 2015/16 and only any excess loss is set against chargeable gains of that year.

      (2)   The amount of chargeable gains for the tax year 2015/16 is computed ignoring the annual exempt amount for the purposes of this relief.

      (3)   Capital losses of the tax year 2015/16 are taken into account, but not brought forward losses, for the purposes of this relief.

      (4)   Hong can specify the amount to be set against chargeable gains, so her annual exempt amount for the tax year 2015/16 is not wasted.

      A   1 and 2
      B   2 and 3
      C   1 and 4
      D   2 and 4   **(2 marks)**

                                                                                                         (Total = 10 marks)

CBE style OT case – Chi (06/14) (amended)   20 mins

This objective test question contains question types which will only appear in a computer-based exam, but this question provides valuable practice for all students whichever version of the exam they are taking.

The following scenario relates to questions 78 to 82.

Chi commenced self-employment on 6 April 2016, and for the year ended 5 April 2017 her trading profit using the normal accruals basis was £53,000, calculated as follows:

	Note	£	£
Revenue	1		72,500
Expenses			
Motor expenses	2	4,400	
Other expenses	3	8,200	
Capital allowances	4	6,900	
			(19,500)
Trading profit			53,000

Notes

1   *Revenue*

      The revenue figure of £72,500 includes receivables of £1,600 which were owed as at 5 April 2017.

2   *Motor expenses*

      The total motor expenses for the year ended 5 April 2017 were £5,500, of which 20% was for private journeys. This proportion has been disallowed in calculating the trading profit. During the year ended 5 April 2017, Chi drove 13,200 business miles.

3   *Other expenses*

      The other expenses figure of £8,200 includes payables of £900 which were owed as at 5 April 2017.

4   *Capital allowances*

Capital allowances consist of an annual investment allowance claim of £4,020 in respect of office equipment purchased on 6 April 2016, and a writing down allowance of £2,880 claimed in respect of Chi's motor car. The motor car had cost £20,000 on 6 April 2016.

Additional information

Chi has no other income for the tax year 2016/17.

78   Based on the trading profit of £53,000 for the year ended 5 April 2017, what is Chi's income tax liability for the tax year 2016/17?

£ [   ]

(2 marks)

79   Based on the trading profit of £53,000 for the year ended 5 April 2017, what are the class 4 national insurance contributions payable by Chi for the tax year 2016/17?

£ [   ]

(2 marks)

80   Which **TWO** of the following statements about the cash basis of assessment are correct?

(1)   The trader must prepare accounts to 5 April each year.

(2)   The trader can deduct capital expenditure on plant and machinery (other than motor cars) as business expenses rather than using capital allowances.

(3)   A trader can start to use the cash basis if his receipts for the tax year do not exceed the value added tax (VAT) registration threshold.

(4)   Under the cash basis, a trader can offset losses against other income or gains.

  ○ 1 and 2
  ○ 2 and 3
  ○ 1 and 4
  ○ 2 and 4

(2 marks)

81   If Chi uses the cash basis and claims fixed profit motor expenses, what is the amount of motor expenses (note 2) which are allowable?

  ○ £4,400
  ○ £5,300
  ○ £5,940
  ○ £8,180

(2 marks)

82   If Chi uses the cash basis, what is the amount of revenue which is chargeable (note 1) and the other expenses (note 3) which are allowable for the year ended 5 April 2017?

    ⭘ Revenue £72,500, other expenses £8,200

    ⭘ Revenue £70,900, other expenses £8,200

    ⭘ Revenue £72,500, other expenses £7,300

    ⭘ Revenue £70,900, other expenses £7,300

(2 marks)

(Total = 10 marks)

83 Michael and Sean (06/12) (amended)   20 mins

You are a trainee chartered certified accountant and your manager has asked for your help regarding two taxpayers who have both made trading losses.

Michael

Michael commenced in self-employment on 1 July 2015, preparing accounts to 5 April. His results for the first two periods of trading were as follows:

		£
Nine-month period ended 5 April 2016	– Trading loss	(25,230)
Year ended 5 April 2017	– Trading profit	9,665

For the tax years 2011/12 to 2013/14 Michael had the following income from employment:

	£
2011/12	45,100
2012/13	19,365
2013/14	50,095

Michael did not have any income during the period 6 April 2014 to 30 June 2015.

Sean

Sean has been in self-employment since 2006, but ceased trading on 31 December 2016. He has always prepared accounts to 31 December. His results for the final five years of trading were as follows:

		£
Year ended 31 December 2012	– Trading profit	21,300
Year ended 31 December 2013	– Trading profit	14,400
Year ended 31 December 2014	– Trading profit	18,900
Year ended 31 December 2015	– Trading profit	3,700
Year ended 31 December 2016	– Trading loss	(23,100)

For each of the tax years 2012/13 to 2016/17 Sean has property business profits of £11,200.

Sean has unused overlap profits brought forward of £3,600.

Required

For each of the two taxpayers, Michael and Sean, identify the loss relief claims that are available to them, and explain which of the available claims would be the most beneficial.

Notes

1   You should clearly state the amount of any reliefs claimed and the rates of income tax saved. However, you are not expected to calculate any income tax liabilities.

2   You should assume that the tax rates and allowances for the tax year 2016/17 apply throughout.

3   The following mark allocation is provided as guidance for this requirement:

Michael, 4½ marks
Sean, 5½ marks   **(10 marks)**

(Total = 10 marks)

84 Samantha (12/07)   20 mins

Samantha has been self-employed since 2003. She has the following income and chargeable gains for the tax years 2014/15 to 2017/18:

	2014/15	2015/16	2016/17	2017/18
	£	£	£	£
Trading profit/(loss)	7,290	42,600	(79,000)	16,285
Building society interest	–	6,100	3,800	2,130
Chargeable gains/(loss)	21,100	23,300	(3,400)	14,100

The chargeable gains are stated **before** taking account of loss relief and the annual exempt amount.

Required

(a)   State the factors that will influence an individual's choice of loss relief claims.   **(3 marks)**

(b)   Calculate Samantha's taxable income and taxable gains for each of the tax years 2014/15, 2015/16, 2016/17 and 2017/18 on the assumption that she relieves the trading loss of £79,000 for the tax year 2016/17 on the most favourable basis.

You should assume that the tax rates and allowances for the tax year 2016/17 apply throughout.   **(7 marks)**

(Total = 10 marks)

85 Martin   20 mins

Assume that it is 1 July 2016.

Martin started trading on 1 January 2016. His profits for the first six months of trading to 30 June 2016 were £3,000 each month. Martin estimates that his profits will be £4,000 each month for the next six months of trading to 31 December 2016 and then £5,000 each month thereafter for the foreseeable future.

Martin has decided to prepare accounts either to 5 April each year (starting with the period ending 5 April 2016) or to 30 April each year (starting with the period ending 30 April 2016).

You have advised Martin that if he chooses 30 April as his accounting date rather than 5 April this will delay the taxation of his trading profits.

Required

(a)   Assuming that Martin chooses 5 April as his accounting date, compute Martin's taxable profits for the periods of account ending 5 April 2016, 5 April 2017 and 5 April 2018.   **(2 marks)**

(b)   Using your answer to part (a), compute Martin's trading income for the tax years 2015/16, 2016/17 and 2017/18 if he chooses 5 April as his accounting date.   **(2 marks)**

(c)   Assuming that Martin chooses 30 April as his accounting date, compute Martin's taxable profits for the periods of account ending 30 April 2016 and 30 April 2017.   **(2 marks)**

(d)   Using your answer to part (c), compute Martin's trading income for the tax years 2015/16, 2016/17 and 2017/18 if he chooses 30 April as his accounting date.   **(3 marks)**

(e)   Using your answer to parts (b) and (d), show why you have advised Martin that if he chooses 30 April as his accounting date rather than 5 April this will delay the taxation of his trading profits.   **(1 mark)**

(Total = 10 marks)

86 Lucy   20 mins

Assume that it is 1 March 2016.

Lucy is considering two work arrangements. She will start her chosen arrangement on 6 April 2016 and will continue with that arrangement for the whole of the tax year 2016/17.

Employment with Red plc

Lucy has been offered employment with Red plc. She would be paid a salary of £35,000 and would be required to work at Red plc's offices.

Lucy would travel from home to Red plc's offices by train and would buy an annual season ticket costing £1,500.

Self employment

Lucy would work for a number of clients at their offices. She would receive fees of £35,000 from her clients in the year to 5 April 2017.

Lucy would travel from home to client offices in her own car. Her business mileage would be 4,600 miles during the year and she estimates this would actually cost 40p per mile.

Lucy would prepare accounts to 5 April 2017 and elect to use the cash basis and fixed rate expenses.

Required

Determine which of the work arrangements would result in Lucy having a higher amount of disposable income after deducting income tax, national insurance contributions and travel costs.   **(10 marks)**

Note. You are expected to calculate the income tax and NIC liability for Lucy for each arrangement and then calculate her disposable income in each case, taking into account her travel costs.

(Total = 10 marks)

87 Daniel, Francine and Gregor (Sep/Dec 15)   20 mins

(a)   Amanda, Beatrice and Claude have been in partnership since 1 November 2010, preparing accounts to 31 October annually. Daniel joined as a partner on 1 May 2016. Profits have always been shared equally. The partnership's recent tax-adjusted trading profits are as follows:

	£
Year ended 31 October 2015	147,000
Year ended 31 October 2016	96,000
Year ended 31 October 2017 (forecast)	180,000

Required:

Calculate Daniel's trading income assessment for the tax year 2016/17.   **(3 marks)**

(b)   Francine is employed by Fringe plc. On 1 August 2016, Fringe plc provided Francine with a loan of £96,000 to help her purchase a holiday cottage. On 1 October 2016, the loan was increased by a further £14,000 so that Francine could renovate the cottage. Francine pays interest at an annual rate of 1.5% on this loan.

The taxable benefit in respect of this loan is calculated using the average method.

Required:

Calculate Francine's taxable benefit for the tax year 2016/17 in respect of the loan from Fringe plc.

(3 marks)

(c)   Gregor has been self-employed since 6 April 2003. He has the following income and chargeable gains for the tax years 2015/16 and 2016/17:

	2015/16 £	2016/17 £
Trading profit/(loss)	14,700	(68,800)
Business property profit/(loss)	4,600	(2,300)
Building society interest (gross)	1,300	900
Chargeable gain/(loss)	(2,900)	17,400

Required:

On the assumption that Gregor relieves his trading loss of £68,800 as early as possible, calculate the amount of trading loss carried forward to the tax year 2017/18.

Note. You should assume that the tax allowances for the tax year 2016/17 apply throughout.   **(4 marks)**

(Total = 10 marks)

88 George (Mar/Jun 16)   20 mins

You should assume that today's date is 1 March 2016.

George is a software developer. He has accepted a one-year contract to update software for Xpee plc.

(1)   The contract will run from 6 April 2016 to 5 April 2017, with a fee of £40,000 payable for the entire year of the contract. A condition of the contract is that George will have to do the work personally and not be permitted to sub-contract the work to anyone else.

(2)   George will work from home, but will have to attend weekly meetings at Xpee plc's offices to receive instructions regarding the work to be performed during the following week.

(3)   George will not incur any significant expenses in respect of the contract apart from the purchase of a new laptop computer for £3,600 on 6 April 2016. This laptop will be used 100% for business purposes.

(4)   During the term of the contract, George will not be permitted to work for any other clients. He will therefore not have any other income during the tax year 2016/17.

(5)   George's tax liability for the tax year 2015/16 was collected through PAYE, so he will not be required to make any payments on account in respect of the tax year 2016/17.

George has several friends who are also software developers. He understands that his employment status is not clear cut but that his income tax liability for the tax year 2016/17 will be the same regardless of whether he is treated as employed or as self-employed. However, George appreciates that there are advantages to being classed as self-employed.

Required:

(a)   List FOUR factors which are indicators of George being treated as an employee in relation to his contract with Xpee plc rather than as self-employed.

Note. You should confine your answer to the information given in the question.   **(2 marks)**

(b)　Calculate George's income tax liability and national insurance contributions for the tax year 2016/17 if he is treated as self-employed in respect of his contract with Xpee plc.　**(4 marks)**

(c)　If George is treated as being an employee of Xpee plc instead of self-employed:

　　(i)　Explain why his income tax liability will be payable earlier.　**(2 marks)**

　　(ii)　Calculate the additional amount of national insurance contributions which he personally will suffer for the tax year 2016/17.　**(2 marks)**

(Total = 10 marks)

89 Joe (B)(12/10) (amended)　　　　29 mins

On 31 December 2016 Joe resigned as an employee of Firstly plc, and on 1 January 2017 commenced employment with Secondly plc. The following information is available for the tax year 2016/17:

Employment with Firstly plc

(1)　From 6 April 2016 to 31 December 2016 Joe was paid a salary of £6,360 per month. In addition to his salary, Joe was paid a bonus of £12,000 on 12 May 2016. He had become entitled to this bonus on 22 March 2016.

(2)　Joe contributed 6% of his monthly gross salary of £6,360 into Firstly plc's HM Revenue and Customs' registered occupational pension scheme.

(3)　On 1 May 2016 Firstly plc provided Joe with an interest free loan of £120,000 so that he could purchase a holiday cottage. Joe repaid £50,000 of the loan on 31 July 2016, and repaid the balance of the loan of £70,000 when he ceased employment with Firstly plc on 31 December 2016.

(4)　During the period from 6 April 2016 to 31 December 2016 Joe's three-year-old daughter was provided with a place at Firstly plc's workplace nursery. The total cost to the company of providing this nursery place was £11,400 (190 days at £60 per day).

(6)　Firstly plc provided Joe with a home entertainment system for his personal use costing £4,400 on 6 April 2016. The company gave the home entertainment system to Joe for free, when he left the company on 31 December 2016, although its market value at that time was £3,860.

Employment with Secondly plc

(1)　From 1 January 2017 to 5 April 2017 Joe was paid a salary of £6,565 per month.

(2)　During the period 1 January 2017 to 5 April 2017 Joe contributed a total of £3,000 (gross) into a personal pension scheme.

(3)　From 1 January 2017 to 5 April 2017 Secondly plc provided Joe with living accommodation. The property has an annual value of £10,400 and is rented by Secondly plc at a cost of £2,250 per month. On 1 January 2017 Secondly plc purchased furniture for the property at a cost of £16,320. The company pays for all of the running costs relating to the property, and for the period 1 January 2017 to 5 April 2017 these amounted to £1,900.

(4)　During the period 1 January 2017 to 5 April 2017 Secondly plc provided Joe with 13 weeks of childcare vouchers costing £100 per week. Joe used the vouchers to provide childcare for his three-year-old daughter at a registered nursery near to his workplace.

Required

Calculate Joe's employment income for the tax year 2016/17.　**(15 marks)**

(Total = 15 marks)

90 Sammi (12/10)

You should assume that today's date is 20 March 2016.

Sammi is a director of Smark Ltd, a profitable company. The company has given her the choice of being provided with a leased company motor car or alternatively being paid additional director's remuneration and then privately leasing the same motor car herself.

Company motor car

The motor car will be provided throughout the tax year 2016/17, and will be leased by Smark Ltd at an annual cost of £27,630. The motor car will be petrol powered, will have a list price of £80,000, and will have an official CO_2 emission rate of 300 grams per kilometre.

The lease payments will cover all the costs of running the motor car except for fuel. Smark Ltd will not provide Sammi with any fuel for private journeys.

Additional director's remuneration

As an alternative to having a company motor car, Sammi will be paid additional gross director's remuneration of £27,000 during the tax year 2016/17. She will then privately lease the motor car at an annual cost of £27,630.

Other information

The amount of business journeys that will be driven by Sammi will be immaterial and can therefore be ignored.

Sammi's current level of director's remuneration is over £150,000 which means that she will pay income tax at the additional rate of 45% in 2016/17. Smark Ltd prepares its accounts to 5 April. The lease of the motor car will commence on 6 April 2016.

Required

(a) Advise Sammi of the income tax and national insurance contribution implications for the tax year 2016/17 if she (1) is provided with the company motor car, and (2) receives additional director's remuneration of £27,000. **(5 marks)**

(b) Advise Smark Ltd of the corporation tax and national insurance contribution implications for the year ended 5 April 2017 if the company (1) provides Sammi with the company motor car, and (2) pays Sammi additional director's remuneration of £27,000.

   Note. You should ignore value added tax (VAT). **(5 marks)**

(c) Determine which of the two alternatives is the more beneficial from each of the respective points of view of Sammi and Smark Ltd. **(5 marks)**

(Total = 15 marks)

91 Simon (12/09)

On 22 April 2016 Simon purchased a derelict freehold house for £127,000. Legal fees of £1,800 were paid in respect of the purchase.

Simon then renovated the house at a cost of £50,000, with the renovation being completed on 9 August 2016. He immediately put the house up for sale, and it was sold on 30 August 2016 for £260,000. Legal fees of £2,600 were paid in respect of the sale.

Simon financed the transaction by a bank loan of £150,000 that was taken out on 22 April 2016 at an annual interest rate of 6%. The bank loan was repaid on 30 August 2016.

Simon had no other income or capital gains for the tax year 2016/17 except as indicated above.

Simon has been advised that whether or not he is treated as carrying on a trade will be determined according to the six following 'badges of trade':

(1) Subject matter of the transaction
(2) Length of ownership
(3) Frequency of similar transactions
(4) Work done on the property
(5) Circumstances responsible for the realisation
(6) Motive

Required

(a) Briefly explain the meaning of each of the six 'badges of trade' listed in the question.

Note. You are not expected to quote from decided cases. **(3 marks)**

(b) Calculate Simon's income tax liability and his Class 2 and Class 4 national insurance contributions for the tax year 2016/17, if he is treated as carrying on a trade in respect of the disposal of the freehold house.

(8 marks)

(c) Calculate Simon's capital gains tax liability for the tax year 2016/17, if he is not treated as carrying on a trade in respect of the disposal of the freehold house. **(4 marks)**

(Total = 15 marks)

92 Na (12/09) (amended)   29 mins

Na commenced self-employment as a hairdresser on 1 January 2014. She had tax adjusted trading profits of £25,200 for the six-month period ended 30 June 2014 and £21,600 for the year ended 30 June 2015.

The following information is available for the tax year 2016/17:

Trading profit for the year ended 30 June 2016

(1) Na's statement of profit or loss for the year ended 30 June 2016 is as follows:

	Note	£	£
Income			63,635
Expenses			
Depreciation		2,635	
Motor expenses	2	2,200	
Professional fees	3	1,650	
Property expenses	4	12,900	
Purchases	5	4,700	
Other expenses	6	16,550	
			(40,635)
Net profit			23,000

(2) Na charges all the running expenses for her motor car to the business. During the year ended 30 June 2016 Na drove a total of 8,000 miles, of which 7,000 were for private journeys.

(3) The figure for professional fees includes £1,260 for legal fees in connection with the grant of a new five-year lease of parking spaces for customers' motor cars.

(4) Na lives in a flat that is situated above her hairdressing studio, and one-third of the total property expenses of £12,900 relate to this flat.

(5) During the year ended 30 June 2016 Na took goods out of the hairdressing business for her personal use without paying for them, and no entry has been made in the accounts to record this. The goods cost £250 (an amount that has been deducted under 'purchases') and had a selling price of £450.

(6) The figure for other expenses of £16,550 includes £480 for a fine in respect of health and safety regulations and £160 for a trade subscription to the Guild of Small Hairdressers.

(7)   Na uses her private telephone to make business telephone calls. The total cost of the private telephone for the year ended 30 June 2016 was £1,200, and 20% of this related to business telephone calls. The cost of the private telephone is not included in the statement of profit or loss expenses of £40,635.

(8)   Capital allowances for the year ended 30 June 2016 are £810.

Other information

(9)   During the tax year 2016/17 Na received interest of £310 from an individual savings account (ISA) and dividends of £1,200 from quoted company shareholdings.

Required

(a)   Calculate the amount of trading profits that will have been assessed on Na for the tax years 2013/14, 2014/15 and 2015/16 respectively, clearly identifying the amount of any overlap profits.   **(5 marks)**

(b)   Calculate Na's tax adjusted trading profit for the year ended 30 June 2016.

Note. Your computation should commence with the net profit figure of £23,000, and should list all of the items referred to in notes (1) to (8) indicating by the use of zero (0) any items that do not require adjustment.   **(7 marks)**

(c)   Calculate Na's income tax liability for the tax year 2016/17.   **(3 marks)**

(Total = 15 marks)

93 Bayle (A) (06/11) (amended)   29 mins

Bayle is self-employed as a lawyer. She is also a director of Acquit & Appeal Ltd. The following information is available for the tax year 2016/17:

Self-employment

(1)   Bayle's statement of profit or loss for the year ended 30 September 2016 is as follows:

	Note	£	£
Revenue	2		318,987
Expenses			
Gifts and donations	3	8,680	
Lease of motor car	4	4,345	
Professional fees	5	3,240	
Property expenses	6	46,240	
Travel expenses	7	16,770	
Other expenses	8	66,410	
			(145,685)
Net profit			173,302

(2)   Revenue includes £2,800 received during May 2016 in respect of an impairment loss that Bayle had written off when calculating her trading profit for the year ended 30 September 2014.

(3)   Gifts and donations are as follows:

	£
Gifts to customers (clocks costing £110 each and displaying Bayle's name)	3,300
Gifts to customers (bottles of champagne costing £40 each and displaying Bayle's name)	2,480
Donations to political parties	2,900
	8,680

(4)   The lease commenced on 1 May 2016, and is in respect of a motor car with CO_2 emissions of 244 grams per kilometre. There is no private use of the motor car.

(5)   The figure of £3,240 for professional fees is in respect of accountancy services, of which £600 is for inheritance tax planning advice.

(6)   Bayle lives in an apartment that is situated above her office, and two-fifths of the total property expenses of £46,240 relate to this apartment.

(7)   The figure of £16,770 for travel expenses includes £520 for parking fines incurred by Bayle.

(8)   The figure for other expenses of £66,410 includes £670 for Bayle's professional subscription to the Law Society, and £960 for her golf club membership fee.

Director's remuneration

(9)   Bayle will be paid gross director's remuneration of £42,000 by Acquit & Appeal Ltd during the tax year 2016/17.

(10)   In addition to her director's remuneration, Bayle received two bonus payments of £6,000 from Acquit & Appeal Ltd during June 2016, both of which were in respect of the year ended 31 December 2015. Bayle became entitled to the first bonus payment of £6,000 on 10 March 2016, and to the second bonus payment of £6,000 on 20 April 2016.

(11)   Acquit & Appeal Ltd deducts PAYE at a flat rate of 45% from all of Bayle's earnings.

Other information

(12)   During the tax year 2016/17 Bayle will receive dividends of £11,000, interest of £5,240 on the maturity of a savings certificate issued by National Savings & Investments (NS&I).

(13)   Bayle owned £160,000 3% Treasury Stock (gilts) which pay interest on 30 June and 31 December each year. She sold the Treasury Stock on 30 September 2016 including interest.

(14)   On 1 November 2016 Bayle made a gross gift aid donation of £5,000.

Required

(a)   Calculate Bayle's tax adjusted trading profit for the year ended 30 September 2016.

        Note. Your computation should commence with the net profit figure of £173,302, and you should also list all of the items referred to in notes (2) to (8) indicating by the use of zero (0) any items that do not require adjustment.   **(6 marks)**

(b)   Calculate the income tax payable by Bayle for the tax year 2016/17.   **(9 marks)**

                                                                                              (Total = 15 marks)

---

94 Flick (A) (06/12) (amended)   29 mins

On 6 April 2016 Flick commenced employment with 3D Ltd. On 1 January 2017 she commenced in partnership with Art Reel running a small cinema, preparing accounts to 30 April. The following information is available for the tax year 2016/17:

Employment

(1)   During the tax year 2016/17 Flick was paid a gross annual salary of £28,030.

(2)   Throughout the tax year 2016/17 3D Ltd provided Flick with living accommodation. The company had purchased the property in 2007 for £89,000, and it was valued at £145,000 on 6 April 2016. The annual value of the property is £4,600.

Partnership

(1)   The partnership's tax adjusted trading profit for the four-month period ended 30 April 2017 is £29,700. This figure is before taking account of capital allowances.

(2)   The only item of plant and machinery owned by the partnership is a motor car that cost £18,750 on 1 February 2017. The motor car has a CO_2 emission rate of 190 grams per kilometre. It is used by Art, and 40% of the mileage is for private journeys.

(3)   Profits are shared 40% to Flick and 60% to Art. This is after paying an annual salary of £6,000 to Art.

Property income

(1) Flick owns a freehold house which is let out furnished. The property was let throughout the tax year 2016/17 at a monthly rent of £660.

(2) During the tax year 2016/17 Flick paid council tax of £1,320 in respect of the property, and also spent £2,560 on building a new extended porch. She spent £500 on a new washer-dryer to replace an old washing machine. A like-for-like replacement of the old washing machine would have cost £350.

Required

(a) Calculate Flick's taxable income for the tax year 2016/17.   **(11 marks)**

(b) List the advantages and disadvantages for the partnership of choosing 30 April as its accounting date rather than 5 April.   **(4 marks)**

(Total = 15 marks)

95 Richard (A) (12/13) (amended)   **29 mins**

(a) On 6 April 2016, Richard commenced in self-employment, running a restaurant. Richard's statement of profit or loss for the year ended 5 April 2017 is as follows:

	Note	£	£
Gross profit			73,440
Expenses			
Motor expenses	1	7,660	
Property expenses	2	16,200	
Repairs and renewals	3	6,420	
Other expenses	4	10,960	
			(41,240)
Net profit			32,200

Notes

1   *Motor expenses*

Motor expenses are as follows:

	£
Cost of running Richard's motor car	4,710
Cost of running a motor car used by the restaurant's chef	2,670
Parking fines incurred by Richard	280
	7,660

Richard's motor car is used 70% for private journeys and the chef's motor car is used 20% for private journeys.

2   *Property expenses*

Richard lives in an apartment which is situated above the restaurant, and one-fifth of the total property expenses of £16,200 relate to this apartment.

3   *Repairs and renewals*

Repairs and renewals are as follows:

	£
Decorating the restaurant	5,100
Decorating the apartment	1,320
	6,420

The property was in a useable state when it was purchased.

4   *Other expenses*

The figure of £10,960 for other expenses includes legal fees of £2,590 in connection with the purchase of the restaurant property. The remaining expenses are all allowable.

Additional information

Advertising

Richard spent £800 in March 2016 on newspaper advertisements prior to opening the restaurant.

Plant and machinery

The following motor cars were purchased during the year ended 5 April 2017:

	Date of purchase	Cost £	CO_2 emission rate
Motor car [1]	6 April 2016	14,000	114 grams per kilometre
Motor car [2]	6 April 2016	16,800	113 grams per kilometre

Motor car [1] is used by Richard and motor car [2] is used by the restaurant's chef.

Required

Calculate Richard's tax adjusted trading profit for the year ended 5 April 2017.

Notes

1   Your computation should commence with the net profit figure of £32,200, and should list all of the items referred to in notes (1) to (4), indicating by the use of zero (0) any items which do not require adjustment.

2   In answering this part of the question you are not expected to take account of any of the information provided in part (b) below. **(8 marks)**

(b)   Richard had three employees working for him in his restaurant during the tax year 2016/17 as follows:

(1)   A chef who was employed throughout the tax year 2016/17 on a gross annual salary of £46,000. The chef was provided with a petrol powered motor car (see the plant and machinery information in part (a) above) throughout the tax year. The list price of the motor car is the same as its cost. Richard did not provide any fuel for private journeys.

(2)   A part-time waitress who was employed for 20 hours per week throughout the tax year 2016/17 on a gross annual salary of £8,000.

(3)   An assistant chef who was employed for eight months from 6 August 2016 to 5 April 2017 on a gross monthly salary of £2,200.

Required

Calculate the employer's class 1 and class 1A national insurance contributions which Richard would have incurred in respect of his employees' earnings and benefit for the tax year 2016/17.

Note. You are not expected to calculate the national insurance contributions suffered by the employees or by Richard in respect of his self-employment. **(7 marks)**

(Total = 15 marks)

96 John (06/13) (amended)   29 mins

John is employed by Surf plc. The following information is available for the tax year 2016/17:

(1)   During the tax year 2016/17, John was paid gross remuneration of £208,318.

(2)   During the tax year 2016/17, John contributed £18,000 into Surf plc's HM Revenue and Customs' registered occupational pension scheme. The company contributed a further £12,000 on his behalf. Both John and Surf plc have made exactly the same contributions for the previous five tax years.

(3)   During the period from 1 November 2016 to 5 April 2017, Surf plc provided John with a petrol powered motor car which has a list price of £28,200 and an official CO_2 emission rate of 186 grams per kilometre. No fuel is provided by Surf plc.

(4) During 2013 Surf plc provided John with a loan which was used to purchase a yacht. The amount of loan outstanding at 6 April 2016 was £84,000. John repaid £12,000 of the loan on 31 July 2016, and then repaid a further £12,000 on 31 December 2016. He paid loan interest of £630 to Surf plc during the tax year 2016/17. The taxable benefit in respect of this loan is calculated using the average method.

(5) During the tax year 2016/17, John made personal pension contributions up to the maximum amount of available annual allowances, including any unused amounts brought forward from previous years. These contributions were in addition to the contributions he made to Surf plc's occupational pension scheme (see note (2)). John has not made any personal pension contributions in previous tax years.

(6) John owns a holiday cottage which is let out as a furnished holiday letting, although the letting does not qualify as a trade under the furnished holiday letting rules. The property business profit for the year ended 5 April 2017 was £16,730.

Required

(a) Calculate John's income tax liability for the tax year 2016/17.   **(12 marks)**

(b) State the tax advantages of a rental property qualifying as a trade under the furnished holiday letting rules.
                                                                                                      (3 marks)

                                                                                          (Total = 15 marks)

97 Ronald (06/14) (amended)   **29 mins**

Ronald is employed and also self-employed. Ronald has tried to prepare his own income tax computation for the tax year 2016/17, but he has found it more difficult than expected. Although the sections which Ronald has completed are correct, there are a significant number of omissions. The omissions are marked as outstanding (O/S). The partly completed income tax computation is as follows:

Ronald – Income tax computation 2016/17

	Note	£
Trading income	1	O/S
Employment income		65,065
Property business profit	2	O/S
Building society interest		1,260
Dividends		O/S
		O/S
Personal allowance		(11,000)
Taxable income		O/S
Income tax		
Non-savings income: £32,000 @ 20%		6,400
Non-savings income: O/S @ 40%		O/S
Savings income: £500 @ 0%		0
Savings income: O/S @ 40%		O/S
Dividend income: O/S @ 0%		0
Dividend income: £800 @ 32.5%		260
O/S		
Income tax liability		O/S
Tax suffered at source		
PAYE		(9,130)
Income tax payable		O/S

Notes

1 *Trading profit*

Ronald commenced self-employment on 1 January 2016. He had a tax adjusted trading profit of £3,840 for the four-month period ended 30 April 2016, and £12,060 for the year ended 30 April 2017. These figures are **before** taking account of capital allowances.

The only item of plant and machinery owned by Ronald is his motor car, which cost £18,000 on 1 September 2016.

The motor car has a CO_2 emission rate of 142 grams per kilometre, and 70% of the mileage driven by Ronald is for private journeys.

2 *Property business profit*

Ronald owns a freehold shop. The shop was purchased on 1 October 2016, and during October 2016 Ronald spent £8,400 replacing the building's roof. The shop was not usable until this work was carried out, and this fact was represented by a reduced purchase price.

On 1 December 2016, the property was let to a tenant, with Ronald receiving a premium of £12,000 for the grant of a 30-year lease. The monthly rent is £960 payable in advance, and during the period 1 December 2016 to 5 April 2017 Ronald received five rental payments.

Due to a fire, £8,600 was spent on replacing the roof of the shop during February 2017. Only £8,200 of this was paid for by Ronald's property insurance.

Ronald paid insurance of £480 in respect of the property. This was paid on 1 October 2016 and is for the year ended 30 September 2017.

Other information

Ronald did not make any personal pension contributions during the tax year 2016/17. He has never been a member of a pension scheme.

Required

(a) Calculate the income tax payable by Ronald for the tax year 2016/17.   **(11 marks)**

(b) Advise Ronald why the maximum gross amount of tax relievable personal pension scheme contribution which he could have made for the tax year 2016/17 is £40,000, and the method by which tax relief would have been given if he had made this amount of contribution.   **(4 marks)**

(Total = 15 marks)

98 Samson and Delilah (Sep/Dec 15) (amended)   29 mins

Samson and Delilah are a married couple. They are both employed by Rope plc, and Delilah is also a partner in a partnership. The following information is available in respect of the tax year 2016/17:

Samson

During the tax year 2016/17, Samson was paid a gross annual salary of £112,000 in respect of his employment with Rope plc.

Delilah

(1) During the tax year 2016/17, Delilah was paid a gross annual salary of £184,000 in respect of her employment with Rope plc.

(2) Throughout the tax year 2016/17, Rope plc provided Delilah with a petrol powered motor car which has a list price of £67,200, and an official CO_2 emission rate of 187 grams per kilometre. Rope plc does not provide Delilah with any fuel for private journeys. Delilah was unable to drive her motor car for a period during the tax year 2016/17 because of a skiing accident, and during this period Rope plc provided her with a chauffeur at a total cost of £9,400.

(3) Rope plc provided all its employees with a hamper of groceries costing £42 each in December 2016.

(4) Delilah spent £70 in July 2016 on traveling by train to visit a customer of Rope plc. This amount was reimbursed by Rope plc in August 2016.

(5) During the tax year 2016/17, Delilah donated £250 (gross) per month to charity under the payroll deduction scheme operated by Rope plc.

(6) Delilah has been in partnership with Esther and Felix for a number of years. The partnership's tax adjusted trading profit for the year ended 31 December 2016 was £93,600. Esther is paid an annual salary of £8,000, with the balance of profits being shared 40% to Delilah, 30% to Esther and 30% to Felix.

(7) During the tax year 2016/17, Delilah paid interest of £6,200 (gross) on a personal loan taken out to purchase her share in the partnership.

(8) During the tax year 2016/17, Delilah made charitable gift aid donations totalling £4,864 (net).

Joint income – Building society deposit account

Samson and Delilah have savings in a building society deposit account which is in their joint names. During the tax year 2016/17, they received building society interest totalling £9,600 from this joint account.

Required

(a) Calculate Samson and Delilah's respective income tax liabilities for the tax year 2016/17.

Note. The following mark allocation is provided as guidance for this requirement:

Samson (4 marks)

Delilah (9 marks)   **(13 marks)**

(b) Calculate Samson's income tax saving for the tax year 2016/17 if the building society deposit account had been in Delilah's sole name instead of in joint names for the entire year.   **(2 marks)**

(Total = 15 marks)

99 Patience (Mar/Jun 16)   29 mins

Patience retired on 31 December 2016, and on that date ceased employment and self-employment. The following information is available in respect of the tax year 2016/17:

Employment

(1) Patience was employed by a private school as a teacher. From 6 April to 31 December 2016, she was paid a salary of £3,750 per month.

(2) During the period 6 April to 31 December 2016, Patience contributed 6% of her monthly gross salary of £3,750 into her employer's HM Revenue and Customs' (HMRC's) registered occupational pension scheme. Patience's employer contributed a further 10% on her behalf.

(3) During the period 6 April to 30 June 2016, Patience's granddaughter was provided with a free place at the private school run by Patience's employer. The normal fee payable would have been £4,600. The additional marginal expense of providing the place for the grandchild was £540.

(4) On 25 June 2016, Patience was given a clock valued at £600 as an award for her 25 years of teaching at her employer's school. She has not previously received any similar awards.

(5) Patience's employer provided her with an interest-free loan so that she could purchase a season ticket for the train to work. The balance of the loan outstanding at 6 April 2016 was £8,000, and Patience repaid the loan in full on 31 December 2016.

Self-employment

(1) Patience was self-employed as a private tutor. Her trading profit for the year ended 31 July 2016 was £14,800. This figure is **after** taking account of capital allowances.

(2) Patience's trading profit for the final five-month period of trading from 1 August to 31 December 2016 was £6,900. This figure is **before** taking account of capital allowances.

(3) The tax written down value of the capital allowances main pool at 1 August 2016 was £2,200. On 10 August 2016, Patience purchased a laptop computer for £1,700.

On the cessation of trading, Patience personally retained the laptop computer. Its value on 31 December 2016 was £1,200. The remainder of the items included in the main pool were sold for £800 on 31 December 2016.

(4) Patience has unused overlap profits brought forward of £3,700.

Personal pension contributions

During the period 6 April to 31 December 2016, Patience contributed a total of £3,600 (net) into a personal pension scheme.

Pension income

During the period 1 January to 5 April 2017, Patience received the state pension of £1,450, a pension of £6,000 from her employer's occupational pension scheme, and a private pension of £3,300. These were the total gross amounts received.

Property

Patience owned two properties which were let out unfurnished until both properties were sold on 31 December 2016. The following information is available in respect of the two properties:

	Property one £	Property two £
Rent received during the tax year 2016/17	3,600	7,200
Sale proceeds on 31 December 2016	122,000	98,000
Allowable revenue expenditure during the tax year 2016/17	(4,700)	(2,600)
Purchase cost	(81,400)	(103,700)

Patience has never occupied either of the two properties as her main residence.

Required:

Calculate Patience's income tax and capital gains tax liabilities for the tax year 2016/17.

Notes

1 You should indicate by the use of zero (0) any items which are not taxable or deductible.

2 The following mark allocation is provided as guidance for this question:

Income tax (13 marks)
Capital gains tax (2 marks)

(Total = 15 marks)

PART C CHARGEABLE GAINS FOR INDIVIDUALS

Questions 100 to 128 cover chargeable gains for individuals, the subject of Chapters 13 to 16 of the BPP Study Text for Paper F6.

MCQ bank – Chargeable gains for individuals 1   20 mins

100   Which **TWO** of the following are exempt assets for CGT purposes?

(1)   Vintage Rolls Royce motor car worth £30,000
(2)   Painting worth £20,000
(3)   Shares held in an Individual Savings Account
(4)   Shop used by a sole trader in his business

A   1 and 2
B   1 and 3
C   2 and 4
D   2 and 3   **(2 marks)**

101   Trudy sold a house in November 2016. She had never lived in the house. Her chargeable gain on the sale was £25,100. Trudy has taxable income of £19,920 in the tax year 2016/17. The house does not qualify for entrepreneurs' relief.

What is Trudy's capital gains tax liability for the tax year 2016/17 assuming that she has no other disposals in that year?

A   £2,712
B   £3,920
C   £5,820
D   £1,745   **(2 marks)**

102   Clive purchased a ten-acre plot of land in May 2010 for £80,000. In January 2017, Clive sold three of the acres for £36,000 with expenses of sale amounting to £1,000. The market value of the remaining seven acres of land in January 2017 was £90,000.

What is Clive's chargeable gain on the disposal of the three acres of land in the tax year 2016/17?

A   £12,600
B   £13,143
C   £11,000
D   £12,143   **(2 marks)**

103   James has the following gains and losses arising from disposals of chargeable assets:

Tax year	2014/15	2015/16	2016/17
	£	£	£
Gains	2,000	4,000	13,900
Losses	(14,000)	(2,000)	(2,000)

The allowable loss carried forward to 2017/18 will be:

A   £nil
B   £2,000
C   £11,200
D   £100   **(2 marks)**

104   Ellen purchased an antique vase for £1,500. In October 2016 she sold the vase for £7,000.

What is Ellen's chargeable gain on the sale of the vase?

A   £Nil
B   £1,000
C   £1,667
D   £5,500

(2 marks)

(Total = 10 marks)

CBE style OTQ bank – Chargeable gains for individuals 2

20 mins

105   Harold bought a painting for £8,500. In December 2016 he sold the painting for £5,000.

What is Harold's allowable loss on the sale of the painting?

£	

(2 marks)

106   Angela purchased a house and lived in it for three years. The house was then unoccupied for five years because Angela went to work outside the UK. She then lived in the house for two years. Angela then went to live with her sister and the house was unoccupied for four years. Angela then lived in the house for the last one year of ownership.

How many years of Angela's 15 year period of ownership of the house will be exempt for the purposes of principal private residence relief?

Select...   ▼
14½ years
14 years
13½ years
15 years

(2 marks)

107   Sascha owned a factory which had always been used in her business. She sold the factory on 14 May 2016 and realised a gain of £60,000. On 12 August 2016, she purchased a 20 year lease on a warehouse using all the proceeds from the sale of the factory. A claim for relief for replacement of business assets was made. The warehouse will continue to be used in Sascha's trade until it is sold on 14 October 2026.

When will the deferred gain of £60,000 become chargeable to capital gains tax?

○ 12 August 2016

○ 14 May 2026

○ 12 August 2026

○ 14 October 2026

(2 marks)

108 Louise has two chargeable gains from the disposal of shares in the tax year 2016/17:

£8,000 – claim made for entrepreneurs' relief

£12,900 – claim not made for entrepreneurs' relief

Louise has taxable income of £33,000 in the tax year 2016/17.

What is Louise's capital gains tax liability for the tax year 2016/17?

£ [   ]

(2 marks)

109 Neil bought 1,000 shares in G plc for £1,500 in October 2004. In November 2006, there was a 1 for 2 bonus issue when the shares had a market value of £2.40 each. In July 2011, there was a 3 for 1 rights issue when the shares had a market value of £3 but were offered to existing shareholders for £2.70 each. Neil took up his full entitlement to shares under the rights issue. Neil sold all of his shares in G plc in February 2017.

What is the cost of the shares sold in February 2017?

£ [   ]

(2 marks)

(Total = 10 marks)

CBE style OT case – Nim (06/09) (amended)   20 mins

This objective test question contains question types which will only appear in a computer-based exam, but this question provides valuable practice for all students whichever version of the exam they are taking.

The following scenario relates to questions 110 to 114

Nim disposed of the following assets during the tax year 2016/17:

(1)   On 20 July 2016 Nim made a gift of 10,000 £1 ordinary shares in Kapook plc to his daughter. On that date the shares were quoted on the Stock Exchange at £3.70 – £3.80. Nim has made the following purchases of shares in Kapook plc:

19 February 2004	8,000 shares for £16,200
6 June 2009	1 for 2 rights issue at £3.65 per share
24 July 2016	2,000 shares for £5,800

Nim's total shareholding was less than 5% of Kapook plc, and so holdover relief is not available.

(2)   On 13 August 2016 Nim transferred his entire shareholding of 5,000 £1 ordinary shares in Jooba Ltd, an unquoted company, to his wife. On that date the shares were valued at £28,200. Nim's shareholding had been purchased on 11 January 2010 for £16,000.

(3)   On 26 November 2016 Nim sold an antique table for net proceeds of £8,700 after deducting the sale costs of £300. The antique table had been purchased for £5,200.

Other information

Nim has unused capital losses of £15,800 brought forward from the tax year 2015/16.

110   What are the deemed proceeds of the shares in Kapook plc sold on 20 July 2016?

    ○ £37,000

    ○ £37,250

    ○ £37,500

    ○ £38,000

(2 marks)

111 What is the total cost of the shares in Kapook plc sold on 20 July 2016?

   ○ £26,333

   ○ £28,500

   ○ £25,667

   ○ £20,533

(2 marks)

112 Which **TWO** of the following statements about capital gains tax for Nim and his wife are correct?

☐ Nim's wife will take the Jooba Ltd shares at market value at the date of the transfer

☐ Nim will have deemed proceeds on the transfer of the Jooba Ltd shares to his wife so that neither a gain nor a loss will arise

☐ The transfer of the Jooba Ltd shares is exempt from capital gains tax because it is between spouses

☐ Nim's wife will not be able to transfer her annual exempt amount to Nim

(2 marks)

113 What is the gain on the sale of the antique table on 26 November 2016?

   ○ £4,500

   ○ £5,000

   ○ £3,500

   ○ £800

(2 marks)

114 Assuming that Nim had chargeable gains of £20,000 in the tax year 2016/17, what is the amount of the loss brought forward from 2015/16 which will be carried forward to 2017/18?

£ [   ]

(2 marks)

(Total = 10 marks)

Aloi, Bon and Dinah (06/11) (amended)   20 mins

The following scenario relates to questions 115 to 119.

On 15 October 2016 Alphabet Ltd, an unquoted trading company, was taken over by XYZ plc. Prior to the takeover Alphabet Ltd's share capital consisted of 100,000 £1 ordinary shares, and under the terms of the takeover the shareholders received for each £1 ordinary share in Alphabet Ltd either cash of £6 per share or one £1 ordinary share in XYZ plc worth £6.50. The following information is available regarding three of the shareholders of Alphabet Ltd:

Aloi

Aloi has been the managing director of Alphabet Ltd since the company's incorporation on 1 January 2011, and she accepted XYZ plc's cash alternative of £6 per share in respect of her shareholding of 60,000 £1 ordinary shares in Alphabet Ltd. Aloi had originally subscribed for 50,000 shares in Alphabet Ltd on 1 January 2011 at their par value, and purchased a further 10,000 shares on 20 May 2012 for £18,600.

On 6 February 2017 Aloi sold an investment property, and this disposal resulted in a chargeable gain against which her annual exempt amount will be set.

For the tax year 2016/17 Aloi has taxable income of £60,000. All her income tax has previously been collected under PAYE so she has not received a notice to file a return for the tax year 2016/17 and so is required to give notice of her chargeability to capital gains tax to HMRC.

Bon

Bon has been the sales director of Alphabet Ltd since 1 February 2016, having not previously been an employee of the company although she had been a shareholder since 1 March 2015. She accepted XYZ plc's share alternative of one £1 ordinary share for each of her 25,000 £1 ordinary shares in Alphabet Ltd. Bon had purchased her shareholding on 1 March 2015 for £92,200.

On 4 March 2017 Bon made a gift of 10,000 of her £1 ordinary shares in XYZ plc to her brother. On that date the shares were quoted on the Stock Exchange at £7.10 – £7.14. Holdover (gift) relief is not available in respect of this disposal.

Dinah

Dinah has been an employee of Alphabet Ltd since 1 May 2015. She accepted XYZ plc's share alternative of one £1 ordinary share for each of her 3,000 £1 ordinary shares in Alphabet Ltd. Dinah had purchased her shareholding on 20 June 2015 for £4,800.

On 13 November 2016 Dinah sold 1,000 of her £1 ordinary shares in XYZ plc for £6,600.

Dinah died on 5 April 2017, and her remaining 2,000 £1 ordinary shares in XYZ plc were inherited by her daughter. On that date these shares were valued at £15,600.

For the tax year 2016/17 Dinah had taxable income of £12,000.

115   Which **TWO** of the following statements are correct about Bon and Dinah's entitlement to entrepreneurs' relief on their disposals of shares in Alphabet Ltd?

(1)   Alphabet Ltd was not Bon's personal company for the requisite time before disposal
(2)   Bon was not an officer or employee of Alphabet Ltd for the requisite time before disposal
(3)   Dinah was not an officer or employee of Alphabet Ltd for the requisite time before disposal
(4)   Alphabet Ltd was not Dinah's personal company for the requisite time before disposal

A   1 and 3
B   2 and 3
C   1 and 4
D   2 and 4   **(2 marks)**

116   What is Aloi's capital gains tax liability on the disposal of her shares in Alphabet Ltd assuming that the gain qualifies for entrepreneurs' relief?

A   £31,000
B   £52,452
C   £29,140
D   £81,592   **(2 marks)**

117   What are the latest dates by which Aloi must:

(1)   Give notice of her chargeability to capital gains tax for the tax year 2016/17 to HMRC?

(2)   Pay her capital gains liability for the tax year 2016/17 in order to avoid interest and penalties?

	Notification	*Payment*
A	5 October 2017	31 January 2018
B	31 December 2017	31 January 2018
C	5 October 2017	31 July 2018
D	31 December 2017	31 July 2018

(2 marks)

118   What is the chargeable gain arising on Bon's gift of her shares in XYZ plc to her brother?

A   £34,320
B   £6,200
C   £34,220
D   £61,200   **(2 marks)**

119 What is Dinah's capital gains tax liability for the tax year 2016/17?

A £648
B Nil
C £900
D £1,134

(2 marks)

(Total = 10 marks)

CBE style OT case – Jerome (Mar/Jun 16) (amended)   20 mins

This objective test question contains question types which will only appear in a computer-based exam, but this question provides valuable practice for all students whichever version of the exam they are taking.

The following scenario relates to questions 120 to 124

Jerome made the following disposals of assets to family members during the tax year 2016/17:

(1) On 28 May 2016, Jerome sold a house to his wife for £140,000. The value of the house at that date was £187,000. Jerome's uncle had originally purchased the house on 14 July 1995 for £45,900. The uncle died on 12 June 2004, and the house was inherited by Jerome. On that date, the house was valued at £112,800. Jerome has never occupied the house as his main residence.

(2) On 24 June 2016, Jerome made a gift of his entire 12% holding of 12,000 £1 ordinary shares in Reward Ltd, an unquoted trading company, to his son. The market value of the shares on that date was £98,400. The shares had been purchased on 15 March 2006 for £39,000. On 24 June 2016, the market value of Reward Ltd's chargeable assets was £540,000, of which £460,000 was in respect of chargeable business assets. Jerome and his son will elect to hold over the gain on this gift of a business asset.

(3) On 7 November 2016, Jerome made a gift of an antique bracelet valued at £12,200 to his granddaughter. Yje antique bracelet had been purchased on 1 September 2001 for £2,100.

(4) On 29 January 2017, Jerome made a gift of nine acres of land valued at £78,400 to his brother. He had originally purchased ten acres of land on 3 November 2005 for £37,800. The market value of the unsold acre of land as at 29 January 2017 was £33,600. The land has never been used for business purposes.

120 What is the base cost of the house for capital gains tax purposes for Jerome's wife?

○ £45,900

○ £187,000

○ £112,800

○ £140,000

(2 marks)

121 What is the amount of hold over relief that can be claimed on the gift of the Reward Ltd shares?

£ [   ]

(2 marks)

122 Match the latest date for submission of the election to hold over the gain on the gift of the Reward Ltd shares and person(s) who must make the election.

31 January 2018		Jerome

5 April 2021		Jerome and his son

Latest date for election	

Person(s) making election	

(2 marks)

123 What is the amount of the chargeable gain on the disposal of the antique bracelet?

- ○ £10,100
- ○ £3,900
- ○ £10,333
- ○ £10,000

(2 marks)

124 What is the amount of the chargeable gain on the disposal of the nine acres of land?

- ○ £66,200
- ○ £40,600
- ○ £44,380
- ○ £51,940

(2 marks)

(Total = 10 marks)

125 Jorge (12/11) (amended)   20 mins

Jorge disposed of the following assets during the tax year 2016/17:

(1)   On 30 June 2016 Jorge sold a house for £308,000. The house had been purchased on 1 January 1999 for £93,000. On 10 June 2006, Jorge had incurred legal fees of £5,000 in relation to a boundary dispute with his neighbour. Throughout the 210 months of ownership the house had been occupied by Jorge as follows:

Months	
34	Occupied
18	Unoccupied – Travelling overseas
24	Unoccupied – Required to work overseas by his employer
11	Occupied
30	Unoccupied – Required to work elsewhere in the United Kingdom by his employer
22	Unoccupied – Travelling overseas
26	Unoccupied – Required to work elsewhere in the United Kingdom by his employer
17	Occupied
12	Unoccupied – Required to work overseas by his employer
13	Unoccupied – Travelling overseas
3	Unoccupied – Lived with sister
210	

Jorge let the house out during all of the periods when he did not occupy it personally. Throughout the period 1 January 1999 to 30 June 2016 Jorge did not have any other main residence.

(2) On 30 September 2016 Jorge sold a copyright for £80,300. The copyright had been purchased on 1 October 2014 for £70,000 when it had an unexpired life of 10 years.

(3) On 6 October 2016 Jorge sold a painting for £5,400. The painting had been purchased on 18 May 2012 for £2,200.

(4) On 29 October 2016 Jorge sold a motor car for £10,700. The motor car had been purchased on 21 December 2014 for £14,600.

Required

Calculate Jorge's taxable gains for the tax year 2016/17. **(10 marks)**

(Total = 10 marks)

126 Winston (06/12) (amended)   20 mins

(a) On 19 May 2016 Winston disposed of a painting, and this resulted in a chargeable gain of £46,360. For the tax year 2016/17 Winston has taxable income of £19,400 after the deduction of the personal allowance.

Winston is considering the sale of a business that he has run as a sole trader since 1 July 2008. The business will be sold for £260,000, and this figure, along with the respective cost of each asset, is made up as follows:

	Sale proceeds £	Cost £
Freehold shop	140,000	80,000
Freehold warehouse	88,000	102,000
Net current assets	32,000	32,000
	260,000	

The freehold warehouse has never been used by Winston for business purposes.

Required

(i) Assuming that Winston does not sell his sole trader business, calculate his capital gains tax liability for the tax year 2016/17. **(3 marks)**

(ii) Calculate Winston's capital gains tax liability for the tax year 2016/17 if he sold his sole trader business on 25 March 2017. **(4 marks)**

(b) On 3 December 2016 Renaldo sold two acres of land at auction for gross proceeds of £92,000. The auctioneers' commission was 5% of the sale price.

Renaldo's wife's father had originally purchased three acres of land on 4 August 2002 for £19,500. He died on 17 June 2009, and the land was inherited by Renaldo's wife. On that date the three acres of land were valued at £28,600.

Renaldo's wife transferred the land to Renaldo on 14 November 2012. On that date the three acres of land were valued at £39,000. The market value of the unsold acre of land as at 3 December 2016 was £38,000.

Required

Compute Renaldo's chargeable gain in respect of the disposal on 3 December 2016. **(3 marks)**

(Total = 10 marks)

127 Mick (06/14) (amended)

20 mins

Mick disposed of the following assets during the tax year 2016/17:

(1)   On 19 May 2016, Mick sold a freehold warehouse for £522,000. The warehouse was purchased on 6 August 2003 for £258,000, and was extended at a cost of £99,000 during April 2005. In January 2009, the floor of the warehouse was damaged by flooding and had to be replaced at a cost of £63,000. The warehouse was sold because it was surplus to the business's requirements as a result of Mick purchasing a newly built warehouse during 2015. Both warehouses have always been used for business purposes in a wholesale business run by Mick as a sole trader.

(2)   On 24 September 2016, Mick sold 700,000 £1 ordinary shares in Rolling Ltd, an unquoted trading company, for £3,675,000. He had originally purchased 500,000 shares in Rolling Ltd on 2 June 2007 for £960,000. On 1 December 2012, Rolling Ltd made a 3 for 2 bonus issue. Mick has been a director of Rolling Ltd since 1 January 2007.

Required

(a)   Assuming that no reliefs are available, calculate the chargeable gain arising from each of Mick's asset disposals during the tax year 2016/17.

Note. You are not required to calculate the taxable gains or the amount of tax payable.   **(4 marks)**

(b)   State which capital gains tax reliefs might be available to Mick in respect of each of his disposals during the tax year 2016/17, and what further information you would require in order to establish if the reliefs are actually available and to establish any restrictions as regards the amount of relief.

Note. For this part of the question you are not expected to perform any calculations.   **(6 marks)**

(Total = 10 marks)

128 Ruby (Sep/Dec 15)

20 mins

You should assume that today's date is 1 March 2017.

(a)   On 27 August 2016, Ruby disposed of a residential investment property and this resulted in a chargeable gain of £45,800.

For the tax year 2016/17 Ruby has taxable income of £17,815.

Required

Calculate Ruby's capital gains tax liability for the tax year 2016/17 if this is her only disposal in that tax year.

(2 marks)

(b)   In addition to the disposal already made on 27 August 2016, Ruby is going to make one further disposal during the tax year 2016/17. The disposal will be of either Ruby's holding of £1 ordinary shares in Pola Ltd, or her holding of 50p ordinary shares in Aplo plc.

Shareholding in Pola Ltd

Pola Ltd is an unquoted trading company in which Ruby has a 10% shareholding. The shareholding was purchased on 14 July 2008 for £23,700 and could be sold for £61,000. Ruby has been an employee of Pola Ltd since 2006.

Shareholding in Aplo plc

Aplo plc is a quoted trading company in which Ruby has a shareholding of 40,000 50p ordinary shares. Ruby received the shareholding as a gift from her father on 27 May 2011. On that date, the shares were quoted on the stock exchange at £2.12 – £2.18. The shareholding could be sold for £59,000.

Neither entrepreneurs' relief nor holdover relief is available in respect of this disposal.

Required

Calculate Ruby's revised capital gains tax liability for the tax year 2016/17, if she also disposes of either (1) her shareholding in Pola Ltd; or alternatively (2) her shareholding in Aplo plc.

Note. The following mark allocation is provided as guidance for this requirement:

Pola Ltd (4½ marks)

Aplo plc (3½ marks)   **(8 marks)**

(Total = 10 marks)

PART D INHERITANCE TAX

Questions 129 to 157 cover inheritance tax, the subject of Chapter 18 of the BPP Study Text for Paper F6.

MCQ bank – Inheritance tax 1

20 mins

129 Gillian owned a 70% shareholding in R Ltd, an unquoted investment company. On 23 July 2016, she gave a 20% shareholding in R Ltd to her son. The values of shareholdings in R Ltd on 23 July 2016 were as follows:

	£
100% shareholding	600,000
70% shareholding	350,000
50% shareholding	200,000
20% shareholding	80,000

What is the diminution in value of Gillian's estate as a result of her gift on 23 July 2016?

A £150,000
B £270,000
C £80,000
D £120,000

(2 marks)

130 Joel and Sunita were a married couple. Sunita died in July 2008 and 65% of her nil rate band of £312,000 (2008/09) was unused. Joel died in May 2016. He had made a potentially exempt transfer (after all available exemptions) of £75,000 in August 2012. Joel left his estate to his sister. Any relevant elections were made.

What is the nil rate band available to set against Joel's death estate?

A £325,000
B £452,800
C £461,250
D £536,250

(2 marks)

131 On 7 July 2011, Paul made a gross chargeable transfer (after all exemptions) of £260,000. On 19 December 2016 he gave £190,000 to a trust. Paul agreed to pay any lifetime IHT due.

How much inheritance tax will be payable by Paul on the December 2016 transfer of value?

A £28,250
B £31,250
C £29,750
D £23,800

(2 marks)

132 Donald made the following transactions in the tax year 2016/17:

(1) A gift of £2,000 to his grand-daughter on the occasion of her marriage.

(2) A sale of a vase to his friend, Alan, for £1,000 which both Donald and Alan believed to be the market value of the vase. The vase was later valued by an auction house as worth £20,000 at the date of the sale.

Ignoring the annual exemption, what is the total value of potentially exempt transfers made by Donald as a result of these gifts?

A £21,000
B Nil
C £2,000
D £19,000

(2 marks)

133 Kirstin gave shares worth £150,000 to a trust on 15 September 2008 and shares worth £600,000 to her brother on 10 July 2013. The nil rate band in 2008/09 was £312,000 and in 2013/14 it was £325,000. Kirstin died on 23 October 2016.

Ignoring the annual exemption, what is the inheritance tax payable on Kirstin's death in relation to her lifetime transfers?

A   £170,000
B   £88,000
C   £136,000
D   £132,160   (2 marks)

(Total = 10 marks)

CBE style OTQ bank – Inheritance tax 2   20 mins

134   Mary made the following gifts in the tax year 2016/17:

(1)   £1,000 on the first day of each month for nine months to her grand-son to pay university living expenses. Mary used income surplus to her living requirements to make these payments.

(2)   £100 to her grand-nephew on his birthday and a further £250 to the same grand-nephew as a Christmas gift.

Ignoring the annual exemption, what is the total value of potentially exempt transfers made by Mary as a result of these gifts?

O £9,350

O £100

O £9,000

O £350   (2 marks)

135   Daniel owned all 1,000 shares in Q Ltd, an unquoted investment company. On 10 October 2016, Daniel gave 300 of his shares in Q Ltd to his daughter. The values of the shares on 10 October 2016 were as follows:

% shareholding	Value per share (£)
76 – 100	150
51 – 75	120
26 – 50	90
1 – 25	30

What is the diminution in value of Daniel's estate as a result of his gift on 10 October 2016 ?

Select...   ▼
£123,000
£27,000
£66,000
£18,000

(2 marks)

136 Susanna died on 19 November 2016. Her estate consisted of a house worth £200,000 (on which there was a repayment mortgage of £60,000) and investments and cash totalling £350,000. Her executors paid funeral expenses of £5,000. Susanna left a cash legacy of £100,000 to her husband and the residue of her estate to her son and daughter. Susanna had not made any lifetime transfers of value.

How much inheritance tax will be payable on Susanna's estate?

£ [   ]

(2 marks)

137 Rodney died on 13 August 2016. In his will he left £200 in cash to each of his five nephews, investments held in ISAs valued at £350,000 to his daughter, and the residue of his estate, which amounted to £520,000, to his wife.

What is the chargeable estate for inheritance purposes?

£ [   ]

(2 marks)

138 Ruth made a chargeable lifetime transfer of £750,000 on 18 June 2016. Ruth died on 10 July 2016.

Match the dates by which the lifetime inheritance tax and the inheritance tax arising as a result of Ruth's death be paid.

31 December 2016		31 January 2017

30 April 2017		30 April 2017

Lifetime tax	

Death tax	

(2 marks)

(Total = 10 marks)

Ning (06/12) (amended)   20 mins

The following scenario relates to questions 139 to 143.

You should assume that today's date is 19 March 2017.

Ning owns the following assets:

(1) Two properties respectively valued at £674,000 and £442,000. The first property has an outstanding repayment mortgage of £160,000, and the second property has an outstanding endowment mortgage of £92,000.

(2) Vintage motor cars valued at £172,000.

(3) Investments in Individual Savings Accounts valued at £47,000, National Savings & Investments savings certificates valued at £36,000, and government stocks (gilts) valued at £69,000.

Ning owes £22,400 in respect of a personal loan from a bank, and she has also verbally promised to pay legal fees of £4,600 incurred by her nephew. Her reasonable funeral expenses will amount to £5,500.

Ning's husband died on 12 March 2007, and 70% of his inheritance tax nil rate band was not used.

On 14 August 2006 Ning had made a gift of £100,000 to her daughter, and on 7 November 2016 she made a gift of £220,000 to her son. These amounts are after taking account of any available exemptions.

The nil rate band for the tax year 2006/07 is £285,000.

139   What is the net value for the two properties in (1) which will be included in the calculation of Ning's chargeable estate were she to die on 20 March 2017?

    A   £1,024,000
    B   £956,000
    C   £933,600
    D   £864,000   **(2 marks)**

140   What is the value of the assets in (2) and (3) which will be included in the calculation of Ning's chargeable estate were she to die on 20 March 2017?

    A   £172,000
    B   £Nil
    C   £324,000
    D   £152,000   **(2 marks)**

141   What is the total amount of deductions (ignoring mortgage debts) which will be taken into account in the calculation of Ning's chargeable estate were she to die on 20 March 2017?

    A   £5,500
    B   £32,500
    C   £10,100
    D   £27,900   **(2 marks)**

142   What is the amount of Ning's own nil rate band for calculating the inheritance tax payable in respect of her estate were she to die on 20 March 2017?

    A   £325,000
    B   £105,000
    C   £5,000
    D   £Nil   **(2 marks)**

143   What is the amount of Ning's husband's nil rate band that Ning's personal representatives could claim were she to die on 20 March 2017 and by when should the claim be made?

	Amount	Claim
A	£227,500	By 31 March 2019
B	£227,500	By 30 September 2017
C	£199,500	By 31 March 2019
D	£199,500	By 30 September 2017

    (2 marks)

(Total = 10 marks)

CBE style OT case – Jimmy (06/11) (amended)

20 mins

This objective test question contains question types which will only appear in a computer-based exam, but this question provides valuable practice for all students whichever version of the exam they are taking.

The following scenario relates to questions 144 to 148.

Jimmy died on 14 February 2017. He had used up his nil rate band at the date of his death by making the following gifts during his lifetime:

(1)   On 2 August 2015 Jimmy made a cash gift to his grandson as a wedding gift when he got married.

(2)   On 9 September 2015 Jimmy gave 200 shares valued at £5 each in J Ltd, an unquoted investment company, to his daughter, Before the gift, Jimmy owned 5,100 shares valued at £30 each in J Ltd. After the gift Jimmy owned 4,900 shares valued at £20 each in J Ltd.

(3)   On 14 November 2015 Jimmy made a cash gift of £800,000 to a trust. Jimmy paid the inheritance tax arising from this gift. Additional inheritance tax was payable on this transfer as a result of Jimmy's death.

At the date of his death Jimmy owned assets valued at £980,000. Under the terms of his will Jimmy left £200,000 to his wife and the residue of his estate to his son.

The nil rate band for the tax year 2015/16 was £325,000.

144   What was the total amount of the exemptions that were deducted in computing the potentially exempt transfer made on 2 August 2015?

    ⭕ £3,000

    ⭕ £8,500

    ⭕ £6,000

    ⭕ £11,000

(2 marks)

145   What is the diminution in value in Jimmy's estate as a result of his gift on 9 September 2015?

    ⭕ £55,000

    ⭕ £4,000

    ⭕ £6,000

    ⭕ £1,000

(2 marks)

146   What was the amount of the inheritance tax paid by Jimmy as a result of his gift made on 14 November 2015?

    £ _____

(2 marks)

147 Match the due date for payment of the additional inheritance tax on the gift made on 14 November 2015 as a result of Jimmy's death and by whom should it be paid.

14 August 2017		Trustees of trust

31 August 2017		Executors of Jimmy's estate

Due date	

By whom paid	

(2 marks)

148 What is the inheritance tax chargeable on Jimmy's death estate as a result of his death on 14 February 2017?

£ [   ]

(2 marks)

(Total = 10 marks)

CBE style OT case – Marcus (Sep/Dec 15) (amended)   20 mins

This objective test question contains question types which will only appear in a computer-based exam, but this question provides valuable practice for all students whichever version of the exam they are taking.

The following scenario relates to questions 149 to 153.

Marcus died on 10 March 2017. He had made the following gifts during his lifetime:

(1)   On 14 January 2008, Marcus made a chargeable lifetime transfer of £315,000 to a trust. The trustees paid the lifetime inheritance tax which arose in respect of this gift.

(2)   On 3 February 2014, Marcus made a chargeable lifetime transfer to another trust. In addition to the gift, Marcus paid the related lifetime inheritance tax on this gift. The gross chargeable lifetime transfer amounted to £491,250.

(3)   On 17 March 2014, Marcus made a gift (a potentially exempt transfer) of 30,000 £1 ordinary shares in Scarum Ltd, an unquoted investment company, to his daughter.

        Before the transfer, Marcus owned all of Scarum Ltd's issued share capital of 100,000 £1 ordinary shares. On 17 March 2014, Scarum Ltd's shares were worth £5 each for a holding of 30%, £9 each for a holding of 70%, and £12 each for a holding of 100%.

(4)   On 29 June 2015, Marcus gave a plot of land worth £100,000 to his wife. Marcus had bought the land in 2008 for £80,000.

The nil rate band for the tax year 2007/08 is £300,000, and for the tax year 2013/14 it is £325,000.

Under the terms of his will, Marcus left his entire estate to his wife. Jerome's wife has not made any gifts during her lifetime. She is intending to remarry.

Ignore the inheritance tax annual exemption.

149 What was the amount of the lifetime inheritance tax paid by the trustees (if any) as a result of the gift made on 14 January 2008?

£ [   ]

(2 marks)

---

150 What was the amount of the lifetime inheritance tax paid by Marcus as a result of the gift made on 3 February 2014?

○ £120,312

○ £33,250

○ £96,250

○ £41,562

(2 marks)

---

151 What was the amount of the taper relief deductible from the additional inheritance tax due as a result of the death of Marcus on the gift made on 3 February 2014?

○ £154,000

○ £38,500

○ £13,300

○ £57,750

(2 marks)

---

152 What was the amount of the potentially exempt transfer made by Marcus on 17 March 2014?

○ £360,000

○ £270,000

○ £150,000

○ £570,000

(2 marks)

---

153 Which **TWO** of the following statements about Jerome and his wife for inheritance tax purposes are correct?

☐ There is no liability for inheritance tax on the transfer of Jerome's estate to his wife because they are treated together as a single chargeable person for inheritance tax.

☐ If Jerome's wife remarries, any unused nil rate band on her death can be transferred to her spouse if they survive her.

☐ The gift of the land on 29 June 2015 by Jerome to his wife is a potentially exempt transfer of £80,000.

☐ The transfer of Jerome's estate to his wife on his death is an exempt transfer.

(2 marks)

(Total = 10 marks)

154 Afiya (12/13) (amended)

20 mins

16/17 (handwritten)

Afiya died on 29 November 2016. She had made the following gifts during her lifetime:

(1) On 14 September 2015, Afiya made a gift of 6,500 £1 ordinary shares in Cassava Ltd, an unquoted *PET* (handwritten) investment company, to her daughter. *15/16* (handwritten) *65%* (handwritten circled)

80% *15% left* (handwritten) Before the transfer Afiya owned 8,000 shares out of Cassava Ltd's issued share capital of 10,000 £1 ordinary shares. On 14 September 2015, Cassava Ltd's shares were worth £3 each for a holding of 15%, £7 each for a holding of 65%, and £8 each for a holding of 80%.

(2) On 27 January 2016, Afiya made a cash gift of £400,000 to a trust. Afiya paid the inheritance tax arising from this gift. *15/16* (handwritten) *CLT* (handwritten)

On 29 November 2016, Afiya's estate was valued at £623,000. Her executors paid funeral expenses of £3,000 on 12 January 2017. Under the terms of her will Afiya left £150,000 to her husband, a specific legacy of £40,000 to her sister, and the residue of the estate to her children.

The nil rate band for the tax year 2015/16 is £325,000.

Required

(a) Calculate the inheritance tax which will be payable as a result of Afiya's death. **(9 marks)**

(b) Calculate the amount of the inheritance which will be received by Afiya's children. **(1 mark)**

(Total = 10 marks)

---

155 Kendra (06/14) (amended)

20 mins

You should assume that today's date is 1 January 2017.

Kendra, aged 93, is unfortunately in poor health with just a few months left to live. She has made no lifetime gifts.

Kendra owns the following assets:

(1) A residential property valued at £970,000. The property is no longer occupied by Kendra, and if it were disposed of during the tax year 2016/17 the disposal would result in a chargeable gain of £174,000 after principal private residence relief.

(2) Building society deposits of £387,000.

(3) Investments in Individual Savings Accounts (ISAs) valued at £39,000 and savings certificates from NS&I (National Savings and Investments) valued at £17,000.

(4) A life assurance policy on her own life. The policy has an open market value of £210,000, and proceeds of £225,000 will be received following Kendra's death.

None of the above valuations are expected to change in the near future. The cost of Kendra's funeral will be £12,800. She also has an outstanding unsecured loan of £1,200 which is due to be repaid on her death.

Under the terms of her will, Kendra has left her entire estate to her children.

The nil rate band of Kendra's husband was fully utilised when he died ten years ago.

For the tax year 2016/17, Kendra will pay income tax at the higher rate.

Required

(a) Calculate the inheritance tax which would be payable if Kendra were to die on 31 March 2017. **(5 marks)**

(b) Advise Kendra why it would not be beneficial to make an immediate lifetime gift of the property valued at £970,000 to her children.

Notes

1. Your answer should take account of both the capital gains tax and the inheritance tax implications of making the gift.

2. For this part of the question you should ignore the capital gains tax annual exempt amount and inheritance tax annual exemptions. **(3 marks)**

(c) Advise Kendra why it might be beneficial for inheritance tax purposes to change the terms of her will so that part of her estate was instead left to her grandchildren rather than her children. **(2 marks)**

(Total = 10 marks)

156 James (Mar/Jun 16)   20 mins

James died on 22 January 2017. He had made the following gifts during his lifetime:

(1) On 9 October 2009, a cash gift of £35,000 to a trust. No lifetime inheritance tax was payable in respect of this gift.

(2) On 14 May 2015, a cash gift of £420,000 to his daughter.

(3) On 2 August 2015, a gift of a property valued at £260,000 to a trust. No lifetime inheritance tax was payable in respect of this gift because it was covered by the nil rate band. By the time of James' death on 22 January 2017, the property had increased in value to £310,000.

On 22 January 2017, James' estate was valued at £870,000. Under the terms of his will, James left his entire estate to his children.

The nil rate band of James' wife was fully utilised when she died ten years ago.

The nil rate band for the tax years 2009/10 and 2015/16 is £325,000.

Required:

(a) Calculate the inheritance tax which will be payable as a result of James' death, and state who will be responsible for paying the tax. **(6 marks)**

(b) Explain why it might have been beneficial for inheritance tax purposes if James had left a portion of his estate to his grandchildren rather than to his children. **(2 marks)**

(c) Explain why it might be advantageous for inheritance tax purposes for a person to make lifetime gifts even when such gifts are made within seven years of death.

Notes

1. Your answer should include a calculation of James' inheritance tax saving from making the gift of property to the trust on 2 August 2015 rather than retaining the property until his death.

2. You are not expected to consider lifetime exemptions in this part of the question. **(2 marks)**

(Total = 10 marks)

157 Alan

Assume that it is 1 December 2016.

Alan acquired quoted shares in Crimson plc in August 2011 at a cost of £375,000. He is now considering whether to give the shares to his daughter, Julie, in the near future or to retain the shares and give them to Julie under the terms of his will. You should assume that Alan will die on 1 April 2020 and that the inheritance tax nil rate band in 2019/20 will be £325,000.

Lifetime gift to Julie

Alan would give the shares to Julie on 10 December 2016 when they are expected to have a value of £450,000. Neither capital gains tax gift relief nor entrepreneurs' relief will be available on this disposal. Alan is a higher rate taxpayer and has no other chargeable assets.

Alan's only previous lifetime transfer was a gift to a trust in December 2012 which resulted in a gross chargeable transfer (after all exemptions) of £55,000.

Gift in will to Julie

Alan would give the shares to Julie on his death in his will when they are expected to have a value of £500,000.

Alan's other assets in his estate would be reduced to a value of nil by his debts so that the gift to Julie would be the only chargeable transfer on his death.

Required

(a) (i) Calculate the capital gains tax payable if the shares in Crimson plc are gifted on 10 December 2016.

(2 marks)

(ii) Calculate the inheritance tax payable if the shares in Crimson plc are gifted on 10 December 2016 and Alan dies on 1 April 2020.

(4 marks)

(b) (i) State the capital gains tax implications of Alan's death in relation to his shareholding in Crimson plc if he retains the shares until his death.

(1 mark)

(ii) Calculate the inheritance tax payable if Alan dies on 1 April 2020 and the shares in Crimson plc are left in his will to Julie.

(2 marks)

(c) Based on your answers in parts (a) and (b), advise Alan whether it would be more tax advantageous to gift the shares in Crimson plc to Julie on 10 December 2016 or to retain them until his death on 1 April 2020 and pass them to Julie in his will.

(1 mark)

(Total = 10 marks)

PART E CORPORATION TAX LIABILITIES

Questions 158 to 190 cover corporation tax liabilities, the subject of Chapters 19 to 23 of the BPP Study Text for Paper F6.

MCQ bank – Corporation tax liabilities 1 — 20 mins

158 J Ltd has deducted the following items in calculating its statement of profit or loss for the year ended 31 December 2017.

	£
Legal expenses relating to the acquisition of a new 40-year lease on its factory	3,000
Cost of arranging a new bank loan to purchase machinery for trade	5,000
Write off of an irrecoverable loan to a former employee	4,000
Donation to local charity with mention of J Ltd's support in programme for fund-raising concert (not a qualifying charitable donation)	100

How much should J Ltd add back to its accounting profit to arrive at its adjusted taxable trading income for the year ended 31 December 2017?

A   £5,100
B   £9,000
C   £7,000
D   £4,000 (2 marks)

159 R Ltd started trading on 1 December 2015 and prepared its first set of accounts to 31 March 2017.

What will R Ltd's accounting periods be for the period of account to 31 March 2017?

A   4 months to 31 March 2016, 12 months to 31 March 2017
B   4 months to 5 April 2016, nearly 12 months to 31 March 2017
C   12 months to 30 November 2016, 4 months to 31 March 2017
D   16 months to 31 March 2017 (2 marks)

160 X Ltd has included a deduction in its accounting profit of £3,200 in respect of the annual leasing cost for a car, which has a recommended list price of £16,000 and CO_2 emissions of 140g/km. The lease of the car started on 1 April 2016 and the car has been used for the whole of the 12-month period ended 31 March 2017.

When preparing the adjusted profit for tax purposes what is the allowable deduction in respect of the leasing cost in the year ended 31 March 2017?

A   £Nil
B   £480
C   £2,720
D   £3,200 (2 marks)

161 K Ltd was incorporated and started trading on 1 July 2016 and prepared its first set of accounts to 31 December 2016. During the six-month accounting period to 31 December 2016, it purchased two vehicles:

		£
28 November 2016	Motor car [1] (CO$_2$ emissions 146g/km)	15,400
2 December 2016	Motor car [2] (CO$_2$ emissions 111g/km)	30,400

Motor car [1] is used 20% for private purposes by a director of K Ltd.

What are the capital allowances to which K Ltd is entitled for the period to 31 December 2016?

A   £4,122
B   £3,352
C   £6,704
D   £3,229   (2 marks)

162 L plc prepares accounts to 31 March each year. L plc sold its 2% holding of shares in S Ltd on 15 November 2016 for £30,000. L plc had purchased the S Ltd shares at a cost of £8,000 in May 2008. The RPI in May 2008 was 215.1 and in November 2016 is assumed to be 263.0. This was the only disposal of a chargeable asset during the year to 31 March 2017.

What is L plc's chargeable gain to be included in its calculation of total profits for the year to 31 March 2017?

A   £22,000
B   £20,219
C   £17,101
D   £9,119   (2 marks)

(Total = 10 marks)

CBE style OTQ bank – Corporation tax liabilities 2   20 mins

163 C plc prepares accounts to 31 December each year. For the year ended 31 December 2015 taxable total profits (after deduction of a £1,000 qualifying charitable donation) were £25,000. For the year ended 31 December 2016 the company made an adjusted trading loss of £40,000 and had other taxable income of £10,000 and made no qualifying charitable donation.

What is the maximum amount of the loss of the accounting period ended 31 December 2016 that the company can claim to carry back to the accounting period ended 31 December 2015?

£ [   ]

(2 marks)

164 D Ltd has the following results:

	12 months to 31 March 2016	9 months to 31 December 2016	12 months to 31 December 2017
	£	£	£
Trading profits/(losses)	45,000	40,000	(160,000)
Property business profits	18,000	15,500	5,000

The company wishes to claim relief for its loss as early as possible.

What is the unused loss carried forward at 31 December 2017?

£ [   ]

(2 marks)

165 R Ltd has the following results for the year ended 31 March 2017:

	£
Trading loss	(15,000)
Interest income	2,000
Qualifying charitable donation	(5,000)
Capital loss	(4,000)

What is the maximum amount that R Ltd could surrender as group relief?

£ [   ]

(2 marks)

166 The D plc group of companies has the following structure.

All companies are resident in the UK except G Inc.

Identify, by clicking on the relevant boxes in the table below, the companies to which E Ltd could surrender a trading loss.

D plc	G Inc
F Ltd	H Ltd

(2 marks)

167 The I plc group of companies has the following structure.

BPP
LEARNING MEDIA

All companies are resident in the UK except L Inc.

Identify, by clicking on the relevant boxes in the table below, the companies to which M Ltd could transfer a capital loss.

I plc	K Ltd
J Ltd	L Inc

(2 marks)

(Total = 10 marks)

Tay Ltd

20 mins

The following scenario relates to questions 168 to 172

Tay Ltd prepares accounts to 31 March each year. In the year to 31 March 2017, it had the following events relating to chargeable assets:

(1) Received insurance proceeds of £180,000 in December 2016 as the result of the destruction of a freehold warehouse in a flood in that month. The warehouse originally cost £140,000 and had an indexed cost in December 2016 of £155,000. Tay Ltd purchased a new warehouse for £162,000 in March 2017.

(2) Received shares and cash on the takeover of Grey Ltd. Tay Ltd had acquired 20,000 shares in Grey Ltd. The shares had an indexed cost in September 2016 of £96,000 when Grey Ltd was taken over by Kline plc. On the takeover, Tay Ltd received one £1 ordinary share in Kline plc worth £4 per share and £2 in cash for each one share held in Grey Ltd.

(3) Sold a piece of machinery which it had used in its trade for £9,000 in July 2016. The machinery had an indexed base cost in July 2016 of £3,500. Capital allowances had been claimed on the machinery.

(4) Sold a plot of land, which it had held as an investment, for £45,000 in October 2016. The land had been acquired in June 2006 for £20,000. Tay Ltd had spent £2,000 on draining the land in January 2010. The indexation factor from June 2006 to October 2016 was 0.324 and from January 2010 to October 2016 was 0.206.

In the year to 31 March 2018, Tay Ltd will dispose of an investment property which will realise a loss. The company wants to know how this loss can be relieved.

168 What is the base cost of the new warehouse purchased in March 2017?

A   £162,000
B   £155,000
C   £144,000
D   £140,000

(2 marks)

169 What was the chargeable gain arising on the takeover of Grey Ltd?

A   £8,000
B   £24,000
C   £16,000
D   £64,000

(2 marks)

170 What was the chargeable gain (if any) arising on the disposal of the machinery?

A   £Nil
B   £5,500
C   £2,500
D   £5,000

(2 marks)

171   What was the chargeable gain arising on the disposal of the plot of land?

    A   £16,520
    B   £15,872
    C   £16,108
    D   £15,548

(2 marks)

172   Which **TWO** of the following statements about the use of the capital loss in the year ended 31 March 2018 are correct?

    (1)   The capital loss can be carried back against chargeable gains made in the year ended 31 March 2017
    (2)   The capital loss can be set against chargeable gains made in the year ended 31 March 2018
    (3)   The capital loss can be set against total profits in the year ended 31 March 2018
    (4)   The capital loss can be carried forward and set against the first available chargeable gains

    A   1 and 2
    B   1 and 3
    C   2 and 4
    D   3 and 4

(2 marks)

(Total = 10 marks)

CBE style OT case – Hyde plc group   20 mins

This objective test question contains question types which will only appear in a computer-based exam, but this question provides valuable practice for all students whichever version of the exam they are taking.

The following scenario relates to questions 173 to 177.

The Hyde plc group has the following structure:

All the group companies prepared accounts to 31 March 2017. However, Greenwich plc intends to change its accounting date to 31 December and will prepare accounts to 31 December 2017.

Hyde plc and Greenwich plc are in a group relief group.

In the year ended 31 March 2017, Greenwich plc had the following results:

	£
Trading loss	(68,000)
Capital loss	(4,000)
Interest income	5,000
Qualifying charitable donations	(3,000)

Greenwich plc will surrender the maximum amount possible for the year ended 31 March 2017 to Hyde plc under group relief.

In the year ended 31 March 2017, Hyde plc had the following results:

	£
Trading loss	(8,000)
Chargeable gain	48,000
Interest income	12,000
Qualifying charitable donations	(1,500)

Hyde plc will make a claim to carry back its trading loss to the year ended 31 March 2016.

Greenwich plc will make a trading loss in the period ended 31 December 2017 and will surrender the maximum amount possible to Hyde plc under group relief.

Regent plc and Primrose plc are in a chargeable gains group. In the year to 31 March 2017, Regent plc sold a factory to Primrose plc for £250,000. The market value of the factory at that date was £300,000. Regent plc had acquired the factory for £100,000. The indexation factor between the date of acquisition and the date of disposal is 0.200.

173 Identify, by clicking on the relevant boxes in the table below, which of the following companies are also members of the Hyde plc group for group relief purposes.

Hampstead plc	Regent plc
Richmond plc	Primrose plc

(2 marks)

174 What is the maximum amount that Greenwich plc could surrender as group relief of the year ended 31 March 2017?

- ○ £68,000
- ○ £70,000
- ○ £71,000
- ○ £75,000

(2 marks)

175 What are the maximum available taxable total profits of Hyde plc that could be group relieved for the year ended 31 March 2017?

Select...   ▼
£58,500
£2,500
£52,000
£50,500

(2 marks)

176 Which **TWO** of the following statements about group relief claims between Hyde plc and Greenwich plc are correct?

☐ A claim for group relief will be ineffective unless Greenwich plc gives a notice of consent

☐ If Hyde plc pays Greenwich plc an amount up to the amount of the loss surrendered, the payment will be deducted from the group relief

☐ A claim for group relief between Greenwich plc and Hyde plc will be available against the whole of the taxable total profits of Hyde plc for the year to 31 March 2018

☐ The claim for group relief would be made on Hyde plc's corporation tax return

(2 marks)

177 What is base cost of the factory acquired by Primrose plc in August 2016?

○ £100,000

○ £120,000

○ £250,000

○ £300,000

(2 marks)

(Total = 10 marks)

178 Do-Not-Panic Ltd (06/08) (amended)   20 mins

Do-Not-Panic Ltd is a trading company. The company commenced trading on 1 January 2016 and its results for the fifteen-month period ended 31 March 2017 are summarised as follows:

(1) The trading profit as adjusted for tax purposes is £285,000. This figure is before taking account of capital allowances.

(2) Do-Not-Panic Ltd purchased a new car with CO_2 emissions of 67 g/km for £9,000 on 10 August 2016, machinery for £8,000 on 19 October 2016 and office equipment for £5,000 on 20 February 2017.

(3) Do-Not-Panic Ltd bought some loan stock on 1 January 2017 as an investment. Interest of £9,500 was received on 31 March 2017 which was also the amount accrued to that date.

(4) On 21 December 2016 Do-Not-Panic Ltd disposed of some investments and this resulted in a capital loss of £4,250. On 28 March 2017 the company made a further disposal and this resulted in a chargeable gain of £39,000.

(5) A qualifying charitable donation of £2,000 was paid on 22 February 2017.

Required

Calculate Do-Not-Panic Ltd's corporation tax liabilities in respect of the fifteen-month period ended 31 March 2017 and advise the company by when these should be paid. The rate of corporation tax in Financial Year 2015 was 20%.

(10 marks)

(Total = 10 marks)

179 Problematic Ltd (06/10) (amended)

20 mins

Problematic Ltd sold the following assets during the year ended 31 March 2017:

(1) On 14 June 2016 16,000 £1 ordinary shares in Easy plc were sold for £54,400. Problematic Ltd had originally purchased 15,000 shares in Easy plc on 26 June 2005 for £12,600. On 28 September 2008 Easy plc made a 1 for 3 rights issue. Problematic Ltd took up its allocation under the rights issue in full, paying £2.20 for each new share issued. The relevant retail prices indexes (RPIs) are as follows:

June 2005	192.2
September 2008	218.4
June 2016 (assumed)	261.2

(2) On 28 January 2017 a freehold factory was sold for £171,000. The indexed cost of the factory on that date was £127,000. Problematic Ltd has made a claim to holdover the gain on the factory against the cost of a replacement leasehold factory under the rollover relief (replacement of business assets) rules. The leasehold factory has a lease period of 20 years, and was purchased on 10 December 2016 for £154,800. The two factory buildings have always been used entirely for business purposes.

Required

(a) Calculate Problematic Ltd's chargeable gains for the year ended 31 March 2017.   **(9 marks)**

(b) Advise Problematic Ltd of the carried forward indexed base cost of the leasehold factory.   **(1 mark)**

(Total = 10 marks)

---

180 Volatile Ltd (12/09) (amended)

20 mins

Volatile Ltd commenced trading on 1 July 2012. The company's results for its first five periods of trading are as follows:

	Period ended 31 December 2012 £	Year ended 31 December 2013 £	Year ended 31 December 2014 £	Period ended 30 September 2015 £	Year ended 30 September 2016 £
Trading profit/(loss)	44,000	(73,800)	95,200	78,700	(186,800)
Property business profit	9,400	6,600	6,500	–	–
Chargeable gain/(loss)	5,100	–	(2,000)	11,700	–
Qualifying charitable donations	(800)	(1,000)	(1,200)	–	–

Required

(a) State the factors that will influence a company's choice of loss relief claims.

Note. You are not expected to consider group relief.   **(2 marks)**

(b) Assuming that Volatile Ltd claims relief for its trading losses as early as possible, calculate the company's taxable total profits for the six-month period ended 31 December 2012, each of the years ended 31 December 2013 and 2014 and the nine-month period ended 30 September 2015. Your answer should also clearly identify the amount of any unrelieved trading losses as at 30 September 2016.   **(8 marks)**

(Total = 10 marks)

181 Acebook Ltd (12/12) (amended)

20 mins

(a) Explain how limited companies can obtain relief for capital losses. **(3 marks)**

Note. You are not expected to explain how groups of companies can obtain relief for capital losses.

(b) On 10 March 2017 Acebook Ltd sold its entire shareholding of 50p ordinary shares in Oogle plc for £3.20 per share. The company had originally purchased 8,000 shares in Oogle plc on 28 June 2003 for £25,200. On 31 October 2006 Oogle plc made a 2 for 1 bonus issue. Then, on 14 February 2008, Oogle plc made a 1 for 5 rights issue. Acebook Ltd took up its allocation under the rights issue in full, paying £4.30 for each new share issued.

Indexation factors are as follows:

June 2003 to October 2006	0.105
June 2003 to February 2008	0.166
June 2003 to March 2017 (assumed)	0.456
October 2006 to February 2008	0.055
October 2006 to March 2017 (assumed)	0.317
February 2008 to March 2017 (assumed)	0.248

Required

Calculate Acebook Ltd's chargeable gain on the disposal on 10 March 2017. **(7 marks)**

(Total = 10 marks)

182 Black Ltd (12/11) and Gastron Ltd (06/09) (amended)

20 mins

(a) Black Ltd owns 100% of the ordinary share capital of White Ltd. The results of Black Ltd and White Ltd for the year ended 31 March 2017 are as follows:

	Black Ltd	White Ltd
	£	£
Trading profit/(loss)	396,800	(351,300)
Property business profit	21,100	26,700
Capital loss	–	(17,200)
Qualifying charitable donations	(4,400)	(5,600)

As at 1 April 2016 Black Ltd had unused trading losses of £57,900, and unused capital losses of £12,600, whilst White Ltd had unused trading losses of £21,800.

Required

Advise Black Ltd as to the maximum amount of group relief that can be claimed from White Ltd in respect of its losses for the year ended 31 March 2017. Clearly identify any losses that cannot be surrendered by White Ltd as part of the group relief claim.

Note. You are not expected to calculate either company's corporation tax liability. **(5 marks)**

(b) Gastron Ltd is a manufacturing company. In the year to 31 March 2017 Gastron Ltd had taxable total profits of £600,000. The taxable total profits included a chargeable gain of £74,800 on the sale of a 1% shareholding. This figure is after taking account of indexation.

Gastron Ltd owns 100% of the ordinary share capital of Culinary Ltd. On 13 February 2017 Culinary Ltd sold a freehold factory and this resulted in a capital loss of £66,000. For the year ended 31 March 2017 Culinary Ltd made no other disposals.

Required

(i) Explain the group relationship that must exist in order for two or more companies to form a group for chargeable gains purposes. **(2 marks)**

(ii) Explain why it would be beneficial for Gastron Ltd and Culinary Ltd to make a joint election to transfer the whole of the capital gain on Gastron Ltd's disposal of shares to Culinary Ltd. **(1 mark)**

(iii) Explain what two other taxation consequences arise as a result of companies being in a chargeable gains group. **(2 marks)**

(Total = 10 marks)

183 Jogger Ltd (A) (12/08) (amended)   29 mins

Jogger Ltd is a manufacturing company. The company's summarised statement of profit or loss for the year ended 31 March 2017 is as follows:

	Note	£	£
Operating profit	1		156,482
Income from investments			
Bank interest	3	8,460	
Loan interest	4	24,600	
Income from property	5	144,000	
Dividends		45,000	
			222,060
Profit from sale of non-current assets			
Disposal of shares	6		102,340
Profit before taxation			480,882

Notes

1 *Operating profit*

   Depreciation of £58,840 has been deducted in arriving at the operating profit of £156,482.

2 *Plant and machinery*

   On 1 April 2016 the tax written down values of plant and machinery were as follows:

	£
Main pool	26,600
Special rate pool	18,800

   The following transactions took place during the year ended 31 March 2017:

		Cost/(proceeds) £
20 July 2016	Sold a special rate pool motor car	(11,700)
31 July 2016	Purchased motor car	11,800
	CO$_2$ emissions 105g/km	
15 August 2016	Purchased new motor car	9,000
	CO$_2$ emissions 65g/km	
30 September 2016	Purchased machinery	500,000
15 December 2016	Purchased computer system	12,500
14 March 2017	Sold a lorry	(8,600)

   The motor car sold on 20 July 2016 for £11,700 originally cost more than this amount. The computer system purchased on 15 December 2016 has a predicted working life of six years and any relevant election has been made. The lorry sold on 14 March 2017 for £8,600 originally cost £16,600.

3 *Bank interest received*

   The bank interest was received on 31 March 2017. The bank deposits are held for non-trading purposes.

4   *Loan interest receivable*

The loan was made for non-trading purposes on 1 July 2016. Loan interest of £16,400 was received on 31 December 2016, and interest of £8,200 was accrued at 31 March 2017.

5   *Income from property*

Jogger Ltd lets out an unfurnished freehold office building that is surplus to requirements. The office building was let throughout the year ended 31 March 2017. On 1 April 2016 Jogger Ltd received a premium of £100,000 for the grant of a ten-year lease, and the annual rent of £44,000 which is payable in advance.

6   *Profit on disposal of shares*

The profit on disposal of shares is in respect of a shareholding that was sold in December 2016 for £150,000. The shares were acquired in August 2006 at a cost of £47,660. The RPI in August 2006 was 199.2 and is assumed to be 263.4 in December 2016.

Required

(a)   Calculate Jogger Ltd's tax adjusted trading loss for the year ended 31 March 2017.

      Notes:

      1   Your computation should start with the operating profit of £156,482.

      2   You should assume that the company claims the maximum available capital allowances.

      3   Ignore VAT.   **(8 marks)**

(b)   Assuming that Jogger Ltd claims relief for its trading loss against total profits, calculate the company's corporation tax liability for the year ended 31 March 2017.   **(7 marks)**

                                                                                        (Total = 15 marks)

184 Mice Ltd (06/10) (amended)   29 mins

Mice Ltd commenced trading on 1 July 2013 as a manufacturing company. The company prepares accounts to 31 March, and its results for the first three periods of trading were as follows:

	Period ended 31 March 2014	Year ended 31 March 2015	Year ended 31 March 2016
	£	£	£
Trading profit	83,200	24,700	51,200
Property business profit	2,800	7,100	12,200
Qualifying charitable donations	(1,000)	(1,500)	–

The following information is available in respect of the year ended 31 March 2017:

Trading loss

Mice Ltd expects to make a trading loss of £180,000.

Property business income

Mice Ltd lets out three freehold office buildings that are surplus to requirements.

The first office building was let throughout the year ended 31 March 2017 at a quarterly rent of £3,200, payable in advance. Mice Ltd paid business rates of £2,200 and insurance of £460 in respect of this property for the year ended 31 March 2017. During June 2016 Mice Ltd repaired the existing car park for this property at a cost of £1,060 and then subsequently enlarged the car park at a cost of £2,640.

The second office building was let on 1 April 2016 to a tenant, with Mice Ltd receiving a premium of £18,000 for the grant of an eight-year lease. The company also received the annual rent of £6,000 which was payable in advance. Mice Ltd paid insurance of £310 in respect of this property for the year ended 31 March 2017.

The third office building was purchased by Mice Ltd on 1 January 2017 and it will be empty until 31 March 2017. The building is to be let from 1 April 2017 at a monthly rent of £640, and on 15 March 2017 Mice Ltd received three months rent in advance. On 1 January 2017 Mice Ltd paid insurance of £480 in respect of this property for the year ended 31 December 2017, and during February 2017 spent £680 on advertising for tenants. Mice Ltd paid loan interest of £1,800 in respect of the period 1 January 2017 to 31 March 2017 on a loan that was taken out to purchase this property.

Loan interest received

On 1 July 2016 Mice Ltd made a loan for non-trading purposes. Loan interest of £6,400 was received on 31 December 2016 and £3,200 will be accrued at 31 March 2017.

Chargeable gain

On 20 December 2016 Mice Ltd sold a piece of freehold land which it acquired in August 2012 at a cost of £28,000. The gross proceeds of sale were £34,844 before legal and selling costs of 5% of the gross proceeds.

The relevant retail price indexes (RPIs) are as follows:

August 2012	243.0
December 2016	263.4

Required

(a) Calculate Mice Ltd's property business profit for the year ended 31 March 2017. **(8 marks)**

(b) Assuming that Mice Ltd claims relief for its trading loss as early as possible, calculate the company's taxable total profits for the nine-month period ended 31 March 2014, and each of the years ended 31 March 2015, 2016 and 2017. **(7 marks)**

(Total = 15 marks)

185 Molten-Metal plc (06/11) (amended)   29 mins

Molten-Metal plc is a manufacturing company. The following information is available for the year ended 31 March 2017:

Trading profit

The tax adjusted trading profit for the year ended 31 March 2017 is £2,170,144. This figure is before making any deductions required for:

(1) Interest payable
(2) Capital allowances.

Interest payable

During the year ended 31 March 2017 Molten-Metal plc paid loan stock interest of £22,500. Loan stock interest payable of £3,700 was accrued at 31 March 2017, with the corresponding accrual at 1 April 2016 being £4,200. The loan is used for trading purposes.

The company also incurred a loan interest expense of £6,800 in respect of a loan that is used for non-trading purposes.

Capital expenditure account

The following items of expenditure have been debited to the capital expenditure account during the year ended 31 March 2017:

1 May 2016 Purchase of a second-hand freehold office building for £428,000. This figure included £31,000 for a ventilation system and £42,000 for a lift. Both the ventilation system and the lift are integral to the office building.

26 June 2016 Purchase of machinery for £186,600. During June 2016 a further £7,700 was spent on building alterations that were necessary for the installation of the machinery.

8 August 2016 A payment of £41,200 for the construction of a new decorative wall around the company's premises.

27 August 2016	Purchase of movable partition walls for £22,900. Molten-Metal plc uses these to divide up its open plan offices, and the partition walls are moved around on a regular basis.
18 November 2016	Purchase of a motor car costing £24,000. This motor car has a CO_2 emission rate of 145 grams per kilometre. This car is used only for business purposes.
28 January 2017	Purchase of a computer costing £2,500. This computer has an expected working life of 5 years. Any relevant election will be made in respect of this asset.
11 March 2017	Purchase of two motor cars each costing £17,300. Each motor car has a CO_2 emission rate of 110 grams per kilometre. One motor car is used by the factory manager, and 60% of the mileage is for private journeys. The other motor car is used as a pool car.

Written down value

On 1 April 2016 the tax written down value of plant and machinery in Molten-Metal plc's main pool was £87,800.

Interest receivable

Molten-Metal plc made a loan for non-trading purposes on 1 August 2016. Loan interest of £9,800 was received on 31 January 2017, and £3,100 was accrued at 31 March 2017.

The company also received bank interest of £2,600 during the year ended 31 March 2017. The bank deposits are held for non-trading purposes.

Required

Calculate Molten-Metal plc's corporation tax liability for the year ended 31 March 2017. Ignore VAT. **(15 marks)**

(Total = 15 marks)

186 Starfish Ltd (A) (12/11) (amended)   29 mins

Starfish Ltd, a retailing company, commenced trading on 1 December 2012. The company initially prepared accounts to 31 March, but changed its accounting date to 31 December by preparing accounts for the nine-month period ended 31 December 2016. Starfish Ltd ceased trading on 31 March 2017.

Starfish Ltd's results for each of its periods of account up to 31 December 2016 are as follows:

	Tax adjusted trading profit/(loss)	Bank interest	Qualifying charitable donations
	£	£	£
Four-month period ended 31 March 2013	(12,600)	600	(800)
Year ended 31 March 2014	64,200	1,400	(1,000)
Year ended 31 March 2015	53,900	1,700	(900)
Year ended 31 March 2016	14,700	0	(700)
Nine-month period ended 31 December 2016	49,900	0	(600)

The company's summarised statement of profit or loss for its final three-month period of trading ended 31 March 2017 is as follows:

	Note	£	£
Gross profit			16,100
Expenses			
Depreciation		25,030	
Donations	1	1,650	
Impairment loss	2	2,000	
Legal fees	3	9,370	
Other expenses	4	168,050	
			(206,100)
Loss before taxation			(190,000)

Notes

1 *Donations*

Donations were made to the following:

	£
A political party	900
A national charity (qualifying charitable donation)	750
	1,650

2 *Impairment loss*

On 31 March 2017 Starfish Ltd wrote off an impairment loss of £2,000 in respect of a trade debt.

3 *Legal fees*

Legal fees were in connection with the following:

	£
Court action for a misleading advertisement	2,020
Issue of 6% loan notes (to raise finance for trading) that was subsequently cancelled	7,350
	9,370

4 *Other expenses*

Other expenses are as follows:

	£
Entertaining customers	3,600
Counselling services provided to employees who were made redundant	8,400
Balance of expenditure (all allowable)	156,050
	168,050

5 *Plant and machinery*

On 1 January 2017 the tax written down values of the company's plant and machinery were as follows:

	£
Main pool	23,600
Special rate pool	13,200

The special rate pool consists of a motor car which has CO_2 emissions of 190 grams per kilometre. The motor car was used 30% privately by a director of Starfish Ltd.

On 10 January 2017 Starfish Ltd purchased a laptop computer for £3,120. This figure is inclusive of value added tax (VAT). Starfish Ltd is registered for VAT.

On 31 March 2017 the company sold all of the items included in the main pool for £31,200, the laptop computer for £1,800, and the motor car for £9,600. These figures are inclusive of VAT where applicable. None of the items included in the main pool was sold for more than its original cost, and all of the items were standard rated.

Required

(a) Calculate Starfish Ltd's tax adjusted trading loss for the three-month period ended 31 March 2017.

   Note. Your computation should commence with the loss before taxation figure of £190,000, and should also list all of the items referred to in notes (1) to (4) indicating by the use of zero (0) any items that do not require adjustment. **(10 marks)**

(b) Assuming that Starfish Ltd claims relief for its trading losses on the most beneficial basis, calculate the company's taxable total profits for the four-month period ended 31 March 2013, the years ended 31 March 2014, 2015 and 2016 and the nine-month period ended 31 December 2016. **(5 marks)**

(Total = 15 marks)

187 Softapp Ltd (12/13) (amended)

Softapp Ltd is a trading company. The company's summarised statement of profit or loss for the year ended 31 March 2017 is as follows:

	Note	£
Operating profit	1	711,475
Other income		
Rental income receivable	2	30,000
Loan interest receivable	3	8,100
Profit on disposal of shares	4	64,900
Finance costs		
Interest payable	5	(67,200)
Profit before taxation		747,275

Notes

1   *Operating profit*

Depreciation of £10,170 and amortisation of leasehold property of £2,500 have been deducted in arriving at the operating profit of £711,475.

2   *Rental income*

Softapp Ltd let out a warehouse surplus to its requirements on 1 October 2016, the monthly rent of £5,000 being payable in advance on the first of each calendar month. The rent due on 1 March 2017 was not received due to the business failure of the tenant. Half of the unpaid rent was received on 10 April 2017 and the rest is irrecoverable.

3   *Loan interest receivable*

The loan was made for non-trading purposes on 1 July 2016. Loan interest of £5,600 was received on 31 December 2016, and interest of £2,500 was accrued at 31 March 2017.

4   *Profit on disposal of shares*

The profit on disposal of shares is in respect of the sale of Softapp Ltd's entire (2%) shareholding in Networked plc on 28 February 2017 for proceeds of £93,219. The shares were acquired on 15 July 2013 at a cost of £30,000. The RPI for July 2013 was 249.7 and the RPI for February 2017 is assumed to be 263.8.

5   *Interest payable*

The interest payable is in respect of the company's 4% loan stock. Interest of £33,600 was paid on 30 September 2016 and again on 31 March 2017. The loan stock was used to finance the company's trading activities.

Additional information

Leasehold property

On 1 January 2017, Softapp Ltd acquired a leasehold office building, paying a premium of £100,000 for the grant of a ten-year lease. The office building was used for business purposes by Softapp Ltd throughout the period 1 January to 31 March 2017.

Plant and machinery

The tax written down value of Softapp Ltd's plant and machinery as at 1 April 2016 was nil.

On 1 September 2016, Softapp Ltd purchased computer equipment at a cost of £175,000.

During October 2016 Softapp Ltd had an extension constructed adjacent to its existing freehold office building, which is used by the company's employees as a staff room.

The total cost of £100,000 for the extension is made up as follows:

	£
Integral to building	
Building costs of extension	61,000
Heating system	3,600
Ventilation system	4,600
Not integral to building	
Furniture and furnishings	29,400
Refrigerator and microwave cooker	1,400
	100,000

Required

Calculate Softapp Ltd's corporation tax liability for the year ended 31 March 2017.

Note. Your computation should commence with the operating profit figure of £711,475. **(15 marks)**

(Total = 15 marks)

188 Long Ltd group (A) (06/14) (amended)   29 mins

Long Ltd owns 100% of the ordinary share capital of both Wind Ltd and Road Ltd. Long Ltd and Road Ltd run freight transport businesses, whilst Wind Ltd provides transport related insurance services.

Long Ltd's shareholding in Wind Ltd was acquired on 1 April 2011 and the shareholding in Road Ltd was acquired on 15 January 2016 when that company was incorporated. Long Ltd and Wind Ltd have prepared accounts for the year ended 31 March 2017, whilst Road Ltd has prepared accounts for the period 1 January 2017 (when the company commenced trading) to 31 March 2017. The following information is available:

Long Ltd

(1)   The operating profit for the year ended 31 March 2017 is £817,820. Depreciation of £10,170 has been deducted in arriving at this figure.

(2)   On 1 April 2016, the tax written down value of the plant and machinery main pool was £44,800. On 10 June 2016, Long Ltd purchased a lorry for £36,800 and a motor car for £15,700. The motor car has a CO_2 emission rate of 122 grams per kilometre. The motor car is used by the managing director of Long Ltd, and 40% of the mileage is for private journeys.

(3)   On 29 July 2016, Long Ltd disposed of a 2% shareholding in an unconnected company. The disposal resulted in a capital loss of £21,300.

(4)   During the year ended 31 March 2017, Long Ltd received a dividend of £41,400 from Wind Ltd, and dividends totalling £32,000 from unconnected companies.

Wind Ltd

(1)   The operating profit for the year ended 31 March 2017 is £59,490. Depreciation of £5,000 has been deducted in arriving at this figure.

(2)   On 1 April 2016, the tax written down value of the plant and machinery main pool was £900. There were no additions or disposals during the year ended 31 March 2017.

(3)   On 18 August 2016, Wind Ltd disposed of a 1% shareholding in an unconnected company. The disposal resulted in a chargeable gain of £29,800. This figure is after taking account of indexation.

Road Ltd

(1)   The operating loss for the three-month period ended 31 March 2017 is £26,100. Donations of £2,800 have been deducted in arriving at this figure. The donations consist of political donations of £400, and qualifying charitable donations of £2,400.

(2)   On 3 October 2016, Road Ltd purchased a new motor car for £11,600. The motor car has a CO_2 emission rate of 65 grams per kilometre.

(3) For the three-month period ended 31 March 2017, loan interest receivable was £4,300. The loan was made for non-trading purposes.

Other information

(1) Long Ltd, Wind Ltd and Road Ltd do not have any other shareholdings in any other company.

(2) Road Ltd is not expected to be profitable for the foreseeable future.

Required

(a) On the assumption that any available reliefs are claimed on the most beneficial basis, calculate the corporation tax liabilities of Long Ltd and Wind Ltd for the year ended 31 March 2017, and of Road Ltd for the three-month period ended 31 March 2017. **(11 marks)**

(b) Explain Ltd whether or not Long Ltd is a large company for the purpose of paying corporation tax by instalments for the year ended 31 March 2017. **(4 marks)**

(Total = 15 marks)

189 Lucky Ltd (Sep/Dec 15) (amended)   29 mins

Lucky Ltd was incorporated on 20 July 2016, and commenced trading on 1 December 2016. The following information is available for the four-month period 1 December 2016 to 31 March 2017:

(1) The operating profit for the four-month period ended 31 March 2017 is £432,600. Advertising expenditure of £4,700 (incurred during September 2016), depreciation of £14,700, and amortisation of £9,000 have been deducted in arriving at this figure.

The amortisation relates to a premium which was paid on 1 December 2016 to acquire a leasehold warehouse on a 12-year lease. The amount of premium assessed on the landlord as income was £46,800. The warehouse was used for business purposes by Lucky Ltd throughout the period ended 31 March 2017.

(2) Lucky Ltd purchased the following assets during the period 20 July 2016 to 31 March 2017:

		£
19 August 2016	Computer	6,300
22 January 2017	Integral features	41,200
31 January 2017	Office equipment	32,900
17 March 2017	Motor car	12,800

The integral features of £41,200 are in respect of expenditure on electrical systems, a ventilation system and lifts which are integral to a freehold office building owned by Lucky Ltd.

The motor car has a CO_2 emission rate of 62 grams per kilometre.

(3) Lucky Ltd made a loan to another company for non-trading purposes on 1 February 2017. Loan interest income of £700 was accrued at 31 March 2017.

Lucky Ltd will make a company car available to its chief executive officer. The car will be purchased, rather than leased, and will be made available to the chief executive officer in December 2017 onwards.

Required:

(a) State when an accounting period starts for corporation tax purposes. **(2 marks)**

(b) Calculate Lucky Ltd's corporation tax liability for the four-month period ended 31 March 2017.

Note. Your computation should commence with the operating profit of £432,600, and should also indicate by the use of zero (0) any items referred to in the question for which no adjustment is required. **(9 marks)**

(c)   Advise Lucky Ltd as to how long it must retain the records used in preparing its self-assessment corporation tax return for the four-month period ended 31 March 2017, and the potential consequences of not retaining the records for the required period.   **(2 marks)**

(d)   Advise Lucky Ltd on the effects of the company car on its taxable total profits for the year ended 31 March 2018.   **(2 marks)**

(Total = 15 marks)

190 Jump Ltd (Mar/Jun 2016)   29 mins

Jump Ltd's summarised statement of profit or loss for the three-month period ended 31 March 2017 is as follows:

	Note	£	£
Revenue			264,900
Operating expenses			
Depreciation		8,100	
Employee costs	1	189,700	
Lease of motor car	2	1,200	
Professional fees	3	7,800	
Other expenses	4	202,800	
			(409,600)
Operating loss			(144,700)
Bank interest receivable			0
Loss before taxation			(144,700)

Notes

1   *Employee costs*

Employee costs are as follows:

	£
Employee training courses	3,400
Employee pension contributions paid	11,600
Cost of annual staff party (for eight employees)	1,500
Balance of expenditure (all allowable)	173,200
	189,700

2   *Lease of motor car*

The lease is in respect of a motor car with CO_2 emissions of 189 grams per kilometre.

3   *Professional fees*

Professional fees are as follows:

	£
Accountancy	2,200
Legal fees in connection with the issue of share capital	3,800
Legal fees in connection with the renewal of a 20-year property lease	1,800
	7,800

4   *Other expenses*

Other expenses are as follows:

	£
Entertaining UK customers	1,700
Entertaining overseas customers	790
Political donations	800
Balance of expenditure (all allowable)	199,510
	202,800

Additional information

Plant and machinery

On 1 January 2017, the tax written down values of Jump Ltd's plant and machinery were as follows:

	£
Main pool	12,100
Special rate pool	5,700

The following motor cars were sold during the three-month period ended 31 March 2017:

	Date of sale	Proceeds	Original cost
		£	£
Motor car [1]	7 January 2017	9,700	9,300
Motor car [2]	29 March 2017	6,100	13,200

The original cost of motor car [1] was added to the special rate pool when it was purchased, and the original cost of motor car [2] was added to the main pool when it was purchased.

Previous results

Jump Ltd's results for its two previous periods of trading are as follows:

	Year ended 31 May 2016	Period ended 31 December 2016
	£	£
Tax adjusted trading profit	78,600	42,400
Bank interest receivable	1,200	0

Group companies

Jump Ltd owns 80% of the ordinary share capital of Hop Ltd and 60% of the ordinary share capital of Skip Ltd.

Hop Ltd commenced trading on 1 August 2016, and for the eight-month period ended 31 March 2017 has taxable total profits of £63,000.

Skip Ltd has been trading for several years and has taxable total profits of £56,000 for the year ended 31 March 2017.

Required:

(a) Calculate Jump Ltd's tax adjusted trading loss for the three-month period ended 31 March 2017.

Notes

1 Your computation should commence with the operating loss figure of £144,700, and should list all of the items referred to in notes (1) to (4), indicating by the use of zero (0) any items which do not require adjustment.

2 You should assume that the company claims the maximum available capital allowances. **(10 marks)**

(b) (i) State the main factor which will influence Jump Ltd's choice of loss relief or group relief claims.
(1 mark)

(ii) Advise Jump Ltd as to the maximum amount of its trading loss which can be relieved against its total profits for the year ended 31 May 2016 and the seven-month period ended 31 December 2016.

(2 marks)

(iii) Advise Jump Ltd as to the maximum amount of its trading loss which can be surrendered as group relief.
(2 marks)

(Total = 15 marks)

PART F VALUE ADDED TAX

Questions 191 to 240 cover value added tax, the subject of Chapters 24 and 25 of the BPP Study Text for Paper F6.

MCQ bank – Value added tax 1

20 mins

191 Jerome is a value added tax (VAT) registered trader who received an order for goods with a 10% deposit on 18 August 2016. The goods were despatched on 26 August 2016 and an invoice was sent on 2 September 2016. The balancing 90% of the payment was received on 10 September 2016.

What are the tax points for the deposit and the balancing payment if Jerome does not use the cash accounting scheme?

	Deposit	Balancing payment
A	18 August 2016	10 September 2016
B	26 August 2016	26 August 2016
C	18 August 2016	2 September 2016
D	2 September 2016	10 September 2016

(2 marks)

192 Alma runs a financial services business making exempt supplies. Barry runs a children's clothing shop making zero rated supplies. Chris runs an adult clothing shop making standard rated supplies.

Who is making taxable supplies and therefore can reclaim input VAT?

A Alma and Barry
B Alma and Chris
C Barry and Chris
D Chris only

(2 marks)

193 L Ltd is registered for value added tax (VAT). On 1 January 2017 L Ltd purchased a motor car costing £18,400 (inclusive of VAT) for the use of its managing director for business and private purposes. The private use is estimated to be 40%. The managing director is provided with free petrol for business and private mileage which cost L Ltd £625 (exclusive of VAT). L Ltd wishes to use the fuel scale charge: the relevant quarterly VAT inclusive scale charge is £361.

What is L Ltd's VAT repayment in respect of the motor car and the fuel for the quarter ended 31 March 2017?

A £1,905
B £3,132
C £65
D £44

(2 marks)

194 N Ltd prepared a value added tax (VAT) return for the quarter ended 31 May 2016 which showed net VAT payable of £2,500.

By which dates should this return have been submitted to HM Revenue and Customs (HMRC) and the payment made to HMRC?

	Return submitted	Payment
A	30 June 2016	30 June 2016
B	7 July 2016	7 July 2016
C	7 July 2016	30 June 2016
D	30 June 2016	7 July 2016

(2 marks)

195 Mick is a value added tax (VAT) registered trader who prepares quarterly value added tax (VAT) returns to 31 March, 30 June, 30 September and 31 December each year. Mick's accounts are prepared annually to 30 September. Mick made a supply of goods amounting to £6,000 on 22 September 2016 with a due date of payment of 10 October 2016. The customer has defaulted on the payment and Mick has written the debt off in his accounts. He does not use the cash accounting scheme.

Which quarterly VAT return is the earliest in which relief for the impaired debt may be claimed?

A   VAT quarter ended 31 December 2016
B   VAT quarter ended 31 March 2017
C   VAT quarter ended 30 June 2017
D   VAT quarter ended 30 September 2017

(2 marks)

(Total = 10 marks)

CBE style OTQ bank – Value added tax 2

39 mins

196 Karen is a sole trader and is registered for value added tax (VAT). In October 2016, Karen sold goods for £8,000 exclusive of VAT. The sale was standard rated. Karen's invoice states that there is a discount of 8% on sales if invoices are paid within 21 days. The invoice for the supply was actually paid 25 days after it was issued.

How much VAT should Karen have added to the sale price of £8,000?

£ [   ]

(2 marks)

197 Olive is a sole trader who is registered for value added tax (VAT). On 10 October 2016 she purchased a motor car for £12,000 (inclusive of VAT) to use for business and private purposes. The private use is estimated to be 30%. On 1 December 2016, the motor car was damaged in an accident and the repairs amounted to £2,000 (inclusive of VAT).

What is the input tax VAT Olive can recover in relation to the motor car for the quarter ended 31 December 2016?

£ [   ]

(2 marks)

198 P Ltd incurred the following expenditure (inclusive of VAT) in the quarter to 31 December 2016:

	£
New car for salesman (20% private use)	14,040
New motor van	10,320
Entertaining UK customers	4,200
Entertaining overseas customers	3,600

How much input VAT can be recovered by P Ltd for the quarter to 31 December 2016?

Select...   ▼
£5,360
£4,192
£3,020
£2,320

(2 marks)

199   Ben has been in business for three years. Due to an upturn in trade, he applied to register for VAT with effect from 1 October 2016. Prior to registration, he had incurred the following VAT expenditure:

	£
Legal fees on an invoice dated 13 January 2016	500
Accountancy fees on an invoice dated 5 September 2016	30
Inventory of spare parts acquired in past two years and still held on 30 September 2016	240

What is the total pre-registration input VAT that can Ben recover in respect of these items?

£ [   ]

(2 marks)

200   In the first year of trading to 31 December 2015 Scott's taxable turnover was £5,000 per month.

For the first seven months of 2016 his turnover was as follows:

	£
January 2016	8,400
February 2016	8,100
March 2016	8,300
April 2016	9,100
May 2016	9,700
June 2016	10,200
July 2016	10,300

You have advised Scott that he is compulsorily required to be registered for VAT.

From what date will Scott be registered for VAT under compulsory registration?

○ 30 July 2016

○ 1 August 2016

○ 30 June 2016

○ 1 July 2016

(2 marks)

201   During the quarter ended 31 December 2016, Rachel makes purchases of office items for her business of £5,700 and spends £420 entertaining UK customers. Her sales for the period are £35,250. All figures are inclusive of VAT and standard rated.

What is Rachel's total VAT liability for the quarter ended 31 December 2016?

£ [   ]

(2 marks)

202   Charlie, a UK VAT registered trader, made a supply of goods in February 2017 to a customer in France who is VAT registered there.

What rate of VAT will Charlie charge on this sale?

○ 0%

○ 20%

○ 1/6

○ 5%

(2 marks)

203 Which **TWO** of the following are features of the VAT cash accounting scheme?

☐ Date of payment or receipt determines the VAT period in which the transaction is dealt with

☐ Only need to submit an annual VAT return

☐ Gives automatic impairment loss relief (bad debt relief)

☐ Payments on account of VAT are required throughout the quarter

(2 marks)

204 Q Ltd is registered for value added tax (VAT) and uses the flat rate scheme. In its VAT quarter ended 30 June 2016 it had a tax inclusive turnover of £120,000. This comprises of standard rated sales of £85,000, zero-rated sales of £25,000 and exempt sales of £10,000. The flat rate scheme percentage for the company's trading sector is 9.5%.

The VAT payable by Q Ltd for the quarter ended 30 June 2016 is:

○ £11,400

○ £10,450

○ £8,075

○ £11,400

(2 marks)

205 Which of the following is a requirement for a business to be allowed to join the value added tax (VAT) flat rate scheme and when must a business leave the scheme?

	Join scheme	*Leave scheme*
○	Tax exclusive annual taxable turnover up to £150,000	Tax inclusive annual taxable turnover over £230,00
○	Tax exclusive annual taxable turnover up to £150,000	Tax exclusive annual taxable turnover over £230,000
○	Tax inclusive annual taxable turnover up to £150,000	Tax inclusive annual taxable turnover up to £150,000
○	Tax inclusive annual turnover of up to £150,000	Tax exclusive annual taxable turnover up to £150,000

(2 marks)

(Total = 20 marks)

CBE style OT case – Anne (06/09) (amended)　　20 mins

This objective test question contains question types which will only appear in a computer-based exam, but this question provides valuable practice for all students whichever version of the exam they are taking.

The following scenario relates to questions 206 to 210

Anne runs a retail clothing shop. She is registered for value added tax (VAT) and is in the process of completing her VAT return for the quarter ended 30 November 2016.

The following information is available (all figures are exclusive of VAT):

(1) Cash sales amounted to £42,000, of which £28,000 was in respect of sales of adult clothing (standard rated) and £14,000 was in respect of sales of children's clothing (zero rated).

(2) Sales invoices totalling £12,000 were issued in respect of credit sales. These sales were all standard rated. Anne states on her invoice that there is a 5% discount for payment within one month of the date of the sales invoice. 90% of the customers pay within this period. The sales figure of £12,000 is stated before any deduction for the 5% discount.

(3) Purchase and expense invoices totalling £19,200 were received from VAT registered suppliers. This figure is made up as follows:

	£
Standard rated purchases and expenses	11,200
Zero rated purchases	6,000
Exempt expenses	2,000
	19,200

Anne pays all of her purchase and expense invoices two months after receiving the invoice.

(4) On 30 November 2016 Anne wrote off two impairment losses that were in respect of standard rated credit sales. The first impairment loss was for £300, and was in respect of a sales invoice due for payment on 15 July 2016. The second impairment loss was for £800, and was in respect of a sales invoice due for payment on 10 April 2016.

Anne does not use the cash accounting scheme but she is considering using the scheme.

206 What is the amount of output tax on cash sales payable by Anne for the quarter ended 30 November 2016?

£ _____

(2 marks)

207 What is the amount of output tax on credit sales payable by Anne for the quarter ended 30 November 2016, taking into account impairment loss relief?

○ £1,910

○ £2,400

○ £2,280

○ £2,292

(2 marks)

208 What is the amount of input tax recoverable by Anne for the quarter ended 30 November 2016?

£ _____

(2 marks)

209 Which **TWO** of the following statements about the cash accounting scheme are correct?

(1) Anne will be permitted to join the scheme if her expected taxable turnover for the next 12 months does not exceed £1,350,000

(2) Anne must pay her 90% of the previous year's net VAT liability during the year by means of nine monthly payments commencing at the end of the fourth month of the year

(3) Anne will be permitted to join the scheme if she is up-to-date with her VAT payments but not necessarily up-to-date with her VAT returns

(4) If the value of Anne's taxable supplies exceeds £1,600,000 in the 12 months to the end of a VAT period she must leave the scheme immediately

○ 1 and 2

○ 2 and 3

○ 1 and 4

○ 2 and 4

(2 marks)

210 Which **TWO** of the following are the advantages of Anne using the cash accounting scheme?

(1) Reduced amount of output VAT payable
(2) Automatic impairment loss relief (bad debt relief)
(3) Only one VAT return each year
(4) Output VAT on 10% of credit sales will be accounted for up to one month later than at present

○ 1 and 2

○ 2 and 3

○ 1 and 4

○ 2 and 4

(2 marks)

(Total = 10 marks)

Auy and Bim (06/10) (amended)   20 mins

The following scenario relates to questions 211 to 215.

Auy and Bim have been in partnership since 6 April 2005 and have been registered for value added tax (VAT) since that date.

In the year ended 5 April 2017 the partnership's summarised statement of profit or loss shows sales revenue of £140,762, which is exclusive of output VAT of £25,600, and expenses of £60,200 which are exclusive of recoverable input VAT of £180 for motor expenses and £140 for other expenses.

The partnership has recently started invoicing for its services on new payment terms, and the partners are concerned about output VAT being accounted for at the appropriate time.

The partnership is considering using the flat rate scheme. The relevant flat rate scheme percentage for the partnership's trade is 14%.

211 Which **TWO** of the following statements about the tax point are correct?

(1) The basic tax point for services is the date that services commence.

(2) If the VAT invoice is issued within 14 days after the basic tax point and payment has not been received before the basic tax point, the invoice date becomes the tax point.

(3) The tax point determines the VAT period in which output tax must be accounted for and credit for input tax will be allowed.

(4) If VAT invoice is issued and payment is received before the basic tax point, the actual tax point is the later of those two dates.

A   1 and 2
B   2 and 3
C   1 and 4
D   2 and 4

(2 marks)

212 What is the total amount of VAT paid by the partnership to HM Revenue & Customs for the year ended 5 April 2017?

A   £25,600
B   £25,420
C   £25,280
D   £25,460

(2 marks)

213 Which **TWO** of the following statements about the flat rate scheme are correct?

(1) Businesses using the scheme must still issue VAT invoices to their VAT registered customers.

(2) Under the scheme, businesses calculate VAT by applying a fixed percentage to their standard rate income only.

(3) Businesses using the scheme cannot reclaim any input tax suffered.

(4) A 1% reduction off the flat rate percentage can always be made by businesses in the first year that they use the flat rate scheme.

A 1 and 2
B 2 and 4
C 2 and 3
D 1 and 3   **(2 marks)**

214 What are the conditions that the partnership must satisfy in order to join and continue to use the VAT flat rate scheme?

	Join	Continue to use
A	Expected taxable turnover (excluding VAT) for the next 12 months does not exceed £230,000	Until its total turnover (including VAT) for the previous year exceeds £1,350,000
B	Expected taxable turnover (excluding VAT) for the next 12 months does not exceed £150,000	Until its total turnover (including VAT) for the previous year exceeds £230,000
C	Expected taxable turnover (excluding VAT) for the next 12 months does not exceed £150,000	Until its total turnover (including VAT) for the previous year exceeds £1,350,000
D	Expected taxable turnover (excluding VAT) for the next 12 months does not exceed £230,000	Until its total turnover (including VAT) for the previous year exceeds £230,000

(2 marks)

215 What is the amount of VAT that would have been paid to HM Revenue & Customs if the partnership had used the flat rate scheme to calculate the amount of VAT payable for the year ended 5 April 2017?

A £23,291
B £19,707
C £22,971
D £28,152   **(2 marks)**

                                                                    (Total = 10 marks)

Aston (06/11) (amended)

The following scenario relates to questions 216 to 220

Aston commenced self-employment on 1 August 2016 providing consultancy services. His sales revenue has been as follows:

		Standard rated £	Zero rated £
2016	August	6,300	–
	September	6,400	–
	October	21,900	4,800
	November	11,700	–
	December	17,100	–
2017	January	13,800	1,200
	February	4,200	–
	March	31,500	3,300
	April	44,600	6,600

Where applicable, the above figures are stated exclusive of value added tax (VAT). Aston only supplies services and all of his supplies are to VAT registered businesses. He does not offer any discount for prompt payment.

Aston wants advice about when he will need to submit his VAT returns and pay the associated VAT due.

The following is a sample of the new sales invoice that Aston is going to issue to his customers:

SALES INVOICE

Aston
111 Long Road
London W1 9MG
Telephone 0207 123 3456

Customer: Faster Motors plc
Address: 22 Short Lane
Manchester M1 8MB

Invoice Date 6 June 2017
Tax Point   6 June 2017

Description of services
Business advice

	£
Total price (excluding VAT)	12,000.00
Total price (including VAT)	14,400.00

You have advised Aston that he also needs to include the rate of VAT for each supply and the amount of VAT payable.

Aston sometimes receives supplies of standard rated services from VAT registered businesses situated elsewhere within the European Union. Aston wants to know how he should account for these services for VAT purposes.

Because of the complexity of the VAT legislation, Aston is concerned that despite his best efforts he will incorrectly treat a standard rated supply as zero-rated, thus understating the amount of VAT payable. He wants to know if such an error will result in a penalty, and if so how much the penalty will be.

216 On what date was Aston liable to be registered for VAT and from what date should Aston's business be registered for VAT?

	Liable for registration	Date of registration
A	28 February 2017	28 February 2017
B	31 January 2017	1 March 2017
C	31 January 2017	28 February 2017
D	28 February 2017	1 March 2017

(2 marks)

217 When must Aston submit his VAT returns and pay the associated VAT?

	Submission	*Payment*
A	One month after the end of the VAT period	One month after the end of the VAT period
B	One month after the end of the VAT period	One month and seven days after the end of the VAT period
C	One month and seven days after the end of the VAT period	One month and seven days after the end of the VAT period
D	One month and seven days after the end of the VAT period	One month after the end of the VAT period

(2 marks)

218 Which **TWO** pieces of information must Aston show on his new sales invoices in order for them to be valid for VAT purposes in addition to those about which you have already advised him?

(1) Date for payment
(2) Aston's VAT registration number
(3) HMRC reference number
(4) An identifying number (invoice number)

A   1 and 2
B   2 and 4
C   2 and 3
D   1 and 3

(2 marks)

219 Which **TWO** of the following statements about when and how Aston should account for VAT in respect of the supplies of services he receives from VAT registered businesses situated elsewhere within the European Union are correct?

(1) The transaction is entered on Aston's VAT return as an output and an input

(2) The tax point is the earlier of the fifteenth day of the month following that in which the service is completed and the date it is paid for

(3) Supplies of services from VAT registered businesses situated elsewhere within the European Union are always zero-rated for the customer

(4) The service is treated as being supplied in the UK since this is where Aston is situated

A   1 and 3
B   2 and 4
C   1 and 4
D   2 and 3

(2 marks)

220 Assuming that Aston incorrectly treats a standard rated supply as zero-rated with the result that the amount of VAT payable is understated, what is the maximum amount of penalty that is likely to be charged by HM Revenue and Customs and the minimum penalty that could be charged as a result of a subsequent unprompted disclosure?

	Maximum penalty	Minimum penalty for unprompted disclosure
A	70% of the VAT underpaid	15% of the VAT underpaid
B	70% of the VAT underpaid	0% of the VAT underpaid
C	30% of the VAT underpaid	15% of the VAT underpaid
D	30% of the VAT underpaid	0% of the VAT underpaid

(2 marks)

(Total = 10 marks)

Starfish Ltd (B) (12/11) (amended)   20 mins

The following scenario relates to questions 221 to 225

Starfish Ltd, a retailing company, ceased trading on 31 March 2017 and deregistered from value added tax (VAT) on that date.

The following information relates to the company's final VAT return for the quarter ended 31 March 2017:

(1) Cash sales revenue amounted to £41,160, of which £38,520 was in respect of standard rated sales and £2,640 was in respect of zero-rated sales.

(2) Sales invoices totalling £2,000 were issued in respect of credit sales revenue. This figure is exclusive of VAT, and the sales were all standard rated. Starfish Ltd states on its invoices that it offers all of its credit sale customers a 4% discount for payment within 14 days of the date of the sales invoice. 60% of the customers paid within this period.

(3) In addition to the above sales revenue, Starfish Ltd sold its remaining inventory on 31 March 2017 for £28,800.

(4) There were no purchases of inventory during the period.

(5) Standard rated expenses amounted to £69,960, of which £4,320 was in respect of entertaining UK customers.

(6) Starfish Ltd wrote off an impairment loss on 31 March 2017 in respect of a sales invoice (exclusive of VAT) that was due for payment on 8 August 2016. Output VAT of £384 was originally paid in respect of this sale.

(7) On 31 March 2017 the company sold all of its machinery for £31,200 and a motor car for £9,600. The motor car was used 30% privately by a director of Starfish Ltd.

Unless otherwise stated, all of the above figures are inclusive of VAT where applicable.

Starfish Ltd did not use the cash accounting scheme for VAT.

221 What is the amount of output tax on credit sales payable by Starfish Ltd for the quarter ended 31 March 2017?

A £384
B £480
C £390
D £325

(2 marks)

222 What is the amount of output tax, other than on credit sales, payable by Starfish Ltd for the quarter ended 31 March 2017?

A £16,420
B £11,620
C £11,220
D £10,000

(2 marks)

223 What is the amount of input tax recoverable by Starfish Ltd for the quarter ended 31 March 2017?

A £12,744
B £11,324
C £10,940
D £11,276

(2 marks)

224 From which date would default interest be payable if Starfish Ltd is late in paying the VAT for the quarter ended 31 March 2017?

A 30 April 2017
B 7 May 2017
C 14 May 2017
D 31 March 2017

(2 marks)

225 Which of the following would be the consequences for VAT if Starfish Ltd had instead sold its entire business as a going concern to a single VAT registered purchaser?

A Output VAT would have been due on the sale of the inventory or the sale of the non-current assets but would be payable by the purchaser.

B No output VAT would have been due on the sale of the inventory but would have been due on the sale of the non-current assets.

C No output VAT would have been due on the sale of the non-current assets but would have been due on the sale of the inventory.

D No output VAT would have been due on the sale of the inventory or the sale of the non-current assets.

(2 marks)

(Total = 10 marks)

CBE style OT case – Long Ltd group (B) (06/14) (amended)

20 mins

This objective test question contains question types which will only appear in a computer-based exam, but this question provides valuable practice for all students whichever version of the exam they are taking.

The following scenario relates to questions 226 to 230.

Long Ltd owns 100% of the ordinary share capital of both Wind Ltd and Road Ltd. Long Ltd and Road Ltd run freight transport businesses, whilst Wind Ltd provides transport related insurance services.

Long Ltd, Wind Ltd and Road Ltd are not registered as a group for value added tax (VAT) purposes, but such a registration is being considered with Long Ltd being the representative member.

The following VAT information is available for the quarter ended 31 March 2017:

Long Ltd

(1)   All of Long Ltd's sales are standard rated for VAT.

(2)   Output VAT of £52,640 was charged in respect of sales. This figure includes output VAT of £1,760 on a deposit received on 28 December 2016. The deposit was in respect of a contract which was completed on 6 January 2017, with a sales invoice being issued on 20 January 2017.

(3)   In addition to the above, Long Ltd also charged output VAT of £1,940 on sales to Wind Ltd and output VAT of £960 on sales to Road Ltd.

(4)   Input VAT of £14,720 was incurred in respect of expenses.

(5)   In addition to the above, Long Ltd has discovered that it has not been claiming for the input VAT of £18 which it has paid each month since 1 January 2011 for the hire of a photocopier.

Wind Ltd

(1)   All of Wind Ltd's sales are exempt from VAT.

(2)   Input VAT of £7,330 was incurred in respect of expenses. This includes input VAT of £1,940 incurred on purchases from Long Ltd.

Road Ltd

(1)   All of Road Ltd's sales are zero rated for VAT.

(2)   Road Ltd registered for VAT on 1 January 2017 and this is the company's first VAT return.

(3)   Input VAT of £3,120 was incurred in respect of expenses. This includes input VAT of £960 incurred on purchases from Long Ltd.

(4)   In addition to the above, Road Ltd incurred input VAT in respect of advertising expenditure as follows:

	£
April 2016	640
November 2016	380
	1,020

226   What is the amount of output tax payable by Long Ltd for the quarter ended 31 March 2017?

£ [   ]

(2 marks)

227   What is the amount of input tax recoverable by Long Ltd for the quarter ended 31 March 2017?

○ £14,720

○ £14,774

○ £14,882

○ £15,638

(2 marks)

228   What is the amount of input tax recoverable by Wind Ltd for the quarter ended 31 March 2017?

£ [   ]

(2 marks)

229 What is the amount of input tax recoverable by Road Ltd for the quarter ended 31 March 2017?

○ £3,120

○ £4,140

○ £3,500

○ £2,540

(2 marks)

230 Which **TWO** of the following statements about the Long Ltd group and VAT group registration are correct?

(1) If Wind Ltd and Road Ltd were both owned by the same individual they would not be able to be included in a group registration.

(2) Supplies of goods or services to Road Ltd from outside the group will be treated as a supply to Long Ltd

(3) Each company in the Long Ltd group must join the VAT group if group registration is applied for

(4) The supplies by Long Ltd to Wind Ltd and Road Ltd would be disregarded for VAT purposes

○ 1 and 3

○ 2 and 4

○ 1 and 4

○ 2 and 3

(2 marks)

(Total = 10 marks)

CBE style OT case – Smart Ltd (Sep/Dec 2015) (amended)

20 mins

This objective test question contains question types which will only appear in a computer-based exam, but this question provides valuable practice for all students whichever version of the exam they are taking.

The following scenario relates to questions 231 to 235.

Smart Ltd commenced trading on 1 September 2016. The company's sales for the first four months of trading were as follows:

2016	£
September	26,000
October	47,000
November	134,000
December	113,000

On 1 November 2016, the company signed a contract valued at £86,000 for completion during November 2016.

All of the above figures are stated exclusive of value added tax (VAT). Smart Ltd only supplies services and all of the company's supplies are standard rated.

Smart Ltd allows its customers 60 days credit when paying for services, and it is concerned that some customers will default on the payment of their debts. The company pays its purchase invoices as soon as they are received.

Smart Ltd does not use either the VAT cash accounting scheme or the annual accounting scheme.

Smart Ltd is concerned about the penalties that could be charged if it makes a careless error in its VAT return resulting in underpaid VAT.

231 Match the dates from which Smart Ltd was required to register for value added tax (VAT) and by when it was required to notify HM Revenue and Customs (HMRC) of the registration.

| 1 November 2016 | | 30 December 2016 |

| 30 November 2016 | | 31 December 2016 |

| Register | |

| Notification | |

(2 marks)

232 Identify, by clicking on the relevant boxes in the table below, which of the following statements about how and when Smart Ltd will have to submit its quarterly VAT returns and pay any related VAT liability are true or false.

Smart Ltd must file its VAT returns online	TRUE	FALSE
Smart Ltd can choose whether to pay the VAT which is due electronically or by cheque	TRUE	FALSE
The deadline for paying any VAT which is due is one month after the end of each quarter	TRUE	FALSE
The deadline for filing the VAT return is one month and seven days after the end of each quarter	TRUE	FALSE

(2 marks)

233 Which **TWO** of the following statements about the tax point for Smart Ltd's supplies of services are correct?

(1) The basic tax point is the date on which the invoice is issued.

(2) The basic tax point is the date on which services are completed.

(3) If a customer pays for services before the basic tax point, the payment date will be the tax point.

(4) If a customer pays for services after the basic tax point, the payment date will be the tax point.

○ 1 and 2

○ 2 and 3

○ 1 and 4

○ 2 and 4

(2 marks)

234 Which **TWO** of the following statements are advantages for Smart Ltd to use the VAT cash accounting scheme?

(1) The scheme will provide automatic relief for an impairment loss should a customer default on the payment of a debt.

(2) Only one VAT return will be required each year so there are fewer occasions to trigger a default surcharge.

(3) There will be reduced VAT administration as Smart Ltd will not be required to issue invoices to its customers.

(4) Output VAT will be accounted for 60 days later than at present, because the scheme will result in the tax point becoming the date when payment is received from customers.

○ 1 and 2

○ 2 and 3

○ 1 and 4

○ 2 and 4

(2 marks)

235 What is the maximum amount of penalty that could be charged by HM Revenue and Customs if Smart Ltd makes a careless error in its VAT return resulting in underpaid VAT and the minimum penalty that could be charged as a result of a subsequent prompted disclosure?

	Maximum penalty	Minimum penalty for prompted disclosure
○	70% of the VAT underpaid	15% of the VAT underpaid
○	70% of the VAT underpaid	0% of the VAT underpaid
○	30% of the VAT underpaid	15% of the VAT underpaid
○	30% of the VAT underpaid	0% of the VAT underpaid

(2 marks)

(Total = 10 marks)

236 Jogger Ltd (B) (12/08) (amended)

20 mins

Jogger Ltd is a manufacturing company and has been registered for value added tax (VAT) since 1 April 2010. From that date until 30 June 2015 the company's VAT returns were all submitted on time. Since 1 July 2015 the company's VAT returns have been submitted as follows:

Quarter ended	VAT paid £	Submitted
30 September 2015	42,700	One month late
31 December 2015	41,200	On time
31 March 2016	38,900	One month late
30 June 2016	28,300	On time
30 September 2016	49,100	On time
31 December 2016	63,800	On time
31 March 2017	89,100	Two months late

Jogger Ltd always pays any VAT that is due at the same time as the related return is submitted.

Required

(a) State, giving appropriate reasons, the default surcharge consequences arising from Jogger Ltd's submission of its VAT returns for the quarter ended 30 September 2015 to the quarter ended 31 March 2017 inclusive, at the times stated. You may assume that Jogger Ltd is not a small business for the purposes of the default surcharge regime. **(6 marks)**

(b) Advise Jogger Ltd why it might be beneficial to use the VAT annual accounting scheme, and state the conditions that it will have to satisfy before being permitted to do so. **(4 marks)**

(Total = 10 marks)

---

237 Flick (B) (06/12) (amended)

20 mins

On 1 January 2017, Flick commenced in partnership with Art running a small cinema.

The partnership voluntarily registered for value added tax (VAT) on 1 January 2017, and immediately began using the flat rate scheme to calculate the amount of VAT payable. The relevant flat rate scheme percentage for the partnership's trade is 12%.

For the quarter ended 31 March 2017 the partnership had standard rated sales of £59,700, and these were all made to members of the general public. For the same period standard rated expenses amounted to £27,300. Both figures are stated inclusive of VAT.

The partnership has two private boxes in its cinema that can be booked on a special basis by privileged customers. Such customers can book the boxes up to two months in advance, at which time they have to pay a 25% deposit. An invoice is then given to the customer on the day of the screening of the film, with payment of the balance of 75% required within seven days. For VAT purposes, the renting out of the cinema boxes is a supply of services.

Required

(a) Explain whether or not it was beneficial for the partnership to have used the VAT flat rate scheme for the quarter ended 31 March 2017.

Notes

1 Your answer should be supported by appropriate calculations.

2 You should ignore the 1% reduction from the flat rate that is available during the first year of VAT registration. **(3 marks)**

(b) Explain whether or not it was financially beneficial for the partnership to have voluntarily registered for VAT from 1 January 2017.

Note. Your answer should be supported by appropriate calculations. **(3 marks)**

(c)   Advise the partnership as to when it should account for output VAT on the renting out of its private boxes to privileged customers.   **(4 marks)**

(Total = 10 marks)

238 Richard (B) (12/13) (amended)   20 mins

On 6 April 2016, Richard commenced in self-employment, running a restaurant.

Richard's sales since the commencement of trading have been as follows:

April to July 2016	£10,500 per month
August to November 2016	£14,000 per month
December 2016 to March 2017	£21,500 per month

These figures are stated exclusive of value added tax (VAT). Richard's sales are all standard rated.

As a trainee Chartered Certified Accountant you have advised Richard in writing that he should be registered for VAT, but he has refused to register because he thinks his net profit is insufficient to cover the additional cost which would be incurred.

Required

(a)   Explain from what date Richard was required to be compulsorily registered for value added tax (VAT) and the VAT implications of continuing to trade after this date without registering.

    Note. You are not expected to explain the VAT penalties arising from late VAT registration.   **(4 marks)**

(b)   Briefly explain from an ethical viewpoint the issues you, as a trainee Chartered Certified Accountant, should consider in order for your firm to deal with Richard's refusal to register for VAT.   **(2 marks)**

(c)   State the circumstances in which a trader can issue a simplified (or less detailed) VAT invoice, when such an invoice should be issued, and FIVE pieces of information which such an invoice must show where the supply is entirely standard rated.   **(4 marks)**

(Total = 10 marks)

239 Clueless Ltd (A) (12/12) (amended)   20 mins

Clueless Ltd is a manufacturing company. It is registered for value added tax (VAT), but currently does not use any of the special VAT schemes. The company has annual standard rated sales of £1,200,000 and annual standard rated expenses of £550,000. Both these figures are exclusive of VAT and are likely to remain the same for the foreseeable future. Clueless Ltd is up to date with all of its tax returns, including those for corporation tax, PAYE and VAT. It is also up to date with its corporation tax, PAYE and VAT payments. However, the company often incurs considerable overtime costs due to its employees working late in order to meet tax return filing deadlines.

Clueless Ltd pays its expenses on a cash basis, but allows customers two months credit when paying for sales. The company does not have any impairment losses.

Clueless Ltd is planning to purchase some new machinery at a cost of £22,000 (exclusive of VAT). The machinery can either be purchased from an overseas supplier situated outside the European Union, or from a VAT registered supplier situated in the European Union. Clueless Ltd is not a regular importer and so is unsure of the VAT treatment for this purchase.

Required

(a)   Explain why Clueless Ltd is entitled to use both the VAT cash accounting scheme and the VAT annual accounting scheme, and why it will probably be beneficial for the company to use both schemes.

    (6 marks)

(b)   Explain when and how Clueless Ltd will have to account for VAT in respect of the new machinery if it is purchased from:

    (i)   A supplier situated outside the European Union

    (ii)   A VAT registered supplier situated elsewhere within the European Union.   **(4 marks)**

(Total = 10 marks)

240 Garfield (Mar/Jun 2016)   **20 mins**

Garfield has been registered for valued added tax (VAT) since 1 April 2010. Garfield has previously completed his VAT returns himself, but for the quarter ended 31 March 2017 there are some items for which he is unsure of the correct VAT treatment.

Garfield's partly completed VAT computation for the quarter ended 31 March 2017 is shown below. All of the completed sections of the computation are correct, with the omissions marked as outstanding (O/S).

	Note	£
Output VAT		
Sales (all standard rated)		22,500
Discounted sale	1	O/S
Equipment	2	O/S
Fuel scale charge		60
Input VAT		
Purchases (all standard rated)		(11,200)
Motor car (purchased on 1 January 2017)		0
Equipment	2	O/S
Impairment losses	3	O/S
Entertaining – UK customers		0
– Overseas customers	4	O/S
Motor expenses	5	O/S
VAT payable		O/S

Unless otherwise stated, all of the figures in the following notes are stated exclusive of VAT.

Notes

1   *Discounted sale*

On 10 February 2017, a sales invoice for £4,300 was issued by Garfield in respect of a standard rated supply. To encourage this previously late paying customer to pay promptly, Garfield offered a 10% discount for payment within 14 days of the date of the sales invoice. The customer paid within the 14-day period.

This invoice has not been taken into account in calculating the output VAT figure of £22,500, and this is the only sale for which Garfield has offered a prompt payment discount.

2   *Equipment*

During the quarter ended 31 March 2017, Garfield acquired some new equipment at a cost of £12,400 from a VAT registered supplier situated in the European Union.

3   *Impairment losses*

On 31 March 2017, Garfield wrote off three impairment losses. Details are as follows:

Amount	Invoice date	Payment due date
£1,400	30 July 2016	29 August 2016
£2,700	12 September 2016	12 October 2016
£1,900	4 October 2016	3 November 2016

4   *Entertaining*

During the quarter ended 31 March 2017, Garfield spent £960 on entertaining overseas customers. This figure is inclusive of VAT.

5   *Motor expenses*

The motor car purchased on 1 January 2017 is used by Garfield 60% for business mileage. During the quarter ended 31 March 2017, Garfield spent £1,008 on repairs to the motor car and £660 on fuel for both his business and private mileage. Both of these figures are inclusive of VAT.

Additional information

Garfield does not use the cash accounting scheme, the annual accounting scheme or the flat rate scheme, but has read that the use of these schemes can be beneficial for small businesses such as his.

Garfield's VAT exclusive annual turnover is currently £450,000, and this is expected to steadily decrease over the coming years. He pays for most of his purchases and expenses on a cash basis, but allows many of his customers 30 days credit when paying for sales.

Required:

(a)   Calculate the amount of value added tax (VAT) payable by Garfield for the quarter ended 31 March 2017.

(7 marks)

(b)   State which VAT schemes Garfield is currently permitted to use, and explain, with supporting reasons, which ONE of the available schemes would appear to be the most beneficial for him to use.

Notes

1   Your answer should be confined to the information given in the question.
2   You are not expected to explain how any of the schemes operate.   **(3 marks)**

(Total = 10 marks)

Answers

MCQ bank – The UK tax system and its administration 1

1 D 2 and 4

Inheritance tax is a progressive tax as the proportion of the wealth that is taxable increases as wealth increases (the amount covered by the nil rate band is charged at 0% and the remainder at 20% or 40%). It is also a redistributive tax as it redistributes wealth.

Inheritance tax is a direct tax and it is not an environmental tax.

2 B 2 and 3

Statutes (Acts of Parliament) and Statutory Instruments have legal force.

HMRC publications such as Revenue and Customs Brief and Extra Statutory Concessions do not have legal force.

3 B By the Upper Tribunal

The Upper Tribunal deals with complex cases which either involve an important issue of tax law or a large financial sum.

4 B Notify by 5 October 2017, payment by 31 January 2018

The chargeable gain arises in the tax year 2016/17 and so Daren must notify HMRC of his chargeability within six months from the end of the tax year. The tax liability must be paid by 31 January following the end of the tax year. There are no payments on account for capital gains tax.

5 A £742

Potential Lost Revenue is the tax payable of £2,120 (40% × £5,300)

The minimum penalty for a prompted, deliberate, but not concealed error is 35% × PLR which is £742.

CBE style OTQ bank – The UK tax system and its administration 2

6

Submission	31 January 2018

Notification	30 April 2019

As the return is filed after the due filing date of 31 January 2018, the notification must be made by the quarter day following the first anniversary of the actual filing date.

7 £5,146

	£
Income tax £(12,500 – 10,000 payments on account)	2,500
Class 2 NIC	146
Class 4 NIC £(2,500 – 2,000 payments on account)	500
Capital gains tax	2,000
Amount to pay on 31 January 2018	5,146

8 £31

£10,000 is paid by the due date of 1 January 2018. The balance of £12,400 is one month late so the interest on late paid tax is £12,400 × 3% × 1/12 = £31.

9   £50,000 due on 14 May 2017

The amount of each of the first three instalments is 3/10 × £500,000 = £150,000. The final instalment is the remaining liability of £500,000 − (3 × £150,000) = £50,000, and is due on the 14th day of the fourth month of the next accounting period.

10   £100

There is a £100 penalty for late return which is submitted within three months of the due date (here 12 months after the end of the period to which the return relates).

Domingo and Fargo

Text references. Chapter 17 deals with self assessment for individuals.

Top tips. Note the difference between record keeping requirements for taxpayers in business and those not in business.

Easy marks. There were easy marks in question 11 for the requirements for filing tax returns.

---

11   B   Domingo 31 October 2017, Fargo 31 January 2018

12   D   Domingo 31 January 2019, Fargo 31 January 2023

Domingo was not in business during 2016/17, so his records must be retained until one year after 31 January following the tax year, which is 31 January 2019.

Fargo was in business during 2016/17, so all of his records (both business and non-business) must be retained until five years after 31 January following the tax year, which is 31 January 2023.

13   D   £3,000

14   C   Balancing payment and first payment on account 31 January 2018, second payment on account 31 July 2018

15   A   Interest £1,800 × 3% × 4/12 = £18

Penalty £1,800 @ 5% = £90 (balancing payment not more than five months after the penalty date).

CBE style OT case – Joe (A)

Text references. Chapter 4 deals with the PAYE system.

Top tips. RTI late filing penalties are relatively new in the F6(UK) syllabus for exams so are highly topical.

Easy marks. The details of the provision of form P45 in question 17 should have been well known.

---

16   The code number for Joe, if he was only entitled to a personal allowance, would be 1100L and Joe's tax code will be applied to his salary when calculating the amount of income tax that has to be paid each month under the PAYE system.

Joe's tax code can be adjusted for unpaid tax on income from earlier years. HMRC may issue amended tax codes during the tax year.

17   31 December 2016 by Firstly plc

Form P45 will show Joe's taxable earnings and income tax deducted up to the date of leaving, together with his tax code at the date of leaving.

18   31 May 2017 by Secondly plc

Form P60 will be prepared by Secondly plc at the end of the tax year. It will show Joe's taxable earnings, income tax deducted, final tax code, national insurance contributions, and Secondly plc's name and address.

19   6 July 2017, cash equivalents of the benefits

20   £400

Secondly plc has over 250 employees so the penalty is £400.

CBE style OT case – Ernest

Text references. Self assessment for individuals is covered in Chapter 17. Ethics are covered in Chapter 1.

Top tips. If your firm ceases to act for a client, it must notify HMRC that it has ceased to act but not the reasons for doing so.

Easy marks. The definitions of tax evasion and tax avoidance required for question 21 should be well known.

21

Tax evasion is illegal	**TRUE**	
Both tax evasion and tax avoidance are illegal		**FALSE**
Tax avoidance involves any legal method of reducing the taxpayer's tax burden	**TRUE**	
Tax evasion always involves providing HM Revenue and Customs with false information		**FALSE**

Tax evasion does not necessarily involve providing HM Revenue and Customs (HMRC) with false information. It could include this situation where Ernest is evading tax by not providing HMRC with information to which is entitled.

22   Ernest should be advised to disclose details of the capital gain to HMRC and If Ernest does not disclose the gain to HMRC, your firm would be obliged to report under the money laundering regulations.

Your firm should also consider ceasing to act for Ernest. If it does cease to act, your firm should notify HMRC that it no longer acts for him although your firm should not provide any reason for this.

23   £12,600

The maximum penalty for an error which is deliberate but not concealed is 70% of potential lost revenue which is £18,000 × 70% = £12,600.

24   £6,300

The minimum penalty for prompted disclosure of an error which is deliberate but not concealed is 35% of potential lost revenue which is £18,000 × 35% = £6,300.

25   £270

The due date for payment was 31 January 2017 so the payment is six months late. The interest payable is therefore £18,000 × 3% × 6/12 = £270.

Thai Curry Ltd

26	C	31 March 2018

The CT return must be submitted one year after the end of the period of account ie by 31 March 2018.

27	D	£3,462

As the return is more than 3 months late the fixed penalty is £200. As the return is more than 6 months late there is also a tax geared penalty of 10% × unpaid tax, ie £32,624 × 10% = £3,262. The total amount of penalties are therefore £(200 + 3,262) = £3,462.

28	A	£32,624 on 1 January 2018

As the company is not large since its profits are below the profit threshold of £1,500,000 it must pay its corporation tax by 9 months and 1 day after the accounting period, ie by 1 January 2018.

29	C	1 and 3

An internal review is a less costly and more effective way to resolve disputes informally than a formal appeal and HMRC must usually carry out the review within 45 days. The internal review will be made by an objective HMRC review officer not previously connected with the case. After the review conclusion is notified, the company has 30 days to appeal to the Tax Tribunal.

30	D	Complex track, Upper tier, Standard track First tier

31 John

Marking scheme

			Marks	
(a)	(i)	Date for notification	1	
		Maximum penalty	1	
		Minimum penalty	1	
				3
	(ii)	Compliance check notification date	1	
		Random basis	1	
		Other reasons	1	
				3

				Marks
(b)	(i)	Saving		1
	(ii)	Charitable support		1
	(iii)	Capital gains reliefs	1	
		Plant and machinery	1	
				2
				10

(a)   (i)   **Notification of chargeability**

John should have given notice to HM Revenue and Customs (HMRC) of his chargeability to income tax for 2015/16 by 5 October 2016.

The maximum penalty for careless late notification is 30% of the Potential Lost Revenue (PLR) to HMRC which will be John's tax payable on the return for 2015/16.

However, if John tells HMRC of his failure to notify within 12 months and John has no reason to believe HMRC has discovered, or is about to discover, the error (unprompted disclosure) as appears to be the case here, the penalty can be reduced by HMRC to 0%.

(ii)   **Compliance check**

If HMRC intend to carry out a compliance check enquiry into John's 2015/16 tax return, it will have to notify him by the first anniversary of the actual filing date.

HMRC have the right to carry out a compliance check enquiry as regards the completeness and accuracy of any return and some returns are selected for a compliance check enquiry at random.

Other returns are selected for a particular reason, for example, if HMRC believes that there has been an underpayment of tax due to the taxpayer's failure to comply with tax legislation.

(b)   (i)   Saving is encouraged by offering individuals tax incentives such as income tax and capital gains tax exemptions on new individual savings accounts and income tax relief on pension contributions.

(ii)   Charitable support is encouraged by giving individuals income tax relief on donations made through the gift aid scheme or by payroll deduction.

(iii)   Entrepreneurs are encouraged to build their own businesses through various capital gains tax reliefs such as entrepreneurs' relief.

Investment in plant and machinery is encouraged through capital allowances.

32 Sugar plc

Text references. Chapter 19 deals with computing the corporation tax liability. Chapter 23 includes payment of tax by companies.

Top tips. The rules on related 51% group companies are still relatively new and so are highly topical.

Easy marks. The calculation of the corporation tax liability in part (c) was straightforward.

Marking scheme

		Marks
(a)	Definition	1
	Honey plc	½
	Molasses plc	½
	Treacle plc	1
		3

			Marks
(b)	*Year ended 31 March 2017*		
	Profit limit	½	
	Taxable total profits	½	
	FII	1	
	Profits, therefore large	½	
	Year ended 31 March 2018		
	Taxable total profits = profits, therefore large	½	
			3
(c)	*Year ended 31 March 2017*		
	Corporation tax	½	
	Date payable	½	
	Year ended 31 March 2018		
	Corporation tax	½	
	Instalments	½	
	Dates payable	2	
			4
			10

(a) A company B is a related 51% group company of another company A, if A is a 51% subsidiary of B (B owns more than 50% of A's ordinary shares directly or indirectly) or B is a 51% subsidiary of A or both A and B are 51% subsidiaries of another company. Honey plc is not a related 51% group company of Sugar plc because Sugar plc only directly owns 45% of the ordinary shares of Honey plc. Molasses plc is a related 51% group company of Sugar plc because Sugar plc directly owns 75% of the ordinary shares of Molasses plc. Treacle plc is related 51% group company of Sugar plc because Sugar plc indirectly owns 75% × 70% = 52.5% of the ordinary shares of Treacle plc.

(b) *Year ended 31 March 2017*

Sugar plc has two related 51% group companies (Molasses plc and Treacle plc) at the end of the previous accounting period. The profit limit is therefore £1,500,000/3 = £500,000. Sugar plc's profits for the year to 31 March 2017 are:

	£
Taxable total profits	470,000
Dividends from non-group companies	50,000
Profits	520,000

Sugar plc is therefore a large company in the year to 31 March 2017.

Year ended 31 March 2018

The profit limit is the same and Sugar plc's taxable total profits of £600,000 are also its profits for these purposes. Sugar plc is therefore a large company in the year to 31 March 2018.

(c) *Year ended 31 March 2017*

	£
Corporation tax liability	
£470,000 × 20%	94,000

Since this is the first year that Sugar plc is a large company, its corporation tax liability will be due in one amount on 1 January 2018.

Year ended 31 March 2018

	£
Corporation tax liability	
£600,000 × 20%	120,000

This is payable in four equal instalments of £30,000. The instalments will have been due on 14 October 2017, 14 January 2018, 14 April 2018 and 14 July 2018.

MCQ bank – Income tax and NIC liabilities 1

33   B   1 only

Suzy is UK resident in the tax year 2016/17 as she is present in the UK for 183 days or more (meets automatic UK test).

Miles is not UK resident in the tax year 2016/17 as he was not previously UK resident and is present in the UK for less than 46 days (meets automatic overseas test).

34   A   £2,500

	£
£3,000 @ 20%	600
£(5,000 – 3,000) = £2,000 @ 0% (Starting rate band)	0
£1,000 @ 0% (Savings income nil rate band)	0
£(12,500 – 2,000 – 1,000) = £9,500 @ 20%	1,900
Tax liability	2,500

35   D   2 and 4

Interest on an NS&I Investment account and interest on UK Government stocks ('gilts') are taxable.

Premium bond prizes and dividends on shares held in an Individual Savings Account are exempt.

36   B   £2,260

	£
Taxable income	12,400
Tax	
£12,400 × 20%	2,480
Less transferred personal allowance tax reducer £1,100 × 20%	(220)
Income tax liability	2,260

37   C   Marion £333, Gerald £167

Marion

	£
Accrued interest deemed received 31.12.16 taxable savings income £20,000 × 5% × 4/12	333

Gerald

	£
Interest received 31.12.16 £20,000 × 5% × 6/12	500
Less relief for accrued interest (amount taxable on Marion) £20,000 × 5% × 4/12	(333)
Taxable savings income	167

38   C   £60,100

	£
£(32,000 + 10,000) = £42,000 @ 20%	8,400
£(150,000 + 10,000) = £(160,000 – 42,000) = £118,000 @ 40%	47,200
£(170,000 – 160,000) = £10,000 @ 45%	4,500
Tax liability	60,100

39   C   £538

	£
Net income	57,000
Less personal pension contributions (gross)	(2,000)
Adjusted net income	55,000
Less threshold	(50,000)
Excess	5,000
÷ £100	50
Child benefit income tax charge: 1% × £1,076 × 50	538

40   C   £22,500

The bonus received on 30 September 2016 is taxable in 2016/17 as the receipts basis applies to employment income.

The gratuity received on 1 December 2016 is taxable as employment income in 2016/17 as it is a reward of the employment even though it was not received from the employer.

41   B   2, 3

Travel from office to visit a client and travel from home to visit a trade fair relevant to the employer's business are qualifying travel expenses.

Travel from home to a workplace to which an employee has been seconded for 36 months does not qualify as travel to a temporary workplace as the secondment exceeds 24 months. Travel from home to a permanent place of work is not a qualifying travel expense.

42   D   £4,600

CO_2 emission (rounded down)	115
Base figure	(95)
	20
Divided by 5	4
Starting percentage	16
Diesel addition	3
Final percentage	23
Benefit £20,000 (list price) × 23%	£4,600

MCQ bank – Income tax and NIC liabilities 2

43   B   £3,300

			£
Use	£3,600 × 20%		720
Gift	Current market value	£1,000	
	or		
	Original value	£3,600	
	less use:		
	2015/16 £720 × 5/12	(300)	
	2016/17	(720)	
		£2,580	
	The greater amount is taken		2,580
Total benefits 2016/17			3,300

Note that the value of the asset when first provided to any employee is used rather than the value when first provided to John.

44 C £8,540

	£	£
Basic benefit		
Annual value		8,000
Market value	93,000	
Less limit	(75,000)	
	18,000	
Additional benefit £18,000 × 3%		540
Total benefits 2016/17		8,540

The value of the accommodation when occupied by Jonas is not relevant as fewer than six years have elapsed since purchase when Jonas first moves in.

45 A £55,000

	£
2016/17 annual allowance	40,000
2015/16 annual allowance £(40,000 − 25,000)	15,000
	55,000

The annual allowance for 2013/14 and 2014/15 are not available as Troy was not a member of a pension scheme in those years.

46 D £300

	£
Rental income £150 × 52	7,800
Less rent a room limit	(7,500)
	300

Luke should elect for the 'alternative basis' under rent a room relief, rather the normal basis which would give taxable property business income of £(150 − 20) = £130 × 52 = £6,760.

47 B £3,800

The replacement of an equivalent model of sofa is allowable as a deduction. It is restricted by the amount of proceeds realised by selling the first sofa.
£(4,000 − 200) £3,800

48 B £1,640

The grant of a new short lease and the purchase of freehold premises are capital and therefore the legal fees on them are not deductible.

The legal fees concerning the employment contract and debt collection are deductible £(720 + £920) = £1,640

49 D £5,400

Depreciation and customer entertaining are not deductible and must be added back. The amount added back is therefore £(3,000 + 2,400) = £5,400.

Staff entertaining is fully deductible (the £150 limit applies to the taxable benefit for the employees).

50 C £20,375

	£
Cash sales	41,000
Invoice sales £(4,000 − 1,500)	2,500
Less: Cash expenses	(20,200)
Motoring expenses 6,500 × 45p	(2,925)
Taxable trading income 2016/17	20,375

51   A   £968

The motor car will be treated as a special rate item and will therefore be entitled to writing down allowance at 8%. The allowance will be restricted because of the private use. The total amount due is:
£22,000 × 8% × 4,950/9,000 = £968

52   C   £84,208

	AIA £	Main pool £	Allowances £
p/e 5.4.17			
Plant	95,000		
AIA £200,000 × 5/12	(83,333)		83,333
Transfer to pool	11,667	11,667	
WDA @ 18% × 5/12		(875)	875
TWDV c/f		10,792	
Allowances			84,208

CBE style OTQ bank – Income tax and NIC liabilities 3

53   £400

	Main pool £	Allowances £
y/e 5.4.17		
TWDV b/f	12,000	
Disposal (limit to cost)	(11,600)	
	400	
WDA – small pool	(400)	400
TWDV c/f	0	

54   6 April 2016 to 5 April 2017

2016/17 is the second year of trading. There is no accounting date ending in this year so the actual basis applies.

55   £13,000

First tax year (2014/15): Actual basis 1.2.15 to 5.4.15

Second tax year (2015/16): First 12 months of trading 1.2.15 to 31.1.16

Third tax year (2016/17): Current year basis 1.12.15 to 30.11.16

Periods of overlap 1.2.15 to 5.4.15 and 1.12.15 to 31.1.16

	£
2/10 × £30,000	6,000
2/12 × £42,000	7,000
	13,000

56   £19,000

	£
y/e 31.12.16	18,000
p/e 31.3.17	3,000
Less overlap profits	(2,000)
	19,000

57

2015/16	£3,000

2016/17	£9,600

	£
2015/16 Actual basis 1.1.16 to 5.4.16	
£9,000 × 3/9	3,000
2016/17 First 12 months 1.1.16 to 31.12.16	
£(9,000 – 3,000)	6,000
£14,400 × 3/12	3,600
	9,600

58   £6,000

	2015/16	2016/17
	£	£
Trading profit	16,000	0
Investment income	3,000	3,000
Total income	19,000	3,000
Less loss relief	(19,000)	(0)
Net income	0	3,000
Less personal allowance	0	(3,000)
Net income	0	0

Loss to carry forward to 2017/18 is £(25,000 – 19,000) = £6,000

A claim should not be made to set the loss against investment income in 2016/17 since this is covered by the personal allowance for that year. It is not possible to restrict the set off of the loss in 2015/16 to preserve the personal allowance.

59   £44,150

	£
1.8.15 to 31.8.15 1/12 × £96,000 × 1/2	4,000
1.9.15 to 31.7.16 Salary 11/12 × £9,000	8,250
1.9.15 to 31.7.16 Profit share	
(11/12 × £[96,000 – 8,250]) × 2/5	31,900
	44,150

60   Robin and Stuart £48,000 Tania £5,600

Robin and Stuart

CYB y/e 31.12.16 £96,000 × 1/2 = £48,000

Tania

Actual basis 1.1.17 – 5.4.17 £112,000 × 1/5 × 3/12 = £5,600

61   £160

	£
Class 2 contributions 14 × £2.80	39
Class 4 contributions £(9,400 – 8,060) × 9%	121
Total contributions	160

62 £310

Class 4 contributions £([13,500 – 2,000] – 8,060) × 9%

$£$

310

CBE style OT case – Ann, Basil and Chloe

Text references. Pensions are covered in Chapter 5. The computation of taxable income and the income tax liability are dealt with in Chapter 2.

Top tips. Remember that higher rate tax relief for personal pension contributions made by higher rate taxpayers is given by increasing the basic rate limit.

Easy marks. There were some easy marks in question 65 for working out a basic tax liability.

63 1 and 2

Individuals can always make gross pension contributions of £3,600 in 2016/17 even if they do no have any relevant earnings in that tax year. Relevant earnings relate both to contributions to personal pension schemes and to occupational pension schemes.

Unused relevant earnings cannot be carried forward. Relevant earnings include trading income, employment income and income from furnished holiday lettings.

64

Employer contributions do not count towards the annual allowance		**FALSE**
The annual allowance can be carried forward for three years to the extent that it is unused in the tax year	**TRUE**	
The annual allowance is available even if the individual is not a member of a pension scheme in a tax year and so can be carried forward		**FALSE**
If tax-relievable pension contributions exceed the annual allowance, there is a charge to income tax	**TRUE**	

65 £16,200

The available annual allowance is £(40,000 + 20,000) = £60,000 and so there is no annual allowance charge for the tax year 2016/17.

Tax £81,000 (32,000 + 49,000) × 20%   £16,200

66 £6,000

The annual allowance must be tapered because Basil's adjusted income before any deduction for the pension contribution is more than £150,000. Basil is still a higher rate taxpayer because his higher rate limit is lifted by the gross pension contribution.

Annual allowance
£40,000 – [½ × £(160,000 – 150,000)]   £35,000

Excess pension contribution over annual allowance
£(50,000 – 35,000) @ 40%   £6,000

67 £720

Maximum personal pension contribution is £3,600 since Chloe has no relevant earnings. The pension tax relief is therefore £3,600 × 20% = £720. This relief will have been given at source. The remaining £4,600 contribution is not given tax relief.

Ae, Bee, Cae, and Eu

Text references. Partnerships are covered in Chapter 11. Assessable trading income is dealt with in Chapter 9 and capital allowances are covered in Chapter 8.

Top tips. Remember that there is no annual investment allowance nor writing down allowance in the final period of account.

Easy marks. There were easy marks in question 70 for working out the trading income assessment.

68 C £32,500

	£
2015/16	
Second year, short period of account (first 12 months trading)	
1 July 2014 to 30 April 2015	
£54,000 × ½	27,000
1 May 2015 to 30 June 2015	
£66,000 × ½ × 2/12	5,500
	32,500

69 D £21,750

	£
Y/e 30 April 2017 – Cae joined 1 July 2016	
1 July 2016 to 30 April 2017	
£87,000 × 10/12 = 72,500 × 1/3	24,167
First year	
Actual basis 1 July 2016 – 5 April 2017	
£24,167 × 9/10	21,750

70 D £61,200

	£
2017/18	
CYB y/e 30.6.17 Trading income	62,775
Less CAs	(1,575)
	61,200

71	A	£3,108	
			£

p/e 30.9.18

	£
TWDV c/f	5,883
Addition	2,400
Disposal	(5,175)
BA	3,108

72	B	£57,908

2017/18

	£
y/e 30.6.17 £(57,600 – 1,292)	56,308
p/e 30.9.17 £(14,400 – 3,000)	11,400
Less overlap profits	(9,800)
	57,908

Fang and Hong

> **Text references.** The basis of assessment for sole traders is covered in Chapter 9. Relief for pre-trading expenditure is described in Chapter 7 and capital allowances in Chapter 8. Trading losses are dealt with in Chapter 10.
>
> **Top tips.** It is important to identify the relevant tax years when dealing with the basis of assessment.
>
> **Easy marks.** The identification of relief for overlap profits in question 74 should have been easy marks.

73	C	2014/15 £30,640, 2015/16 £45,960

Tax year	Basis of assessment	£
2014/15	Actual – 1 August 2014 to 5 April 2015	
	£45,960 × 8/12	30,640
2015/16	12 months to accounting date in tax year	
	y/e 31 July 2015	45,960

74	B	Against trading income on cessation.

75	D	Trading expenditure: treated as incurred on 1 August 2014, Computer equipment: addition for capital allowances purposes based on its market value at 1 August 2014

76	B	£31,000

	£
Trading profit	29,700
Less trading loss brought forward	(2,600)
	27,100
Property business profit	3,900
	31,000
Less trading loss carried back	(31,000)
Net income	0

77   A   The trading loss is first set against general income of the tax year 2015/16 and only any excess loss is set against chargeable gains of that year and The amount of chargeable gains for the tax year 2015/16 is computed ignoring the annual exempt amount for the purposes of this relief.

Both capital losses of the tax year 2015/16 and brought forward losses are taken into account for the purposes of this relief. Hong cannot specify the amount to be set against chargeable gains, so her annual exempt amount for the tax year 2015/16 is not wasted.

CBE style OT case – Chi

78   £10,400

	£
Trading income/net income	53,000
Less personal allowance	(11,000)
Taxable income	42,000
Tax	
£32,000 @ 20%	6,400
£10,000 (42,000 – 32,000) @ 40%	4,000
	10,400

79   £3,345

	£
£(43,000 – 8,060) = £34,940 @ 9%	3,145
£(53,000 – 43,000) = £10,000 @ 2%	200
Total Class 4 contributions	3,345

80   2 and 3

The trader can deduct capital expenditure on plant and machinery (other than motor cars) as business expenses rather than using capital allowances. A trader can start to use the cash basis if his receipts for the tax year do not exceed the value added tax (VAT) registration threshold.

Accounts can be prepared to any date in the tax year as for the normal basis of assessment. Cash basis traders cannot offset losses against other income or gains, they can only carry them forward against profits of the cash basis trade.

81   £5,300

	£
10,000 miles @ 45p	4,500
3,200 miles @ 25p	800
	5,300

Capital allowances are not relevant, since purchases of equipment are deducted as an expense. The running and capital costs of owning a motor car are replaced by the deduction based on statutory mileage allowances.

82   Revenue £70,900, other expenses £7,300

Revenue £(72,500 – 1,600)	£70,900
Other expenses £(8,200 – 900)	£7,300

83 Michael and Sean

> **Text references.** Chapter 10 deals with trading losses.
>
> **Top tips.** Remember that if a taxpayer claims loss relief against general income, the benefit of the personal allowance may be lost.
>
> **Easy marks.** There were some easy marks for identifying the possible loss relief claims.

Michael

The loss of £25,230 for 2015/16 can be claimed against general income for the three preceding years, under early years loss relief, earliest year first, since it is incurred in the first four years of trading.

The loss relief claim will therefore be £19,365 in 2012/13 and £(25,230 – 19,365) = £5,865 in 2013/14.

For 2012/13 this will waste Michael's personal allowance, with the balance of the claim of £(19,365 – 11,000) = £8,365 saving income tax at the basic rate of 20%.

For 2013/14 Michael has income of £(50,095 – 11,000 – 32,000) = £7,095 subject to income tax at the higher rate of 40%, so the claim of £5,365 will save tax at the higher rate.

Alternatively, Michael could have carried the trading loss forward against future trading profits, but the trading profit of £9,665 for 2016/17 is covered by the personal allowance, and there is no information regarding future trading profits.

Tutorial note

A claim for loss relief against general income for 2015/16 and/or 2014/15 is not possible since Michael does not have any income for either of these years.

Sean

The unused overlap profits brought forward are added to the loss for the year ended 31 December 2016, so the total loss for 2016/17 is £(23,100 + 3,600) = £26,700.

The whole of the loss can be claimed as a terminal loss since it is for the final 12 months of trading. The claim is against trading income for the year of the loss (2016/17 – nil) and the three preceding years, latest first.

The terminal loss claim will therefore be £3,700 in 2015/16, £18,900 in 2014/15 and £(26,700 – 3,700 – 18,900) = £4,100 in 2013/14.

The property business profits are sufficient to utilise Sean's personal allowance for each year, so the loss relief claims will save income tax at the basic rate of 20%.

BPP
LEARNING MEDIA

Alternatively, Sean could have initially claimed loss relief against his general income for 2016/17 and/or 2015/16, but this would have wasted his personal allowance in those years.

84 Samantha

Text references. Chapter 10 deals with trading losses.

Top tips. You should use the standard layout for losses: set up the columns and lines required and then slot in the numbers. A loss memorandum is also useful as a double check that you have used the losses correctly.

Easy marks. There were easy marks for setting out the trading income and gains stated in the question and using the personal allowance and annual exempt amount.

Marking scheme

		Marks
(a)	Rate of tax	1
	Timing of relief	1
	Waste of personal allowance/annual exempt amount	1
		3
(b)	Trading income	½
	Trading loss relief carried forward	1
	Building society interest	½
	Trading loss relief against general income	1
	Personal allowance	½
	Gains	½
	Capital loss relief carried forward	1
	Trading loss relief against gains	1
	Annual exempt amount	1
		7
		10

(a) Factors that will influence an individual's choice of loss relief claim are:

(i) The rate of income tax or capital gains tax at which relief will be obtained, with preference being given to income charged at the additional rate of 45%, then the higher rate of 40%.

(ii) The timing of the relief obtained, with a claim against general income/capital gains of the current year or preceding year resulting in earlier relief than a carry forward claim against future trading profits.

(iii) The extent to which the income tax personal allowance and the capital gains tax annual exempt amount will be wasted by using a claim against general income/capital gains.

(b) **Samantha – Taxable income**

	2014/15 £	2015/16 £	2016/17 £	2017/18 £
Trading income	7,290	42,600	0	16,285
Less trading loss relief carried forward	(0)	(0)	(0)	(7,000)
	7,290	42,600	0	9,285
Building society interest	0	6,100	3,800	2,130
	7,290	48,700	3,800	11,415
Less trading loss relief against general income (N)	(0)	(48,700)	(0)	(0)
Net income	7,290	0	3,800	11,415
Less personal allowance	(7,290)	(0)	(3,800)	(11,000)
Taxable income	0	0	0	415

Samantha – Taxable gains

	2014/15 £	2015/16 £	2016/17 £	2017/18 £
Gains	21,100	23,300	0	14,100
Less trading loss relief against gains (note)	(0)	(23,300)	(0)	(0)
	21,100	0	0	14,100
Less capital loss carried forward	(0)	(0)	(0)	(3,000)
	21,100	0	0	11,100
Less annual exempt amount	(11,100)	(0)	(0)	(11,100)
Taxable gains	10,000	0	0	0

Note.

Loss relief has been claimed against general income and gains for 2015/16 since this gives relief at the earliest date and at the highest rates of tax. No claim should be made to set the loss against general income in 2016/17 since this is already covered by the personal allowance for that year.

Trading loss memorandum

	£
Loss 2016/17	79,000
Less used 2015/16 (income)	(48,700)
used 2015/16 (gains	(23,300)
Available for c/f	7,000
Less used 2017/18	(7,000)
Loss unused	0

85 Martin

Text references. Chapter 9 deals with basis of assessment.

Top tips. It is important to follow the requirements carefully as they will lead you through the computations so that you can reach a conclusion for part (e).

Easy marks. You should have been able to identify that the actual basis applied for the tax year 2015/16 whichever accounting date was chosen.

			Marks
(a)	p/e 5 April 2016	½	
	y/e 5 April 2017	1	
	y/e 5 April 2018	½	
			2
(b)	2015/16	1	
	2016/17	½	
	2017/18	½	
			2
(c)	p/e 30 April 2016	½	
	y/e 30 April 2017	1½	
			2
(d)	2015/16	1	
	2016/17	1	
	2017/18	1	
			3
(e)	Explanation		1
			10

(a) **Martin's taxable profits for the periods of account ending 5 April 2016, 5 April 2017 and 5 April 2018**

Period of account	Working	Taxable profits £
1.1.16 – 5.4.16	£3,000 × 3	9,000
6.4.16 – 5.4.17	£3,000 × 3 + £4,000 × 6 + £5,000 × 3	48,000
6.4.17 – 5.4.18	£5,000 × 12	60,000

(b) **Martin's taxable income for the tax years 2015/16, 2016/17 and 2017/18 if he chooses 5 April**

Year	Basis period	Taxable profits £
2015/16	1.1.16 – 5.4.16 – actual basis	9,000
2016/17	6.4.16 – 5.4.17 – current year basis	48,000
2017/18	6.4.17 – 5.4.18 - current year basis	60,000
Total		117,000

(c) **Martin's taxable profits for the periods of account ending 30 April 2016 and 30 April 2017**

Period of account	Working	Taxable profits £
1.1.16 – 30.4.16	£3,000 × 4	12,000
1.5.16 – 30.4.17	£3,000 × 2 + £4,000 × 6 + £5,000 × 4	50,000

(d) **Martin's taxable income for the tax years 2015/16, 2016/17 and 2017/18 if he chooses 30 April**

Period of account	Basis period	Working	Taxable profits £
2015/16	1.1.16 – 5.4.16: actual basis	£12,000 × 3/4	9,000
2016/17	1.1.16 – 31.12.16: first 12 months	£12,000 + £50,000 × 8/12	45,333
2017/18	1.5.16 – 30.4.17: current year basis		50,000
Total			104,333

(e) If Martin chooses 30 April as his accounting date, £(117,000 – 104,333) = £12,667 less trading income will be taxable in the tax years 2015/16, 2016/17 and 2017/18 than if he chooses 5 April.

86 Lucy

Text references. Chapter 2 deals with the income tax computation. Chapter 3 covers employment income and Chapter 7 covers trading income. National insurance contributions are dealt with in Chapter 12.

Top tips. Travel from home to work is not an allowable expense for tax purposes for an employee.

Easy marks. There were some easy marks for basic income tax and NIC computations for both the employment and self-employment work arrangements.

Marking scheme

	Marks
Employee	
Income tax payable	1½
Class 1 NIC	1½
Income	1
Self employed	
Income tax payable	2
Classes 2 and 4 NIC	2
Income	1½
Determination of working pattern with higher disposable income	½
	10

Disposable income if Lucy is employee

	£
Income tax	
Employment income/net income	35,000
Less personal allowance	(11,000)
Taxable income	24,000
Income tax @ 20%	4,800

	£
Class 1 NIC	
Salary	35,000
Less primary threshold	(8,060)
	26,940
Class 1 NIC @ 12%	3,233

	£
Disposable income	
Salary	35,000
Less income tax	(4,800)
Class 1 NIC	(3,233)
travel costs	(1,500)
	25,467

Disposable income if Lucy is self employed

	£
Income tax	
Fees received	35,000
Less fixed rate mileage 4,600 @ 45p per mile	(2,070)
Trading income/net income	32,930
Less personal allowance	(11,000)
Taxable income	21,930
Income tax @ 20%	4,386

	£	£
Classes 2 and 4 NIC		
Class 2 NIC £2.80 × 52		146
Class 4 NIC		
Trading income	32,930	
Less lower limit	(8,060)	
	24,870	
Class 4 NIC @ 9%		2,238
Total NICs		2,384

	£
Disposable income	
Fees received	35,000
Less income tax	(4,386)
Classes 2 and 4 NICs	(2,384)
travel costs 4,600 @ 40p	(1,840)
	26,390

Lucy will therefore have a higher disposable income by £(26,390 – 25,467) = £923 if she undertakes the self employed work arrangement.

87 Daniel, Francine and Gregor

Text references. Partnerships are the subject of Chapter 11. Employment benefits are covered in Chapter 4. Trading losses are dealt with in Chapter 10.

Top tips. In part (a) it is important to realise that Daniel is treated as commencing a trade and therefore his trading income assessment for 2016/17 is on an actual basis. In part (c), remember that a trading loss can be relieved against total income in the tax year of the loss and the preceding tax year and can also be extended against chargeable gains.

Easy marks. There were some easy marks in part (b) for dealing with the interest paid by Francine on her loan.

Examiner's comments. This question had three separate scenarios, of which the first and third were fairly well answered and the second was less well answered.

The first scenario in part (a) involved three individuals who were in partnership, preparing accounts to 31 October annually. A fourth partner joined mid-way through an accounting period and the requirement was to calculate the new partner's trading income assessment for his first tax year as a partner. Although many candidates demonstrated satisfactory knowledge here – a large number wasted a significant amount of time by also performing calculations for the three existing partners, despite the requirement only concerning the new partner.

The second scenario in part (b) involved an employee who was provided with a beneficial loan part-way through the tax year. The loan was subsequently increased before the end of the tax year. The basic idea behind this question was that candidates had to calculate the benefit using the average method (they were instructed to use this method), with the interest actually paid to the employer being calculated on a strict basis. However, many candidates failed to read the requirement carefully and thus ignored the instruction to use the average basis when calculating the taxable benefit. In addition, many candidates failed to use proper workings and accordingly became confused mid-way through their calculations.

The third scenario in part (c) involved a self-employed taxpayer who had made a trading loss in the tax year. On the assumption that the taxpayer relieved his trading loss as early as possible, the requirement was to calculate the amount of trading loss carried forward to the next tax year. Once again, many candidates' workings were not well-laid out. Many candidates prepared tax computations for both years for which figures were provided, before realising that all that was required was a loss memorandum. The set off of the brought forward capital loss against the current year chargeable gain was also often overlooked.

Marking scheme

			Marks
(a)	1 May 2016 to 31 October 2016	1½	
	1 November 2016 to 5 April 2017	1½	
			3
(b)	Average loan	1½	
	Interest paid	1½	
			3
(c)	2015/16 claim against total income	1	
	2016/17 claim against total income	1	
	claim against chargeable gain	1½	
	Loss carried forward	½	4
			10

(a)   **Daniel – Trading income assessment 2016/17**

	£
1 May 2016 to 31 October 2016	
£96,000 × ¼ × 6/12	12,000
1 November 2016 to 5 April 2017	
£180,000 × ¼ × 5/12	18,750
	30,750

Tutorial note

Daniel joined as a partner on 1 May 2016, so the commencement rules apply to him for 2016/17. The basis period is the 11-month period from 1 May 2016 to 5 April 2017.

(b)   **Francine – Beneficial loan 2016/17**

	£	£
$\dfrac{96,000 + (96,000 + 14,000)}{2} \times 3\% \times 8/12$		2,060
Interest paid £96,000 at 1.5% × 2/12	240	
£110,000 at 1.5% × 6/12	825	
		(1,065)
Taxable benefit		995

(c)   **Gregor – Trading loss carried forward**

	£
Trading loss	68,800
2015/16 – Claim against total income	
£(14,700 + 4,600 + 1,300)	(20,600)
2016/17 – Claim against total income	(900)
– Claim against chargeable gain (working)	(14,500)
Loss carried forward to 2017/18	32,800

Working – Claim against chargeable gain

The loss relief claim against the chargeable gain is restricted to £14,500 (chargeable gain of £17,400 less the capital loss brought forward of £2,900).

Tutorial note

Gregor can claim loss relief against his total income and chargeable gains for 2015/16 and 2016/17.

88 George

Text references. Employment income is covered in Chapter 3. National insurance contributions are dealt with in Chapter 12.

Top tips. Use your tax tables for all the national insurance limits and rates.

Easy marks. There were some easy marks in part (a) for working out the income tax liability and in part (c) the comparison of the national insurance contributions gets some easy credit even if you have made errors in the main calculations.

Examiner's comments. In part (a), most candidates missed the fact that the taxpayer would not incur any significant expenses in respect of the contract and would not be taking any significant financial risk. Many candidates incorrectly gave the payment of tax under PAYE for the previous year as an indicator.

Part (b) was well answered, but many candidates produced extremely long answers for what should have been a simple set of workings. For example, the capital allowance was simply a 100% annual investment allowance on the purchase of a new asset and did not require a detailed capital allowances computation.

In part (c), as regards the payment aspect, most candidates just referred to PAYE without any further relevant detail. Very few appreciated that the due date under the self-employed basis was simply 31 January following the tax year – payments on account not being required because the previous year's tax liability was collected under PAYE.

Marking scheme

				Marks
(a)	Factors indicative of employment (½ mark each)			2
(b)	Income		½	
	Capital allowances		1	
	Personal allowance		½	
	Income tax		½	
	Class 2		½	
	Class 4		1	
				4
(c)	(i)	PAYE	1	
		Self-assessment	1	
				2
	(ii)	Class 1	1½	
		Additional NIC	½	
				2
				10

(a) The contract is for a relatively long period of time.
George is required to do the work personally.
Xpee plc exercises control over George via the weekly meetings and instructions.
George will not incur any significant expenses in respect of the contract.
George will only be working for Xpee plc.
George is not taking any significant financial risk.

Note. Four items only required.

(b) **George – Income tax liability 2016/17**

	£
Income	40,000
Capital allowances – annual investment allowance	(3,600)
Trading income	36,400
Less personal allowance	(11,000)
Taxable income	25,400

Income tax
£25,400 × 20%   5,080

George – National insurance contributions 2016/17

Class 2 national insurance contributions will be £146 (52 × £2.80).

Class 4 national insurance contributions will be £2,551 (28,340 (36,400 – 8,060) × 9%).

(c) (i) If George is treated as employed in respect of his contract with Xpee plc, then the company will be required to deduct tax under PAYE every time that George is paid during 2016/17.

If treated as self-employed, George's income tax liability for 2016/17 would not be payable until 31 January 2018.

(ii) If George is treated as employed in respect of his contract with Xpee plc, then his class 1 national insurance contributions for 2016/17 will be £3,833 (31,940 (40,000 – 8,060) at 12%).

The additional amount of national insurance contributions which he will suffer for 2016/17 is therefore £1,136 (3,833 – 146 – 2,551).

Tutorial note:

For income tax purposes, capital allowances will reduce employment income in the same way that they are deducted in calculating the trading profit. However, there is no deduction for capital allowances when it comes to calculating class 1 national insurance contributions.

89 Joe (B)

Text references. Chapters 3 and 4 deal with employment income and employment benefits.

Top tips. Don't forget to show that you know if a benefit is exempt by including it in your computation with a zero.

Easy marks. There were some easy marks for basic employment benefit computations such as the living accommodation.

Marking scheme

		Marks
Salary – Firstly plc		½
Occupational pension scheme contributions		1
Bonus		½
Salary – Secondly plc		½
Personal pension contributions		½
Beneficial loan	– Average method	1½
	– Strict method	1½
Workplace nursery		1
Home entertainment system	– Use	1½
	– Acquisition	1½
Living accommodation		2
Furniture		1½
Running costs		½
Childcare vouchers		1
		15

Joe – Employment income 2016/17

	£
Salary – Firstly plc (6,360 × 9)	57,240
Pension contributions (57,240 × 6%) (N2)	(3,434)
	53,806
Bonus (N1)	0
Salary – Secondly plc (6,565 × 3)	19,695
Beneficial loan (W1)	1,775
Workplace nursery (N3)	0
Home entertainment system – Use (W2)	660
– Acquisition (W2)	3,860
Living accommodation (W3)	6,750
Furniture (W3)	816
Running costs	1,900
Childcare vouchers (W4)	936
Employment income	90,198

Workings

1   *Loan benefit*

     The benefit of the beneficial loan using the average method is £1,900 ((120,000 + 70,000)/2 = 95,000 at 3% × 8/12).

     Using the strict method the benefit is £1,775 ((120,000 at 3% × 3/12) + (70,000 at 3% × 5/12)).

     Joe will therefore elect to have the taxable benefit calculated according to the strict method.

2   *Home entertainment system*

     The benefit for the use of the home entertainment system is £660 (4,400 × 20% × 9/12).

     The benefit for the acquisition of the home entertainment system is the market value of £3,860, as this is greater than £3,740 (4,400 – 660).

3   *Living accommodation and furniture*

     The benefit for the living accommodation is the higher of the annual value of £2,600 (10,400 × 3/12) and the rent paid of £6,750 (2,250 × 3).

     The benefit for the use of the furniture is £816 (16,320 × 20% × 3/12).

4   *Childcare vouchers*

     The exemption for childcare vouchers is £28 per week since Joe is a higher rate employee. The benefit for the provision of the vouchers is therefore £936 ((100 – 28) = 72 × 13).

Notes

1   The bonus of £12,000 will have been treated as being received during 2015/16 as Joe became entitled to it during that tax year.

2   The personal pension contributions will increase Joe's basic rate tax limit and are therefore irrelevant as regards the calculation of employment income.

3   The provision of a place in a workplace nursery does not give rise to a taxable benefit.

90 Sammi

Text references. Chapter 4 deals with employment benefits. National insurance contributions are covered in Chapter 12. Computing taxable total profits and computing corporation tax are dealt with in Chapter 19.

Top tips. Use headings to show the examination team which of two options you are dealing with.

Easy marks. There were easy marks for computing the car benefit and computing the national insurance contributions.

		Marks
(a)	**Company motor car**	
	Car benefit	2
	Income tax	1
	NIC implications	½
	Additional director's remuneration	
	Income tax	½
	Class 1 NIC	1
		5

(b) **Company motor car**
Class 1A NIC 1
Allowable leasing costs 1
Corporation tax saving 1
Additional director's remuneration
Class 1 NIC 1
Corporation tax saving 1
                                                                                    5

(c) **Sammi**
Director's remuneration   – Net of tax income 1
                             – Overall result 1
Conclusion 1
Smark Ltd
Director's remuneration 1
Conclusion 1
                                                                                    5
                                                                                   15

(a) **Sammi – Company motor car**

The list price used in the car benefit calculation is £80,000. The relevant percentage is restricted to a maximum of 37% (16% + 41% (300 – 95 = 205/5) = 57%).

Sammi will therefore be taxed on a car benefit of £29,600 (80,000 x 37%).

Sammi's marginal rate of income tax is 45%, so her additional income tax liability for 2016/17 will be £13,320 (29,600 at 45%).

There are no national insurance contribution implications for Sammi.

Tutorial note

There is no fuel benefit as fuel is not provided for private journeys.

Sammi – Additional director's remuneration

Sammi's additional income tax liability for 2016/17 will be £12,150 (27,000 at 45%).

The additional employee's Class 1 NIC liability will be £540 (27,000 at 2%).

Tutorial note

Sammi's director's remuneration exceeds the upper earnings limit of £43,000, so her additional class 1 NIC liability is at the rate of 2%.

(b) **Smark Ltd – Company motor car**

The employer's Class 1A NIC liability in respect of the car benefit will be £4,085 (29,600 at 13.8%).

The motor car has a CO_2 emission rate in excess of 130 grams per kilometre, so only £23,486 (27,630 less 15%) of the leasing costs are allowed for corporation tax purposes.

Smark Ltd's corporation tax liability will be reduced by £5,514 (23,486 + 4,085 = 27,571 at 20%).

Smark Ltd – Additional director's remuneration

The employer's Class 1 NIC liability in respect of the additional director's remuneration will be £3,726 (27,000 at 13.8%).

Smark Ltd's corporation tax liability will be reduced by £6,145 (27,000 + 3,726 = 30,726 at 20%).

(c) **More beneficial alternative for Sammi**

Under the director's remuneration alternative, Sammi will receive additional net of tax income of £14,310 (27,000 – 12,150 – 540).

However, she will have to lease the motor car at a cost of £27,630, so the overall result is additional expenditure of £13,320 (27,630 – 14,310).

If Sammi is provided with a company motor car then she will have an additional tax liability of £13,320, so she is in exactly the same financial position.

Most beneficial alternative for Smark Ltd

The net of tax cost of paying additional director's remuneration is £24,581 (27,000 + 3,726 – 6,145).

This is more beneficial than the alternative of providing a company motor car since this has a net of tax cost of £26,201 (27,630 + 4,085 – 5,514).

91 Simon

> **Text references.** The badges of trade are discussed in Chapter 7 which also deals with the computation of trading profit. Chapter 2 deals with the computation of taxable income and the income tax computation. Chapter 13 covers computation of chargeable gains for individuals.
>
> **Top tips.** Think carefully about what costs are allowable as part of trading expenses in part (b) and, alternatively, as part of the cost of the asset in part (c). Not all the expenses are allowable in both cases.
>
> **Easy marks.** The question gave you the badges of trade in part (a) so it should have been easy marks to comment on them.

			Marks
(a)	Subject matter	½	
	Length of ownership	½	
	Frequency of transactions	½	
	Work done	½	
	Circumstances of realisation	½	
	Profit motive	½	
			3
(b)	Income	½	
	Acquisition of house	½	
	Legal fees on acquisition	½	
	Renovation costs	½	
	Legal fees on sale	½	
	Loan interest	1	
	Personal allowance	½	
	Income tax liability	1	
	Class 4 NICs	1½	
	Class 2 NICs	1½	
			8
(c)	Sale proceeds	½	
	Legal fees on sale	½	
	Cost of house	½	
	Legal fees on acquisition	½	
	Enhancement expenditure	½	
	Loan interest – not allowable	½	
	Annual exempt amount	½	
	Capital gains tax liability	½	
			4
			15

(a)   **Badges of trade**

Subject matter

Some assets are commonly held as investments for their intrinsic value, for example an individual may buy shares for dividend income produced by them or may buy a painting to enjoy it as a work of art. A subsequent disposal of an investment asset usually produces a capital gain. Where the subject matter of a transaction is not an investment asset, any profit on resale is usually a trading profit.

Length of ownership

If items purchased are sold soon afterwards, this indicates trading transactions.

Frequency of transactions

Transactions which may, in isolation, be of a capital nature will be interpreted as trading transactions where their frequency indicates the carrying on of a trade.

Work done

When work is done to make an asset more marketable, or steps are taken to find purchasers, this is likely to be indicative of trading.

Circumstances of realisation

A forced sale, for example to realise funds for an emergency, is not likely to be treated as trading.

Motive

The absence of a profit motive will not necessarily preclude a tax charge as trading income, but its presence is a strong indication that a person is trading.

(b)   **Simon – Income tax and NICs for 2016/17 if trading**

	£	£
Income		260,000
Less: costs incurred		
house	127,000	
legal fees on acquisition	1,800	
renovation	50,000	
legal fees on sale	2,600	
loan interest		
£150,000 × 6% × 4/12	3,000	
		(184,400)
Trading income/Net income		75,600
Less personal allowance		(11,000)
Taxable income		64,600
Income tax		
£32,000 @ 20%		6,400
£32,600 @ 40%		13,040
Income tax liability		19,440
Class 4 NICs		
£(43,000 – 8,060) = £34,940 @ 9%		3,145
£(75,600 – 43,000) = £32,600 @ 2%		652
Total Class 4 NICs		3,797
Class 2 NICs		
£2.80 × 19 weeks (N)		53

Note. Marks were awarded for any reasonable attempt at calculating the number of weeks. ½ mark was deducted if 52 weeks were used.

(c)   **Simon – Capital gains tax 2016/17 if not trading**

	£	£
Sale proceeds		260,000
Less legal fees on sale		(2,600)
Net proceeds of sale		257,400
Less: cost of house	127,000	
legal fees on acquisition	1,800	
renovation	50,000	
loan interest (N)	0	
		(178,800)
Chargeable gain		78,600
Less annual exempt amount		(11,100)
Taxable gain		67,500
Capital gains tax		
£32,000 @ 18%		5,760
£(67,500 – 32,000) = 35,500 @ 28%		9,940
Capital gains tax liability		15,700

Note. The loan interest is a revenue expense and so is not allowable in computing the chargeable gain.

92 Na

Text references. Assessment of trading profits is covered in Chapter 9. Adjustment of trading profit is in Chapter 7. The computation of taxable income and the income tax liability is dealt with in Chapter 2.

Top tips. As you deal with each adjustment to profit, tick it off in the question – this method should ensure that you do not miss out any item and thus lose marks.

Easy marks. The computation of the income tax liability in part (c) should have been easy marks.

		Marks
(a)	First tax year trading profits	1
	Second tax year trading profits	1½
	Third tax year trading profits	½
	Overlap profits	2
		5
(b)	Net profit	½
	Depreciation	½
	Motor expenses	1
	Legal fees	½
	Property expenses	1
	Own consumption	1
	Fine	½
	Trade subscription	½
	Private telephone	1
	Capital allowances	½
		7
(c)	Trading profit	½
	Individual savings account interest (exempt)	½
	Dividends	½
	Personal allowance	½
	Income tax liability	1
		3
		15

(a) **Na – Trading profits 2013/14, 2014/15 and 2015/16**

Year	Basis period	Working	Taxable Profits £
2013/14	1.1.14 – 5.4.14	£25,200 × 3/6	12,600
2014/15	1.1.14 – 31.12.14 (N)	£25,200 + £21,600 × 6/12	36,000
2015/16	1.7.14 – 30.6.15		21,600

Note: because the accounting period ending in the second tax year is less than twelve months, the basis period for that year is the first twelve months of trading.

Overlap profits

Overlap period	Working	Overlap profits £
1.1.14 – 5.4.14	£25,200 × 3/6	12,600
1.7.14 – 31.12.14	£21,600 × 6/12	10,800

(b) **Na – Tax adjusted trading profit for year ended 30 June 2016**

	£	£
Net profit		23,000
Add: depreciation	2,635	
motor expenses – private use 7,000/8,000 × £2,200	1,925	
professional fees – lease (N)	1,260	
property expenses – private use 1/3 × £12,900	4,300	
purchases – goods taken for own use (selling price)	450	
other expenses – fine	480	
other expenses – trade subscription	0	
		11,050
		34,050
Less: telephone – business use 20% × £1,200	240	
capital allowances	810	(1,050)
Tax adjusted trading profit		33,000

Note. Legal expenses relating to the **grant** of a short lease are not allowable.

(c) **Na – Income tax liability for 2016/17**

	Non-savings income £	Dividend income £	Total £
Trading income (part (b))	33,000		
UK dividends		1,200	
Net income (ISA interest is exempt)	33,000	1,200	34,200
Less: personal allowance	(11,000)		
Taxable income	22,000	1,200	23,600

	£
Income tax	
Non-savings income	
£22,000 @ 20%	4,400
Dividend income	
£1,200 @ 0%	0
Tax liability	4,400

93 Bayle (A)

> **Text references.** Adjustment of profit is dealt with in Chapter 7. Employment income is covered in Chapter 3. Taxable income and the income tax liability are dealt with in Chapter 2.
>
> **Top tips.** You must start your adjustment of profit computation with the net profit. Don't forget to include any items which do not require adjustment (such as the impairment loss) with a zero.
>
> **Easy marks.** There were plenty of easy marks for the adjustment of profit computation with standard items such as gifts to customers which should have been well-known.

Marking scheme

			Marks
(a)	Impairment loss	½	
	Gifts to customers	1	
	Donations to political parties	½	
	Lease of motor car	1	
	Personal tax advice	½	
	Property expenses	1	
	Parking fines	½	
	Professional subscription	½	
	Golf membership fee	½	
			6
(b)	Trading profits	½	
	Employment income: salary	½	
	Employment income: bonus payments	1	
	Interest from savings certificates	½	
	Interest from government stock	2	
	Dividends	½	
	Personal allowance	½	
	Income tax	2½	
	Tax suffered at source	1	
			9
			15

(a) Bayle – Trading profit for the year ended 30 September 2016

		£
Net profit		173,302
Add: Impairment loss		0
Gifts to customers – Clocks		3,300
– Bottles of champagne		2,480
Donations to political parties		2,900
Lease of motor car £4,345 × 15%		652
Personal tax advice		600
Property expenses £46,240 × 2/5		18,496
Parking fines		520
Professional subscriptions		0
Golf club membership fee		960
Taxable trading profit		203,210

Tutorial notes

1   The recovered impairments loss will have been allowed as a deduction when originally written off, so the recovery is now taxable. Therefore no adjustment is required.

2   Gifts to customers are only an allowable deduction if they cost less than £50 per recipient per tax year, are not of food, drink, tobacco or vouchers for exchangeable goods and carry a conspicuous advertisement for the trader making the gift.

3   The motor car has a CO_2 emission rate in excess of 130 grams per kilometre, so 15% of the leasing costs are not allowed.

(b)   **Bayle – Income tax computation 2016/17**

	Non-savings income £	Savings income £	Dividend income £	Total £
Trading profit (from (a) above)	203,210			
Employment income £(42,000 + 6,000)	48,000			
Interest from savings certificates (exempt)		0		
Interest from gilts (W)		3,600		
Dividends			11,000	
Net income	251,210	3,600	11,000	265,810
Less: personal allowance	(0)	(0)	(0)	
Taxable income	251,210	3,600	11,000	265,810

Working

	£
Interest received 30.6.16	
£160,000 × 3% × 6/12	2,400
Accrued interest deemed received 31.12.16 for period 1.7.16 to 30.9.16	
£160,000 × 3% × 3/12	1,200
Total taxable as savings income	3,600

Tax	£
£(32,000 + 5,000) = 37,000 @ 20%	7,400
£(150,000 + 5,000 − 37,000) = 118,000 @ 40%	47,200
£(251,210 + 3,600 − 118,000 − 37,000) = 99,810 @ 45%	44,914
£5,000 @ 0%	0
£(11,000 − 5,000) = 6,000 @ 38.1%	2,286
Income tax liability	101,800
Tax suffered at source	
PAYE £48,000 @ 45%	(21,600)
Income tax payable	80,200

Tutorial notes

1   The bonus payment of £6,000 that Bayle became entitled to on 10 March 2016 will have been treated as being received during 2015/16.

2   Interest received on maturity of savings certificates issued by National Savings and Investments is exempt.

3   No personal allowance is available as Bayle's adjusted net income of £260,810 (£265,810 less gift aid donation of £5,000) exceeds £122,000.

4   The basic rate and the higher rate limits are increased by the gross gift aid donation of £5,000.

5   The savings income nil rate band is not available to additional rate taxpayers.

94 Flick (A)

Marking scheme

			Marks	
(a)	Salary		½	
	Living accommodation	– Annual value	½	
		– Additional benefit	2	
	Trading profit	– Profit share	2	
		– Assessment	1	
		– Capital allowances	2	
	Property business profit	– Rent receivable	½	
		– Council tax	½	
		– Porch	½	
		– Washer-dryer	1	
	Personal allowance		½	
				11
(b)	Interval		1	
	Tax planning		1	
	Basis period rules more complicated		1	
	Profit assessed in the year of cessation		1	
				4
				15

(a) Flick – Taxable income 2016/17

		Non-savings income £
Employment income		
Salary		28,030
Living accommodation	– Annual value	4,600
	– Additional benefit (W1)	2,100
		34,730
Trading profit (W2)		8,220
Property income (W3)		6,250
Net income		49,200
Less personal allowance		(11,000)
Taxable income		38,200

Workings

1   *Living accommodation additional benefit*

	£
Market value	145,000
Less limit	(75,000)
	70,000

Additional benefit £70,000 × 3%	2,100

Tutorial note

Since the property was acquired more than 6 years before being provided to Flick, the market value at the date it was provided to her is used as the cost of providing the benefit, instead of the original cost.

2   *Trading profit*

First work out the capital allowances for the partnership.

	Motor car	Allowances @ 60%
	£	£
Purchase	18,750	
WDA @ 8% × 4/12	(500)	300
TWDV c/f	18,250	

Tutorial note

The partnership's motor car has CO_2 emissions over 130 g/km and therefore qualifies for writing down allowance at the rate of 8%.

Flick's share of the partnership's trading profit for the period ended 30 April 2017 is then calculated as follows.

	£
Trading profit	29,700
Less capital allowances	(300)
	29,400
Less salary paid to Art £6,000 × 4/12	(2,000)
Profits available for profit sharing	27,400
Profit share for Flick £27,400 × 40%	10,960
Flick's trading income for 2016/17 £10,960 × 3/4	8,220

Tutorial note

Flick's basis period for 2016/17 is 1 January 2017 to 5 April 2017 since this is her first year of trading.

3   *Property business profit*

	£	£
Rent receivable £660 × 12		7,920
Less council tax	1,320	
porch	0	
washer-dryer	350	
		(1,670)
		6,250

Tutorial note

The cost of building the porch is not allowable as it is capital expenditure. Only the cost of a like for like replacement of the washing machine is allowable, not the improvement of the washer-dryer.

(b)   **Advantages**

The interval between earning profits and paying the related tax liability will be 11 months longer. This can be particularly beneficial where profits are rising.

It will be possible to calculate taxable profits well in advance of the end of the tax year, making it much easier to implement tax planning and make pension contributions.

Disadvantages

The application of the basis period rules is more complicated.

The amount of profit assessed in the year of cessation could potentially be quite high as the basis period will be up to 23 months in length. Although overlap profits are deductible, these might be insignificant if the opening years' profits are low.

95 Richard (A)

> **Text references.** The adjustment of profit is covered in Chapter 7 and capital allowances in Chapter 8. National insurance contributions are the subject of Chapter 12.
>
> **Top tips.** Don't forget to deduct the employment allowance in part (b).
>
> **Easy marks.** The adjustment of profit in part (a) should have yielded good marks. The national insurance computations in part (b) were not too difficult.

			Marks
(a)	*Adjustment of profit*		
	Motor expenses:	Richard	1
	Motor expenses:	chef	½
	Parking fines		½
	Property expenses		1
	Decorating:	restaurant	½
	Decorating:	apartment	½
	Other expenses		½
	Advertising: pre-trading expenditure		1
	Capital allowances:	motor car [1] addition	½
		motor car [2] addition	½
		motor car [2] WDA	½
		motor car [1] WDA	1
			8
(b)	Class 1:	chef	1
		waitress	½
		assistant chef: monthly threshold	1
		assistant chef: NICs	1½
		employment allowance	1
	Class 1A:	car benefit percentage	1
		car benefit	½
		NICs	½
			7
			15

(a) **Richard – Trading profit for the year ended 5 April 2017**

	£
Net profit per accounts	32,200
Add: motor expenses – Richard £4,710 × 70% (private use)	3,297
motor expenses – Chef	0
parking fines for Richard	280
property expenses – apartment £16,200 × 1/5 (private use)	3,240
decorating – restaurant	0
decorating – apartment (private use)	1,320
other expenses – legal fees (capital)	2,590
	42,927
Less: advertising: pre-trading expenditure	(800)
capital allowances (W)	(3,780)
Tax adjusted trading profit	38,347

Tutorial note

The redecoration of the restaurant is a trading expense since the property was in a useable state when it was purchased (*Odeon Associated Theatres Ltd v Jones 1971*).

The advertising is pre-trading expenditure incurred within seven years before commencement and is treated as having been made on 6 April 2016.

Working – capital allowances

	Main pool	Private use motor car	Allowances
Additions	£	£	£
Motor car [1]		14,000	
Motor car [2]	16,800		
WDA @ 18%	(3,024)		3,024
WDA @ 18%		(2,520) × 30%	756
TWDV c/f	13,776	11,480	
Allowances			3,780

Tutorial note

Both motor cars have CO_2 emissions between 76 and 130 grams per kilometre, and therefore qualify for writing down allowances at the rate of 18%. The private use of a motor car by an employee is irrelevant, since such usage will be assessed on the employee as a benefit.

(b) **Richard – National insurance contributions (NIC) as employer**

Class 1 employer's contributions

	£
Chef: £(46,000 – 8,112) = £37,888 × 13.8%	5,229
Waitress less than secondary threshold	0
Assistant chef: £(2,200 – 676(W)) = £1,524 × 13.8% × 8	1,682
	6,911
Less employment allowance	(3,000)
Total Class 1 employer's contributions	3,911

Working – Monthly secondary threshold

£8,112 ÷ 12 = £676

Tutorial note

The alternative approach for the assistant chef using the annual earnings threshold and then taking 8/12ths of an annual NIC figure is acceptable.

Class 1A contributions

£3,192 (W) × 13.8%   £440

Working – Car benefit

Amount by which CO_2 emissions exceed base level: (110 (rounded down) − 95) = 15/5 = 3.
Car benefit percentage is 3 + 16 = 19%.

Car benefit is £16,800 (list price) × 19% = £3,192.

96 John

Text references. Chapter 2 deals with the computation of taxable income and the income tax liability. Pensions are covered in Chapter 5. Employment income is dealt with in Chapters 3 and 4.

Top tips. Make sure you distinguish between occupational pension contributions (which are given tax relief at all rates by being deducted in the computation of employment income) and personal pension contributions (which are given basic rate relief by the taxpayer making a net contribution and higher and additional rate relief by increasing the basic rate and higher rate limits).

Easy marks. In part (a), there were some easy marks for working out the car benefit but you needed to watch out for the restricted availability.

Marking scheme

		Marks
(a)	Remuneration	½
	Occupational pension contributions	1
	Car benefit	
	Relevant percentage	1
	Available for 5 months	1
	Beneficial loan	
	Outstanding loan at end of tax year	1
	Average loan	1
	Interest paid	½
	Property business profit	½
	Personal allowance – not available	½
	Personal pension contributions	
	Unused allowances	1½
	Available allowance 2016/17	1½
	Increase in basic and higher rate limits	1
	Tax liability	
	Basic rate	½
	Higher rate	½
		12
(b)	Capital allowances	1
	Relevant earnings	1
	Capital gains reliefs	1
		3
		15

(a)   **John – Income tax computation 2016/17**

	£	Non-savings income £
Employment income		
Remuneration		208,318
Less occupational pension contributions		(18,000)
Car benefit (W1)	3,995	190,318
Beneficial loan (W2)	1,530	
		5,525
Property business profit		16,730
Net income		212,573
Less personal allowance		(0)
Taxable income		212,573

Tutorial note

No personal allowance is available as John's adjusted net income of £(212,573 –20,000) = £192,573 exceeds £122,000.

Tax

	£
On non-savings income	
£52,000 (W3) @ 20%	10,400
£118,000 (170,000 (W3) – 52,000) @ 40%	47,200
£42,573 (212,573 – 170,000) @ 45%	19,158
	£76,758

Workings

1   *Car benefit*

The relevant percentage for the car benefit is 16% + 18% (185 – 95 = 90/5) = 34%.

The motor car was available during the period 1 November 2016 to 5 April 2017, so the benefit for 2016/17 is £(28,200 × 34% × 5/12) = £3,995.

2   *Beneficial loan*

John repaid £(12,000 + 12,000) = £24,000 of the loan during 2016/17, so the outstanding balance at 5 April 2017 is £(84,000 – 24,000) = £60,000.

The benefit calculated using the average method (specified in the question) is as follows:

	£
$\dfrac{84,000+60,000}{2} \times 3\%$	2,160
Less interest paid	(630)
Taxable benefit	1,530

3   *Effect of personal pension contributions on tax limits*

John has adjusted income which is higher than £150,000 in the tax year 2016/17 so his annual allowance is reduced (tapered) for 2016/17 by £1 for every £2 the adjusted income exceeds £150,000. However the annual allowance is not reduced to less than £10,000.

Unused allowances can be carried forward for three years.

The maximum gross personal pension contribution possible in 2016/17 is as follows:

	£
2016/17 (tapered)	
£40,000 – ½ × £(212,573 – 150,000) = £8,714	
(minimum £10,000)	10,000
2015/16, 2014/15 (2 × £40,000 – tapering only from 2016/17)	80,000
2013/14	50,000
Occupational pension contributions already made	
£(18,000 + 12,000) × 4	(120,000)
Personal pension contribution allowable	20,000

John's basic and higher rate limits will be increased by this gross personal pension contributions to £(32,000 + 20,000) = £52,000 and £(150,000 +20,000) = £170,000.

(b) **Furnished holiday lettings**

Furniture and equipment purchased for use in the furnished holiday letting will qualify for capital allowances instead of replacement furniture relief.

The profit from the furnished holiday letting will qualify as relevant earnings for pension tax relief purposes.

Capital gains tax entrepreneurs' relief, relief for replacement of business assets and gift relief for business assets will potentially be available on a disposal of the furnished holiday letting.

97 Ronald

Text references. Assessable trading income is covered in Chapter 9 and capital allowances in Chapter 8. Property business income is the subject of Chapter 6. The computation of taxable income and the income tax liability will be found in Chapter 2. Pensions are the subject of Chapter 5.

Top tips. You could work out the amount of dividend income by adding back the dividend income nil rate band of £5,000 to the dividend included in the computation.

Easy marks. There were some easy marks in part (a) for working out the income tax liability as the question outlined the computation required and the rates of tax.

Marking scheme

		Marks
(a)	Trading profit: p/e 30 April 2016 assessable trading profit	½
	Trading profit p/e 30 April 2017: capital allowances	1½
	Trading profit p/e 30 April 2017: assessable trading profit	1
	Property business income: premium assessable	1
	Property business income: rent receivable	1
	Property business income: roof replacement	1
	Property business income: roof repairs	1
	Property business income: insurance	1
	Dividends	1
	Figures given	1
	Tax @ 40%	1
		11

		Marks
(b)	No annual allowances for previous years	1
	Annual allowance 2016/17	1
	Basic rate relief	1
	Higher rate relief	1
		4
		15

(a) Ronald – Income tax computation 2016/17

	Non-savings income	Savings income	Dividend income	Total
	£	£	£	£
Trading income (W1)	11,592			
Employment income	65,065*			
Property business income (W2)	8,240			
Building society interest		1,260*		
Dividends £(800 + 5,000)			5,800	
Net income	84,897	1,260	5,800	91,957
Less personal allowance	(11,000)*			
Taxable income	73,897	1,260	5,800	80,957

	£
Income tax	
Non-savings income	
£32,000 @ 20%	6,400*
£41,897 (73,897 – 32,000) @ 40%	16,759
Savings income	
£500 @ 0%	0*
£760 (1,260 – 500) @ 40%	304
Dividend income	
£5,000 @ 0%	0*
£800 (5,800 – 5,000) @ 32.5%	260*
Income tax liability	23,723
Tax suffered at source	
PAYE	(9,130)*
Income tax payable	14,593

* Figures provided in question

Tutorial note

The amount of dividends are not given, but as the dividend income nil rate band of £5,000 is available and only £800 is being taxed at the higher rate, the total dividends must be £(5,000 + 800) = £5,800.

Workings

1 *Trading profit*

	£	£
Period ended 30 April 2016		3,840
Period ended 30 April 2017	12,060	
Capital allowances £18,000 × 8% × 30%	(432)	
	11,628	
× 8/12		7,752
		11,592

2   *Property business income*

	£	£
Premium received		12,000
Less £12,000 × 2% × (30 – 1)		(6,960)
		5,040
Rents receivable £960 × 4		3,840
		8,880
Roof replacement	0	
Roof repairs £(8,600 – 8,200)	400	
Insurance £480 × 6/12	240	
		(640)
Property business profit		8,240

Tutorial note

The initial replacement cost of the shop's roof is not deductible, being capital in nature, as the building was not in a usable state when purchased and this fact was reflected in the reduced purchase price.

(b)   Ronald was not a member of a pension scheme prior to 2016/17, so the annual allowances for 2013/14, 2014/15 and 2015/16 are not available.

Although net relevant earnings are £(11,592 + 65,065) = £76,657, the maximum amount of tax relievable personal pension contribution is effectively restricted to the annual allowance of £40,000 for 2016/17.

Personal pension contributions are made net of basic rate tax, so Ronald would have paid £32,000 (£40,000 less 20%) to the pension company.

Higher rate tax relief would have been given by increasing Ronald's basic rate tax limit for 2016/17 by £40,000, being the gross amount of the pension contribution.

98 Samson and Delilah

Text references. The income tax computation is covered in Chapter 2. Chapters 3 and 4 deal with employment income and taxable and exempt benefits. Partnerships are the subject of Chapter 11.

Top tips. Trivial benefits (not exceeding £50) are new in Finance Act 2016 so are highly examinable.

Easy marks. There were some easy marks for dealing with the car benefit and computing income tax.

Examiner's comments. Part (a) of the question was a typical income tax liability calculation (for both the husband and wife), and it was generally very well answered. Part (b) of the question involved income tax planning, requiring a calculation of the husband's income tax saving for the tax year if the building society deposit account had been in his wife's sole name instead of in joint names for the entire year. Given that the husband's personal allowance restriction would be reduced, the answer was simply the amount of interest [after deducting the savings nil rate band of £500] at 60%. However, half page answers were quite common. Once again, working at the margin (where appropriate) could have saved an enormous amount of time.

Marks

(a) *Samson*

Salary	½
Building society interest	½
Personal allowance	1
Income tax	2
Delilah	
Salary	½
Payroll giving	1
Car benefit	1
Chauffeur	½
Hamper	½
Business travel	½
Trading profit	1
Building society interest	½
Deductible interest	1
Personal allowance not available	½
Income tax	2
	13

(b) Transfer part of account from Samson to Delilah

2
___
15

(a) **Samson – Income tax computation 2016/17**

	Non-savings income £	Savings income £	Total £
Employment income – Salary	112,000		
Building society interest £9,600/2		4,800	
Net income	112,000	4,800	116,800
Less Personal allowance (W)	(2,600)		
Taxable income	109,400	4,800	114,200

Income tax

	£
£32,000 × 20%	6,400
£77,400 (109,400 – 32,000) × 40%	30,960
£500 × 0% (savings rate nil rate band)	0
£4,300 (4,800 – 500) × 40%	1,720
Income tax liability	39,080

Working

Samson's adjusted net income exceeds £100,000, so his personal allowance of £11,000 is reduced to £2,600 (11,000 – 8,400 ((116,800 – 100,000)/2)).

Delilah – Income tax computation 2016/17

	Non-savings income £	Savings income £	Total £
Employment income (W1)	213,248		
Trading profit £85,600 (93,600 – 8,000) × 40%	34,240		
Building society interest £9,600/2		4,800	
Total income	247,488	4,800	252,288
Less interest paid	(6,200)		
Net income/taxable income	241,288	4,800	246,088

Workings

1   *Employment income*

	£
Salary	184,000
Less charitable payroll deductions £250 × 12	(3,000)
	181,000
Car benefit (W2)	22,848
Chauffeur	9,400
Hamper	0
Reimbursement of travel to visit client	0
Employment income	213,248

2   *Car benefit*

The relevant percentage for the car benefit is 34% (16% + (185 – 95)/5).

The motor car was available throughout 2016/17 so the benefit is £22,848 (67,200 × 34%).

Income tax	£
£38,080 (W) × 20%	7,616
£118,000 (156,080 – 38,080) × 40%	47,200
£90,008 (246,088 – 156,080) × 45%	40,504
Income tax liability	95,320

Working

Delilah's basic and higher rate tax limits are increased by £4,864 × $\frac{100}{80}$ = £6,080 to £38,080 (32,000 + 6,080) and £156,080 (150,000 + 6,080) in respect of the charitable gift aid donations.

Tutorial notes

1   The car benefit does not cover the cost of a chauffeur, so this is an additional benefit.

2   The hamper is a trivial benefit as it does not exceed £50.

3   There is an automatic exemption for reimbursement of business expenses such as the train travel by Delilah (which would be a taxable benefit under general principles) provided that the expense would have been a deductible expense for the employee.

4   The loan interest paid of £6,200 is deductible because the loan was used by Delilah for a qualifying purpose.

5   No personal allowance is available as Delilah's adjusted net income of £240,008 (246,088 – 6,080) exceeds £122,000.

6   No savings nil rate band is available as Delilah is an additional rate taxpayer.

(b)   If the building society deposit account had been in Delilah's sole name instead of in joint names for the entire year, this would have saved Samson income tax of £2,580 (£4,300 × 60%).

Tutorial note

Because of the loss of the personal allowance, Samson's effective marginal rate of income tax is 60% on the savings income not covered by the savings nil rate band.

99 Patience

Text references. Employment income is covered in Chapters 3 and 4 and national insurance contributions in Chapter 12. Assessable trading income is covered in Chapter 9 and capital allowances in Chapter 8. Property business income is the subject of Chapter 6. The computation of taxable income and the income tax liability will be found in Chapter 2. Pensions are the subject of Chapter 5.

Top tips. There are no writing down allowances or annual investment allowance in the final year of trading. Remember that gains on the disposal of residential property are taxed at 18% and 28% if they are not covered by the annual exempt amount and principle private residence relief.

Easy marks. Recognising the exempt benefits and mentioning them in your answer is important to get some easy marks.

Examiner's comments. Two aspects to this question caused particular difficulty. Firstly, many candidates treated the pension income (state pension, employer's occupational pension scheme and a private pension) as exempt income. Secondly, the format in which information was given for two properties caused a certain amount of confusion, with the information relevant for income tax and the capital gains tax details being shown within the one table; candidates being required to separate out the relevant information for income tax and capital gains tax purposes. Here figures were often duplicated, with, for example, revenue expenditure being (correctly) deducted as an expense in calculating the property business profit, but then also (incorrectly) deducted in calculating chargeable gains.

Marking scheme

		Marks
Salary		1
Pension contribution	Patience	½
Pension contribution	Employer	½
School place		1
Long-service award		½
Beneficial loan		½
Trading income	Y/e 31.7.16	½
	p/e 31.12.16	½
	Overlap relief	1
Capital allowances	TWDV brought forward	½
	Laptop	½
	Disposal proceeds	1
	Balancing allowance	½
Property business profit	Rent received	½
	Expenditure	½
Pension income		1
Personal allowance		½
Increase basic rate limit		1
Income tax liability		1
Capital gains	Property one	½
	Property two	½
	Annual exempt amount	½
	CGT payable	½
		15

Patience – Income tax computation 2016/17

		£
Employment income		
Salary £3,750 × 9		33,750
Pension contributions	Patience £33,750 × 6%	(2,025)
	Employer	0
		31,725
School place		540
Long-service award		0
Beneficial loan		0
Trading income (W1)		16,100
Pension income £(1,450 + 6,000 + 3,300)		10,750
Property business income (W3)		3,500
Net income		62,615
Less personal allowance		(11,000)
Taxable income		51,615

Income tax

	£
£36,500 (W4) × 20%	7,300
£15,115 (51,615 − 36,500) × 40%	6,046
Income tax liability	13,346

Tutorial notes:

1 An employer contribution to a pension scheme is not a taxable benefit.

2 The taxable benefit on the provision of the school place is the additional marginal cost to the employer, not the normal fee payable.

3 A non-cash long-service award is not a taxable benefit if it is for a period of service of at least 20 years, and the cost of the award does not exceed £50 per year of service.

4 There is no taxable benefit if beneficial loans do not exceed £10,000 during the tax year.

Workings

1 *Trading income*

	£	£
Year ended 31 July 2016		14,800
Period ended 31 December 2016	6,900	
Balancing allowance (W2)	(1,900)	
		5,000
		19,800
Relief for overlap profits		(3,700)
		16,100

2 *Capital allowances*

	Main pool	Allowances
	£	£
WDV brought forward	2,200	
Addition – Laptop computer	1,700	
Proceeds £(1,200 + 800)	(2,000)	
Balancing allowance	(1,900)	1,900

3   *Property business income*

		£
Rent received £(3,600 + 7,200)		10,800
Expenditure £(4,700 + 2,600)		(7,300)
Property business income		3,500

4   *Basic rate limit*

Patience's basic rate tax limit is increased by £4,500 to £36,500 (32,000 + 4,500 (3,600 × 100/80)) in respect of the personal pension contributions.

Patience – Capital gains tax computation 2016/17

		£	£
Property one	Disposal proceeds	122,000	
	Less cost	(81,400)	
			40,600
Property two	Disposal proceeds	98,000	
	Less cost	(103,700)	
			(5,700)
Net chargeable gains			34,900
Less annual exempt amount			(11,100)
Taxable gains			23,800
Capital gains tax			
£23,800 × 28%			6,664

MCQ bank – Chargeable gains for individuals 1

100   B   1 and 3

Motor vehicles suitable for private use and investments held in individual savings accounts (ISAs) are both exempt assets.

101   A   £2,712

	£
Chargeable gain	25,100
Less annual exempt amount	(11,100)
Taxable gains	14,000

Tax

	£
£(32,000 – 19,920) = 12,080 × 18% (residential property)	2,174
£(14,000 – 12,080) = 1,920 × 28% (residential property)	538
Total capital gains tax	2,712

102   D   £12,143

The amount of the cost attributable to the part sold is:

$$\frac{£36,000}{£36,000 + £90,000} \times £80,000 = £22,857$$

	£
Proceeds £(36,000 – 1,000)	35,000
Less cost (see above)	(22,857)
Gain	12,143

103   C   £11,200

	2014/15	2015/16	2016/17		
	£	£	£		
Gains	2,000	4,000	13,900		
Losses	(14,000)	(2,000)	(2,000)		
	(12,000)	2,000	11,900		
c/f	12,000	12,000	(800)	c/f	11,200
			11,100 AEA		

Current period losses must be set against current period gains. Brought forward losses are only set against current period gains in so far as they bring them down to the annual exempt amount.

104   C   £1,667

	£
Proceeds	7,000
Less cost	(1,500)
Gain	5,500

The maximum gain is 5/3 × £(7,000 – 6,000) = £1,667

The chargeable gain is the lower of £5,500 and £1,667, so it is £1,667.

105 £2,500

	£
Deemed proceeds	6,000
Less cost	(8,500)
Loss	(2,500)

106 14½ years

	Exempt years	Chargeable years	Total years
Actual occupation	3		3
Deemed occupation – any time employed overseas	5		5
Actual occupation	2		2
Deemed occupation – up to 3 years any reason	3		3
Unoccupied		½	½
Last 18 months of ownership	1½		1½
Totals	14½	½	15

107 12 August 2026

When a depreciating asset is purchased to replace a non-depreciating asset the gain on the sale is deferred until the earliest of:

The sale of the depreciating asset – 14 October 2026

Ceasing to use the depreciating asset in a business – not applicable here

The ten-year anniversary of the purchase of the depreciating asset – 12 August 2026

108 £1,160

Gains subject to entrepreneurs' relief are taxed at 10%. Other gains will be reduced by the annual exempt amount and then taxed in this case, at 20%, because Louise has taxable income in excess of the basic rate limit of £32,000. The capital gains tax (CGT) payable is therefore:

Tax	£
£8,000 × 10%	800
£(12,900 − 11,100) = 1,800 × 20%	360
Total capital gains tax	1,160

109 £13,650

	Number	Cost £
Purchase October 2004	1,000	1,500
Bonus issue November 2006		
1 for 2 bonus issue	500	0
	1,500	1,500
Rights issue July 2011		
3 for 1 rights issue @ £2.70	4,500	12,150
	6,000	13,650
Disposal February 2017	(6,000)	(13,650)

CBE style OT case – Nim

110   £37,500

The shares in Kapook plc are valued at 3.70 + ½ × (3.80 – 3.70) = £3.75 so the deemed disposal proceeds are 10,000 × £3.75 = £37,500.

111   £26,333

The disposal is first matched against the purchase on 24 July 2016 (this is within the following 30 days) and then against the shares in the share pool. The cost of the shares disposed of is, therefore, £26,333 (5,800 + 20,533).

Share pool	No. of shares	Cost
	£	£
Purchase 19 February 2004	8,000	16,200
Purchase 6 June 2009 1 for 2 @ £3.65 per share	4,000	14,600
	12,000	30,800
Disposal 20 July 2016 £30,800 × 8,000/12,000	(8,000)	(20,533)
Balance c/f	4,000	10,267

112   2 and 4

Nim will have deemed proceeds on the transfer of the Jooba Ltd shares to his wife so that neither a gain nor a loss will arise on the transfer. Nim's wife will not be able to transfer her annual exempt amount to Nim.

Nim's wife will take the Jooba Ltd shares with a cost equal to the deemed proceeds ie the original cost to Nim. The spouse exemption applies for inheritance tax, not capital gains tax.

113   £3,500

	£
Net proceeds	8,700
Less cost	(5,200)
Gain	3,500

The maximum gain is 5/3 × £([8,700 + 300] – 6,000) = £5,000. The chargeable gain is the lower of £3,500 and £5,000, so it is £3,500.

114   £6,900

The set off of the brought forward capital losses is restricted to £8,900 (20,000 – 11,100) so that chargeable gains are reduced to the amount of the annual exempt amount. Capital losses carried forward are therefore £(15,800 – 8,900) = £6,900.

Aloi, Bon and Dinah

> **Text references.** Entrepreneurs' relief is dealt with in Chapter 15. Shares are covered in Chapter 16. Transfers on death, computing chargeable gains and the calculation of capital gains tax will be found in Chapter 13.
>
> **Top tips.** Par value means the face value of the shares. Aloi therefore had a cost of £50,000 for her first 50,000 £1 shares in Alphabet Ltd.
>
> **Easy marks.** The dates in question 117 should have been well known.

115　D　2 and 4

Bon only became a director on 1 February 2016, so this qualifying condition was not met for one year prior to the date of disposal. Her shareholding of 25% (25,000/100,000 × 100) satisfies the minimum required holding of 5% for Alphabet Ltd to be her personal company and this qualifying condition was met for one year prior to the date of disposal.

Dinah was an employee for more than one year prior to the disposal but her shareholding of 3% (3,000/100,000 × 100) is less than the minimum required holding of 5%.

116　C　£29,140

	£
Gain qualifying for entrepreneurs' relief	
Ordinary shares in Alphabet Ltd	
Proceeds of sale (60,000 × £6)	360,000
Less cost £(50,000 + 18,600)	(68,600)
Gain	291,400
CGT @ 10% on £291,400	29,140

117　A　Notification 5 October 2017, payment 31 January 2018.

118　A　£34,320

	£
Deemed proceeds of sale (10,000 × £7.12 (W1))	71,200
Less cost (W2)	(36,880)
Gain	34,320

Workings

1　The shares in XYZ plc are valued at 7.10 + ½ × (7.14 − 7.10) = £7.12.

2　Following the takeover, Bon received 25,000 shares in XYZ plc. The cost of the original shareholding is passed on to the new shareholding so the cost attributable to the 10,000 shares sold is £36,880 (92,200 × 10,000/25,000).

119　B　Nil

There is no CGT liability on the sale of the XYZ plc shares as the gain of £5,000 (6,600 − (4,800 × 1,000/3,000)) is less than the annual exempt amount.

The transfer of the XYZ plc shares on Dinah's death is an exempt disposal

CBE style OT case – Jerome

120 £112,800

The disposal of the house does not give rise to a gain or a loss because it is a transfer between spouses. The base cost of the house for Jerome's wife is therefore Jerome's base cost which was the value of the house at the uncle's death

121 £50,600

	£
Deemed proceeds	98,400
Less cost	(39,000)
Gain before hold over relief	59,400

Hold over relief is restricted to £50,600 (£59,400 × 460,000/540,000), being the proportion of chargeable business assets to chargeable assets.

122

Latest date for election	5 April 2021

Person(s) making election	Jerome and his son

123 £10,100

	£
Proceeds	12,200
Less cost	(2,100)
Chargeable gain	10,100

The maximum gain is 5/3 × £(12,200 − 6,000) = £10,333. The chargeable gain is the lower of £10,330 and £10,100, so it is £10,100.

124 £51,940

	£
Proceeds	78,400
Less cost (W)	(26,460)
Chargeable gain	51,940

Working

The amount of the cost attributable to the part sold is:

$$\frac{£78,400}{£78,400 + £33,600} \times £37,800 = £26,460$$

125 Jorge

Marking scheme

	Marks
House	
Proceeds	½
Cost	½
Enhancement expenditure	½
Period of exemption	3
Principal private residence exemption	1
Letting exemption	1
Copyright	
Proceeds	½
Cost	1½
Painting	½
Motor car	½
Annual exempt amount	½
	10

Jorge – Taxable gains computation 2016/17

	£
House (W1)	0
Copyright (W4)	24,300
Painting – exempt as proceeds and cost £6,000 or less	0
Motor car – exempt asset so loss not allowable	0
Chargeable gains	24,300
Less annual exempt amount	(11,100)
Taxable gains	13,200

Workings

1   *House*

	£
Proceeds	308,000
Less cost	(93,000)
Less enhancement expenditure (defending title to property)	(5,000)
Gain	210,000
Less principal private residence exemption (W2)	(188,000)
letting exemption (W3)	(22,000)
Gain after exemptions	0

2   *Principal private residence exemption*

	Exempt months	Chargeable months	Total months
Actual occupation	34		34
Deemed occupation – up to 3 years any reason	18		18
Deemed occupation – any time employed overseas	24		24
Actual occupation	11		11
Deemed occupation – up to 4 years working elsewhere in UK	30		30
Deemed occupation – up to 3 years any reason balance (36 – 18) = 18, (22 – 18) = 4 chargeable	18	4	22
Deemed occupation – up to 4 years working elsewhere in UK balance (48 – 30) = 18, (26 – 18) = 8 chargeable	18	8	26
Actual occupation	17		17
Working overseas (12 – [18 – 3 – 13]) = 10 chargeable		10	10
Last 18 months – always treated as period of occupation	18		18
Totals	188	22	210

Principal private residence exemption £210,000 × 188/210   £188,000

Tutorial note

In calculating the principal private residence exemption, any periods of absence while working overseas, a maximum of four years absence while working elsewhere in the UK, and a maximum of three years absence for any reason are treated as deemed occupation, usually provided that they are preceded and followed by a period of actual occupation. The second period working overseas is therefore not a period of deemed occupation as it was not followed by a period of actual occupation.

Alternative approach

An alternative approach to calculate the chargeable months as follows:

Total period of ownership	210
Less actual occupation (34 + 11 + 17)	(62)
Deemed occupation – any reason up to 3 years	(36)
– employed overseas without limit	(24)
– working in UK up to 4 years	(48)
Last 18 months – always treated as period of occupation	(18)
Chargeable months	22

3   *Letting exemption*

Lowest of:

(i)	Gain in letting period £210,000 × 22/210	£22,000
(ii)	Gain exempt under PPR (W2)	£188,000
(iii)	Maximum exemption	£40,000

Therefore letting exemption is   £22,000

4   *Copyright*

	£
Proceeds	80,300
Less cost £70,000 × 8/10 (N)	(56,000)
Gain	24,300

Tutorial note

The copyright is a wasting asset. The cost of £70,000 must therefore be depreciated based on an unexpired life of ten years at the date of acquisition and an unexpired life of eight years at the date of disposal.

126 Winston

Text references. Chapter 13 covers transfers on death, computing chargeable gains, transfers between spouses, part disposals and CGT liability. Chapter 15 includes entrepreneurs' relief.

Top tips. Losses on assets not qualifying for entrepreneurs' relief and the annual exempt amount should be deducted to produce the lowest CGT liability. This means that they should be deducted from gains taxed at 20% in priority to gains taxed at 10%.

Easy marks. The calculation of capital gains tax in part (a)(i) was straightforward.

Marking scheme

				Marks
(a)	(i)	Annual exempt amount	1	
		Unused basic rate band	½	
		Capital gains tax	1½	
				3
	(ii)	Freehold shop	½	
		Painting	½	
		Capital loss	1	
		Annual exempt amount	½	
		Capital gains tax	1½	
				4
(b)		Net proceeds	1	
		Cost – probate value taken over on transfer from spouse	1	
		Apportionment of cost	1	
				3
				10

(a) (i) **Winston – CGT liability 2016/17**

	£
Chargeable gain on painting	46,360
Less annual exempt amount	(11,100)
Taxable gain	35,260

		£
CGT liability:	£(32,000 – 19,400) = 12,600 @ 10%	1,260
	£(35,260 – 12,600) = 22,660 @ 20%	4,532
		5,792

(ii) **Winston – Revised CGT liability 2016/17**

	£
Gain qualifying for entrepreneurs' relief	
Gain on freehold shop £(140,000 – 80,000)	60,000
Gain not qualifying for entrepreneurs' relief	
Painting	46,360
Less allowable loss on warehouse £(102,000 – 88,000)	(14,000)
Net gain	32,360
Less annual exempt amount	(11,100)
Taxable gain	21,260

	£
CGT liability: £60,000 @ 10%	6,000
£21,260 @ 20%	4,252
	10,252

Tutorial notes

1   The capital loss on the sale of the freehold warehouse and the annual exempt amount are set against the chargeable gain from the sale of the painting as this saves CGT at the higher rate of 20%. Although the warehouse is being sold with the business, it was never actually used in the business, and so this aspect of the sale does not qualify for entrepreneurs' relief. If it had been used in the business, the loss of £14,000 would have been deducted from the gain on the shop to give a net gain on sale of the business of £46,000. CGT would then be charged on £46,000 at 10%.

2   The unused basic rate tax band of £12,600 is effectively used by the gain qualifying for entrepreneurs' relief of £60,000 even though this has no effect on the 10% tax rate.

(b)   **Renaldo – Chargeable gain 3 December 2016**

	£
Gross proceeds	92,000
Less auctioneers' commission (cost of disposal) £92,000 × 5%	(4,600)
Net proceeds	87,400
Less cost £28,600 × $\dfrac{92,000}{92,000+38,000}$	(20,240)
Chargeable gain	67,160

Tutorial notes

1   The cost of the land is £28,600 which is the value when Renaldo's father-in-law died. Renaldo would have taken over this cost when his wife transferred the land to him.

2   The gross proceeds of sale are used in the part disposal fraction.

127 Mick

Text references. The computation of chargeable gains for individuals is covered in Chapter 13. Shares are the subject of Chapter 16. Business reliefs are deal with in Chapter 15.

Top tips. In part (b) you need to think about how you would use replacement of business asset relief and entrepreneurs' relief to identify the missing information.

Easy marks. The share pool in part (a) should have scored easy marks.

Marking scheme

		Marks
(a)	*Warehouse*	
	Disposal proceeds	½
	Cost	½
	Extension	½
	Floor	½
	Shares in Rolling Ltd	
	Disposal proceeds	½
	Purchase	½
	Bonus issue	½
	Disposal cost	½
		4

		Marks
(b)	*Warehouse*	
	Replacement of business assets relief	1
	Acquisition date of new warehouse	1
	Cost of new warehouse	1
	Shares in Rolling Ltd	
	Entrepreneurs' relief	1
	Rolling Ltd share capital	1
	Previous claims	1
		6
		10

(a) **Mick – Chargeable gains 2016/17**

Freehold warehouse

	£	£
Disposal proceeds		522,000
Less: cost	258,000	
enhancement expenditure: extension	99,000	
enhancement expenditure: floor	0	
		(357,000)
Chargeable gain		165,000

Tutorial note

The cost of replacing the warehouse's floor is revenue expenditure as the floor is a subsidiary part of the property.

Shares in Rolling Ltd

	£
Disposal proceeds	3,675,000
Less cost (W)	(537,600)
Chargeable gain	3,137,400

Working – share pool

	Number	Cost £
Purchase June 2007	500,000	960,000
Bonus issue December 2012		
500,000 × 3/2	750,000	0
Disposal September 2016	1,250,000	960,000
960,000 × 700,000/1,250,000	(700,000)	(537,600)
Balance carried forward	550,000	422,400

(b) **Freehold warehouse**

Replacement of business assets relief (rollover relief) may be available in respect of the chargeable gain arising on the disposal of the freehold warehouse.

The acquisition date of the replacement warehouse is required, since relief will only be available if this is after 19 May 2015 (one year before the date of disposal).

The cost of the replacement warehouse is required, since relief will be restricted if the sale proceeds of £522,000 have not been fully reinvested.

Shares in Rolling Ltd

Entrepreneurs' relief may be available in respect of the chargeable gain arising on the disposal of the shares in Rolling Ltd.

Details of Rolling Ltd's share capital are required, since relief will only be available if Mick had the minimum required holding (and voting rights) of 5%.

Details of any previous entrepreneurs' relief claims made by Mick are required, since there is a lifetime limit of £10 million of gains.

128 Ruby

Text references. The computation of chargeable gains and capital gains tax is covered in Chapter 13. Business reliefs are the subject of Chapter 15 and shares are dealt with in Chapter 16.

Top tips. The annual exempt amount should be set against gains which do not qualify for entrepreneurs' relief in priority to those which do qualify for the relief.

Easy marks. There were easy marks in part (a) for a basic computation of capital gains tax.

Examiner's comments. Part (a) of the question was well answered.

In part (b), the main problem was that candidates did not appreciate that both disposals would impact on the capital gains tax payable in respect of the disposal of the investment property. The disposal of the shares in the unquoted trading company (qualifying for entrepreneur's relief) would utilise the remaining basic rate tax band, meaning that the 28% rate was now applicable. The capital loss arising on the disposal of the shares in the quoted trading company would be offset against the chargeable gain on the investment property. Another common problem was the 50p nominal value of the shares in the quoted trading company. This did not impact on the calculation of the capital loss, although many candidates incorrectly divided their cost figure by two.

		Marks
(a)	Annual exempt amount	½
	CGT at 18%	1
	CGT at 28%	½
		2
(b)	*Pola Ltd*	
	Disposal proceeds	½
	Cost	½
	Investment property	½
	Annual exempt amount (best use)	1
	CGT at 10%	1
	CGT at 28%	1
	Apola plc	
	Disposal proceeds	½
	Cost	1½
	Investment property	½
	Annual exempt amount	½
	CGT at 18%	½
		8
		10

(a) **Ruby's CGT liability**

	£
Chargeable gain on investment property	45,800
Less annual exempt amount	(11,100)
	34,700

Capital gains tax

£14,185 (32,000 – 17,815) @ 18% (residential property)	2,553
£20,515 (34,700 – 14,185) @ 28% (residential property)	5,744
	8,297

(b) **Choice of disposal**

Shareholding in Pola Ltd

	Entrepreneurs' relief £	No entrepreneurs' relief £
Pola Ltd shares £(61,000 – 23,700)	37,300	
Investment property (part (a))		45,800
Less annual exempt amount (best use)		(11,100)
	37,300	34,700

Capital gains tax

£37,300 @ 10%	3,730	
£34,700 @ 28%		9,716

Total CGT £(3,730 + 9,716) 13,446

Shareholding in Aplo plc

	£
Apolo plc shares £59,000 – (40,000 × £2.15(W))	(27,000)
Investment property (part (a))	45,800
Less annual exempt amount	(11,100)
Taxable gain	7,700

Capital gains tax

£7,700 @ 18%	1,386

Working

The Aplo plc shares are valued at £2.12 + ½ × (£2.18 – £2.12) = £2.15.

MCQ bank – Inheritance tax 1

129 A £150,000

	£
Before the gift: 70% shareholding	350,000
After the gift: 50% shareholding	(200,000)
Transfer of value	150,000

130 C £461,250

	£
Sunita's unused nil rate band £325,000 × 65%	211,250
Joel's nil rate band	325,000
	536,250
Less used against Joel's PET now chargeable	(75,000)
Available nil rate band to set against Joel's death estate	461,250

Sunita's nil rate band is increased pro-rata to that available at the time of Joel's death.

131 C £29,750

	£
Gift	190,000
Less AE × 2 (16/17 + 15/16 b/f)	(6,000)
	184,000
Less nil rate band available £(£325,000 – 260,000)	(65,000)
	119,000
IHT @ $^{20}/_{80}$	£29,750

132 B Nil

The gift to the granddaughter is covered by the marriage exemption of £2,500 by a remoter ancestor. There was no gratuitous intent on the sale at undervalue of the vase so there is no charge to inheritance tax on this transaction.

133 C £136,000

	£
PET on 10.7.13 PET now chargeable	600,000
Less nil rate band available £(£325,000 – 150,000)	(175,000)
	425,000
IHT @ 40%	170,000
Less taper relief (3 to 4 years) @ 20%	(34,000)
Death tax payable on lifetime transfer	136,000

The chargeable lifetime transfer on 15 September 2008 is cumulated with the later PET since it was made in the 7 years before that transfer.

CBE style OTQ bank – Inheritance tax 2

134 £350

The gifts to the grandson are exempt as normal expenditure out of income because they are part of the normal expenditure of the donor, made out of income and left the donor with sufficient income to maintain her usual standard of living.

The small gifts exemption only applies to gifts up to £250 per donee per tax year. If gifts total more than £250 the whole amount is chargeable. Since the gifts to the grandnephew totalled £(100 + 250) = £350 in 2016/17, this exemption does not apply.

135 £66,000

	£
Before the gift: 100% shareholding 1,000 × £150	150,000
After the gift: 70% shareholding 700 × £120	(84,000)
Transfer of value	66,000

136 £24,000

	£
House (net of mortgage) £(200,000 – 60,000)	140,000
Investments and cash	350,000
	490,000
Less funeral expenses	(5,000)
	485,000
Less exempt gift to spouse	(100,000)
Chargeable death estate	385,000
Less available nil rate band (no lifetime transfers)	(325,000)
	60,000
IHT @ 40%	24,000

137 £351,000

	£
Cash to nephews £200 × 5	1,000
ISA investments	350,000
Chargeable estate	351,000

The small gifts exemption only applies to lifetime transfers. The ISA exemption only applies for income tax and capital gains tax. The residue to the wife is covered by the spouse exemption.

138

Lifetime tax	30 April 2017

Death tax	31 January 2017

The due date for the lifetime tax is the later of 30 April just after the end of the tax year of the transfer and six months after the end of the month of the transfer. The due date for additional tax on death is six months from the end of the month of death.

Ning

139   B   £956,000

	£
Property one	674,000
Less repayment mortgage	(160,000)
	514,000
Property two	442,000
	956,000

There is no deduction in respect of the endowment mortgage as this will be repaid upon death by the life assurance element of the mortgage.

140   C   £324,000

	£
Motor cars	172,000
Investments £(47,000 + 36,000 + 69,000)	152,000
	324,000

There are no exempt assets for inheritance tax.

141   D   £27,900

	£
Bank loan	22,400
Nephew's legal fees	0
Funeral expenses	5,500
	27,900

The promise to pay the nephew's legal fees is not deductible as it is purely gratuitous (not made for valuable consideration).

142   B   £105,000

The potentially exempt transfer on 14 August 2006 is exempt from inheritance tax as it was made more than seven years before 20 March 2017.

The potentially exempt transfer on 7 November 2016 will utilise £220,000 of the nil rate band, so only £(325,000 – 220,000) = £105,000 is available against the death estate.

143   A   Amount £227,500, Claim by 31 March 2019

Ning's personal representatives could claim her deceased husband's unused nil rate band of £325,000 × 70% = £227,500. The time limit for the claim is two years from the end of the month of Ning's death ie by 31 March 2019.

CBE style OT case – Jimmy

144 £8,500

	£
Marriage exemption	2,500
Annual exemption 2015/16	3,000
Annual exemption 2014/15 b/f	3,000
	8,500

145 £55,000

	£
Before the gift: 5,100 shares × £30	153,000
After the gift: 4,900 shares × £20	(98,000)
Diminution in value	55,000

146 £118,750

	£
Net transfer of value (Jimmy pays IHT)	800,000

IHT	£325,000	× 0% =	Nil
	£475,000	× 20/80 =	118,750
	£800,000		118,750

147

Due date	31 August 2017

By whom paid	Trustees of trust

148 £312,000

	£
Death estate	980,000
Less spouse exemption	(200,000)
Chargeable death estate	780,000
£780,000 × 40%	312,000

The nil rate band has been used up by the lifetime transfers (stated in question) so the chargeable death estate is all taxed at 40%.

CBE style OT case – Marcus

Text references. Inheritance tax is dealt with in Chapter 18.

Top tips. In question 153, do not mix up the rules for transfers between spouses for capital gains tax (no gain/no loss transfer) and inheritance tax (exempt transfer).

Easy marks. There were some easy marks for a basic inheritance tax computation in questions 149 provided that you remembered that the nil rate band at the date of the transfer should be used.

149 £3,000

				£
IHT	£300,000	× 0% =		Nil
	£15,000	× 20% =		3,000
	£315,000			3,000

150 £96,250

				£
IHT	£10,000	(325,000 – 315,000) × 0% =		Nil
	£481,250	× 20% =		96,250
	£491,250			96,250

Although Marcus pays the inheritance tax due, since the gross chargeable transfer is given, in order to work out the tax he pays, this is 20% of the excess over the available nil rate band.

151 £38,500

				£
IHT	£10,000	× 0% =		Nil
	£481,250	× 40% =		192,500
	£491,250			192,500
Taper relief (3 to 4 years) @ 20%				38,500

152 £570,000

		£
Before: 100,000 × £12		1,200,000
After: 70,000 × £9		(630,000)
Potentially exempt transfer of value		570,000

153 If Jerome's wife remarries, any unused nil rate band on her death can be transferred to her spouse if they survive her and the transfer of Jerome's estate to his wife on his death is an exempt transfer.

Married couples (and registered civil partnerships) are not chargeable persons for inheritance tax (IHT) purposes, because each spouse (or civil partner) is taxed separately.

The gift of the land on 29 June 2015 by Jerome to his wife is an exempt transfer.

154 Afiya

Marking scheme

			Marks
(a)	**Lifetime transfers**		
	14 September 2015	Value of shares before transfer	1
		Value of shares after transfer	1
		Annual exemption 2015/16	½
		Annual exemption 2014/15 brought forward	½
	27 January 2016	Nil rate band	½
		Balance @ 20/80	1
	Additional liabilities arising on death		
	14 September 2015	Potentially exempt transfer now chargeable	1
	27 January 2016	Gross chargeable transfer	½
		Nil rate band	½
		Balance @ 40%	½
		Lifetime tax already paid	½
	Death tax		
	Value of estate		½
	Spouse exemption		½
	Charge @ 40%		½
			9
(b)	Residue of estate		1
			10

(a) **Afiya – Inheritance tax on death**

Lifetime transfers

14 September 2015

	£
Value of shares held before transfer 8,000 × £8	64,000
Less value of shares held after transfer 1,500 × £3	(4,500)
Transfer of value	59,500
Less: annual exemption 2015/16	(3,000)
annual exemption 2014/15 b/f	(3,000)
Potentially exempt transfer	53,500

27 January 2016

	£
Net chargeable transfer	400,000

IHT	
325,000 × 0%	0
75,000 × 20/80 (donor pays tax)	18,750
400,000	18,750
Gross chargeable transfer £(400,000 + 18,750)	418,750

Additional tax on lifetime transfer on death of donor

14 September 2015

Potentially exempt transfer of £53,500 becomes chargeable as donor dies within seven years.

Within nil rate band at death, no tax to pay.

27 January 2016

Nil rate band available £(325,000 – 53,500) = <u>£271,500</u>.

	£
Gross chargeable transfer	<u>418,750</u>

IHT	
271,500 × 0%	0
<u>147,250</u> × 40%	58,900
<u>418,750</u>	<u>58,900</u>
No taper relief (death within three years of transfer)	
Less lifetime tax paid	<u>(18,750)</u>
Additional tax payable on death	<u>40,150</u>

Death estate

	£
Assets at death	623,000
Less funeral expenses	<u>(3,000)</u>
Value of estate for IHT purposes	620,000
Less exempt legacy to spouse	<u>(150,000)</u>
Chargeable estate	<u>470,000</u>
IHT liability £470,000 × 40%	<u>188,000</u>

(b)   Afiya's children will inherit the residue of £(620,000 – 150,000 – 40,000 – 188,000) = <u>£242,000</u>.

155 Kendra

Text references. Inheritance tax is covered in Chapter 18.

Top tips. Lifetime gifts may involve both inheritance tax and capital gains tax. Sometimes it will be preferable for a gift to be made on death since there is no capital gains tax charge on death and the assets will pass to the beneficiary at death (probate) value.

Easy marks. The calculation of the death estate should have been easy marks.

		Marks
(a)	Property	½
	Building society deposits	½
	ISAs	½
	NS&I certificates	½
	Proceeds of life assurance policy	1
	Funeral expenses	½
	Loan	½
	Inheritance tax	<u>1</u>
		5

			Marks
(b)	No IHT benefit	1½	
	No CGT benefit	1½	
			3
(c)	Skip a generation	1	
	Avoids double charge to IHT	1	
			2
			10

(a) **Kendra – Inheritance tax on death**

	£
Property	970,000
Building society deposits	387,000
Individual Savings Accounts	39,000
NS&I certificates	17,000
Proceeds of life policy	225,000
Gross estate	1,638,000
Less funeral expenses	(12,800)
loan	(1,200)
Net estate	1,624,000

Inheritance tax

£325,000 @ 0%	0
£1,299,000 @ 40%	519,600
Inheritance tax liability	519,600

(b) As the property is not expected to increase in value in the near future, there is no inheritance tax benefit in making a lifetime gift. Kendra would need to live for three more years for taper relief to be available.

Also, a lifetime gift would result in a capital gains tax liability of £48,720 (£174,000 at 28%) for 2016/17, whereas a transfer on death would be an exempt disposal.

(c) It can be beneficial to skip a generation so that gifts are made to grandchildren rather than children, particularly if the children already have significant assets.

This avoids a further charge to inheritance tax when the children die. Gifts will then only be taxed once before being inherited by the grandchildren, rather than twice.

156 James

Text references. Chapter 18 deals with inheritance tax.

Top tips. When working out the inheritance death tax on the lifetime transfer, remember to look back seven years from the date of the lifetime transfer (not the date of death) to see whether there are any previous transfers to cumulate.

Easy marks. The nil rate band is used up on the first gift so the calculation of the inheritance tax on the CLT and death estate are easy.

		Marks
(a)	Potentially exempt transfer (after annual exemptions)	1
	Nil rate band available	1½
	Inheritance tax	½
	Daughter to pay	½
	Chargeable lifetime transfer	½
	Inheritance tax	½
	Trustees to pay	½
	Death estate – IHT liability	½
	James' personal representatives to pay	½
		6
(b)	Avoidance of double taxation	2
(c)	Taper relief	½
	Lifetime transfer values fixed	½
	IHT saving	1
		2
		10

(a) **James – Inheritance tax arising on death**
Lifetime transfers within seven years of death
14 May 2015

		£
Gift		420,000
Less: annual exemption	2015/16	(3,000)
annual exemption	2014/15 b/f	(3,000)
Potentially exempt transfer		414,000

Inheritance tax liability	£296,000 (W) @ 0%	0
	£118,000 @ 40%	47,200
		47,200

James' daughter will be responsible for paying the inheritance tax of £47,200.

2 August 2015

	£
Chargeable lifetime transfer	260,000

	£
Inheritance tax liability £260,000 @ 40%	104,000

The trustees will be responsible for paying the inheritance tax of £104,000.

Death estate

	£
Chargeable estate	870,000

	£
Inheritance tax liability £870,000 @ 40%	348,000

The personal representatives of James' estate will be responsible for paying the inheritance tax of £348,000.

Working – Available nil rate band

	£	£
Nil rate band at date of death		325,000
Gift 9 October 2009	35,000	
Less: annual exemption 2009/10	(3,000)	
annual exemption 2008/09 b/f	(3,000)	(29,000)
Nil rate band available		296,000

(b) Skipping a generation avoids a further charge to inheritance tax when the children die. Gifts will then only be taxed once before being inherited by the grandchildren, rather than twice.

(c) Even if the donor does not survive for seven years, taper relief will reduce the amount of IHT payable after three years.

The value of potentially exempt transfers and chargeable lifetime transfers are fixed at the time they are made.

James therefore saved inheritance tax of £20,000 (£(310,000 – 260,000) @ 40%) by making the lifetime gift of property.

157 Alan

Text references. The calculation of chargeable gains and the computation of capital gains tax are covered in Chapter 13. Chapter 18 deals with inheritance tax.

Top tips. When working out the inheritance death tax on the lifetime transfer, remember to look back seven years from the date of the lifetime transfer (not the date of death) to see whether there are any previous transfers to cumulate.

Easy marks. There were some easy marks in part (a)(i) for basic computation of capital gains tax. You should also have been able to identify the use of annual exemptions in part (a)(ii). The computation of inheritance tax on the death estate in part (b)(ii) was straightforward.

Marking scheme

				Marks
(a)	(i)	*CGT on lifetime gift*		
		Chargeable gain	1	
		Annual exempt amount	½	
		CGT payable	½	
				2
	(ii)	*IHT on lifetime gift*		
		Identify no lifetime tax on PET	½	
		Gift	½	
		Annual exemptions	1	
		Nil rate band at death	1	
		Death tax	½	
		Taper relief	½	
				4
(b)	(i)	CGT on death		1
	(ii)	*IHT on death*		
		Transfer of value	½	
		Nil rate band at death	1	
		Death tax	½	
				2
(c)		Conclusion		1
				10

(a) (i) *CGT payable on lifetime gift 10 December 2016*

	£
Proceeds (market value)	450,000
Less cost	(375,000)
Chargeable gain	75,000
Less annual exempt amount	(11,100)
Taxable gain	63,900
CGT on £63,900 @ 20% (higher rate taxpayer)	12,780

(ii) *IHT payable on lifetime gift 10 December 2016 if Alan dies on 1 April 2020*

Potentially exempt transfer (PET) on 10 December 2016. No lifetime inheritance tax.

Value of PET £450,000 less £3,000 (AE 2016/17) and £3,000 (AE 2015/16) = £444,000.

PET becomes chargeable when Alan dies within seven years.

Lifetime transfer of value of £55,000 in seven years before 10 December 2016 (transfers after 10 December 2009). Nil rate band of £(325,000 – 55,000) = £270,000 available to compute death tax.

	£
£270,000 × 0%	0
£174,000 × 40%	69,600
£444,000	69,600
Less taper relief @ 20% (3 to 4 years)	(13,920)
Death tax payable	55,680

(b) (i) *CGT on death*

The transfer of the Crimson plc shares on Alan's death is an exempt disposal and Julie will take the shares at their value at Alan's death (probate value).

(ii) *IHT payable on death estate*

No lifetime transfers of value in seven years before 1 April 2020 (transfers after 1 April 2013). Nil rate band (at date of death) of £325,000 available.

Value of death estate is £500,000.

Death tax payable is:

	£
£325,000 × 0%	0
£175,000 × 40%	70,000
£500,000	70,000

(c) Based on the answers to parts (a) and (b), it would be more tax advantageous for Alan to gift the Crimson plc shares to Julie in his lifetime because this would result in an overall tax saving of:

£([12,780(CGT) + 55,680(IHT)] – [0(CGT) + 70,000(IHT)])   £1,540

Tutorial note

Mark will be awarded for any *sensible* conclusion based on your own answers in parts (a) and (b).

MCQ bank – Corporation tax liabilities 1

158 C £7,000

Legal expenses in respect of leases are only allowable if they relate to the **renewal** of a short lease. The cost of arranging a bank loan for trade purposes is allowable. A debt written off in respect of a former employee is accounted for under the non-trade loan relationship rules as it does not relate to the trade of the company. A small donation to a local charity with publicity would normally be allowable as being for the purposes of the trade. The amount to add back is therefore £(3,000 + £4,000) = £7,000.

159 C 12 months to 30 November 2016, 4 months to 31 March 2017

If the company has a long period of account it is divided into one period of 12 months and one of the remainder.

160 C £2,720

	£
Leasing cost	3,200
£3,200 × 15% disallowance	(480)
Allowable deduction	2,720

161 B £3,352

	Main pool £	Special rate pool £	Allowances £
Additions	30,400	15,400	
WDA 8% × 6/12		(616)	616
18% × 6/12	(2,736)		2,736
TWDV c/f / Allowances	27,664	14,784	3,352

Do not forget to pro-rate writing down allowances in a short accounting period. No adjustment is made for private use by a director for a company

162 B £20,219

	£
Proceeds	30,000
Less cost	(8,000)
Unindexed gain	22,000
Less indexation allowance	
$\dfrac{(263.0 - 215.1)}{215.1} \times £8,000$	(1,781)
Indexed gain	20,219

Companies are not entitled to the annual exempt amount.

CBE style OTQ bank – Corporation tax liabilities 2

163 £26,000

C plc must make a current year loss claim against total profits if it wishes to make a claim to carry a loss back. A company is permitted to carry back to 12 months only, against total profits (ie before qualifying charitable donations). Therefore the maximum carry back is the total profits in the year to 31 December 2015 ie £(25,000 + 1,000) = £26,000. This is less than the loss remaining, of £30,000, following the current year claim.

164 £83,750

	£
Loss	160,000
Less loss relief y/e 31.12.17	(5,000)
Less loss relief p/e 31.12.16 (40,000 + 15,500)	(55,500)
Less loss relief y/e 31.3.16 3/12 × (45,000 + 18,000)	(15,750)
Loss c/f	83,750

165 £18,000

	£
Trading loss	15,000
Excess qualifying charitable donation £(5,000 − 2,000)	3,000
Capital loss	0
Amount that can be surrendered as group relief	18,000

166

D plc	
F Ltd	

Group relief can be made to UK companies only, so not to G Inc, and where there is a ≥75% direct and indirect holding by the controlling company. D plc only has a (80% × 90%) = 72% interest in H Ltd.

167

I plc	K Ltd
J Ltd	

Losses can only be transferred to UK companies where there is a ≥ 75% direct interest at each level and >50% indirect holding by the top company. I plc has a (75% × 75%) = 56.25% interest in M Ltd.

Tay Ltd

Text references. Chargeable gains for companies is the subject of Chapter 20.

Top tips. The application of the rules for damaged assets in Question 168 is similar to rollover relief for replacement of business assets.

Easy marks. The chattels rules in Question 170 should have been well known.

168 B £155,000

	£
Proceeds	180,000
Less indexed cost	(155,000)
Gain	25,000
Gain immediately chargeable £(180,000 − 162,000)	(18,000)
Deduction from base cost of new warehouse	7,000

The base cost of the new warehouse is £(162,000 − 7,000) = £155,000.

169 A £8,000

	Market value £	Indexed cost £	Gain £
20,000 £1 Ordinary shares @ £4 each	80,000	64,000	
£40,000 (20,000 × £2) cash	40,000	32,000	8,000
	120,000	96,000	

170 D £5,000

Although the general rules is that wasting chattels are exempt, there is an exception for assets used for the purpose of a trade in respect of which capital allowances have been or could have been claimed. The usual chattel rules therefore apply as follows:

	£
Proceeds	9,000
Less cost	(3,500)
Gain	5,500

The maximum gain is $5/3 \times £(9,000 - 6,000) = £5,000$.

The chargeable gain is the lower of £5,500 and £5,000, so it is £5,000.

171 C £16,108

	£
Proceeds	45,000
Less cost	(20,000)
enhancement (drainage)	(2,000)
Unindexed gain	23,000
Less indexation on cost £20,000 × 0.324	(6,480)
indexation on enhancement £2,000 × 0.206	(412)
Chargeable gain	16,108

172 C 2 and 4

The capital loss can be set against chargeable gains made in the year ended 31 March 2018 and the capital loss can be carried forward and set against the first available chargeable gains.

Capital losses cannot be carried back and cannot be set against profits other than chargeable gains.

CBE style OT case – Hyde plc group

Text references. Groups are the subject of Chapter 22.

Top tips. Make sure you know the difference between the rules for relationships between companies for group relief and those applying to chargeable gains groups.

Easy marks. The identification of the base cost of the factory in Question 177 should have been easy marks if you remembered that transfers between chargeable gains group companies are on a no gain, no loss basis.

173

Hampstead plc	Regent plc
	Primrose plc

A company is in a group relief group where there is a ≥75% direct and indirect holding by the controlling company (Hyde plc). Hyde plc has a (95% × 80%) = 76% interest in Primrose Ltd but only has a (85% × 85%) = 72.25% interest in Richmond Ltd.

174 £70,000

	£
Trading loss	68,000
Excess qualifying charitable donations £(5,000 – 3,000)	2,000
Maximum group relief	70,000

175   £50,500

	£
Chargeable gain	48,000
Interest income	12,000
Trading loss	(8,000)
Qualifying charitable donations	(1,500)
Available taxable total profits	50,500

Hyde plc is assumed to use its own current year losses in working out the taxable total profits against which it may claim group relief, even if it does not in fact claim relief for current losses against total profits. Group relief is set against taxable total profits after all other reliefs for the current period such as qualifying charitable donations.

176   A claim for group relief will be ineffective unless Greenwich plc gives a notice of consent. The claim for group relief would be made on Hyde plc's corporation tax return.

Any payment by Hyde plc for group relief, up to the amount of the loss surrendered, is ignored for all corporation tax purposes. A claim for group relief between Greenwich plc and Hyde plc will be available against 9/12ths of the taxable total profits of Hyde plc for the year to 31 March 2018, since surrendered losses must be set against taxable total profits of a corresponding accounting period (1 April 2017 to 31 December 2017).

177   £120,000

	£
Cost	100,000
Indexation allowance to date of transfer £100,000 × 0.200	20,000
Base cost for Primrose plc	120,000

The transfer of assets within a chargeable gains group is on a no gain/ no loss basis including indexation to the date of the transfer.

178 Do-Not-Panic Ltd

Text references. Chapter 19 cover computing taxable total profits and the corporation tax liability. Payment of corporation tax is covered in Chapter 23.

Top tips. Split out the long period correctly into the two accounting periods. Remember it is always the first twelve months and then the balance (in this case three months).

Easy marks. Allocating the figures between the two accounting periods should be straightforward.

Marking scheme

		Marks
Trading profit		1
Capital allowances	– year ended 31 December 2016	2
Capital allowances	– period ended 31 March 2017	1½
Interest income	– period ended 31 March 2017	1
Capital gains		1
Qualifying charitable donation – period ended 31 March 2017		1
Corporation tax	– year ended 31 December 2016	1
	– period ended 31 March 2017	½
Due dates		1
		10

Do-Not-Panic Ltd – Corporation tax liabilities for the fifteen-month period ended 31 March 2017

	Year ended 31 December 2016 £	Period ended 31 March 2017 £
Trading profit (12:3)	228,000	57,000
Capital allowances (W)	(17,000)	(5,000)
	211,000	52,000
Interest income (accruals basis)	–	9,500
Capital gains (39,000 – 4,250)	–	34,750
	211,000	96,250
Less qualifying charitable donation	–	(2,000)
Taxable total profits	211,000	94,250

	FY 2015/FY 2016 £	FY 2016
y/e 31.12.16		
Rates for FY 2015 and FY 2016 are both 20% so can be dealt with together		
FY 2015/FY 2016		
£211,000 × 20%/CT for y/e 31.12.16	42,200	

p/e 31.3.17
FY 2016

£94,250 × 20%		18,850
Due dates	1 October 2017	1 January 2018

Working

Capital allowances

	FYA £	AIA £	Main pool £	Allowances £
Y/e 31 December 2016				
Addition qualifying for AIA				
Machinery		8,000		
AIA		(8,000)		8,000
Transfer to main pool		0	0	
Addition not qualifying for AIA but qualifying for FYA				
Car	9,000			
FYA	(9,000)			9,000
Transfer to main pool	0		0	
Allowances				17,000
P/e 31 March 2017				
TWDV b/f			0	
Addition qualifying for AIA				
Equipment		5,000		
AIA £200,000 × 3/12 = £50,000 maximum		(5,000)		5,000
Transfer to main pool		0	0	
TWDV c/f			0	
Allowances				5,000

179 Problematic Ltd

Marking scheme

			Marks
(a)	**Easy plc**		
	FA 1985 pool – Purchase		½
	– Rights issue		1
	– Indexation		2
	– Disposal		1
	Chargeable gain		1½
	Freehold factory		
	Disposal proceeds		½
	Indexed cost		½
	Rollover relief		2
			9
(b)	**Leasehold factory**		1
			10

(a) **Easy plc shares**

FA85 pool

	No. of shares	Cost £	Indexed cost £
Purchase 26.6.05	15,000	12,600	12,600
Index to September 2008			
$\dfrac{(218.4-192.2)}{192.2} \times £12,600$			1,718
Rights issue 1 for 3 @ £2.20	5,000	11,000	11,000
c/f	20,000	23,600	25,318
Index to June 2016			
$\dfrac{(261.2-218.4)}{218.4} \times £25,318$			4,962
			30,280
Sale	(16,000)	(18,880)	(24,224)
C/f	4,000	4,720	6,056

Gain	£
Proceeds	54,400
Less cost	(18,880)
	35,520
Less indexation £(24,224 – 18,880)	(5,344)
Chargeable gain	30,176

Freehold factory

	£
Proceeds	171,000
Less indexed cost	(127,000)
	44,000
Less gain deferred on purchase of leasehold factory £(44,000 – 16,200)	(27,800)
Chargeable gain (amount not reinvested £(171,000 – 154,800))	16,200

(b)   The leasehold factory is a depreciating asset, so there is no adjustment to the base cost of £154,800.

Tutorial note

When a replacement asset is a depreciating asset then the gain is not rolled over by reducing the cost of the replacement asset. Instead, the gain is deferred until it crystallises on the earliest of:

- The disposal of the replacement asset.
- The date the replacement asset is no longer used in the business.
- Ten years after the acquisition of the replacement asset which in this case is 10 December 2026.

180 Volatile Ltd

Text references. Corporation tax losses are covered in Chapter 21.

Top tips. Don't forget to set up a loss memorandum for each loss so that you can see how the loss is utilised.

Easy marks. You should have been able to state at least one of the principles of claiming loss relief in part (a).

(a)   **Choice of loss relief**

The two factors that will influence a company's choice of loss relief claims are:

- How quickly relief will be obtained: loss relief against total profits is quicker than carry forward loss relief.

- The extent to which relief for qualifying charitable donations might be lost.

(b) **Volatile Ltd**

	P/e 31.12.12 £	Y/e 31.12.13 £	Y/e 31.12.14 £	P/e 30.9.15 £
Trading income	44,000	0	95,200	78,700
Less carry forward loss relief	(0)	(0)	(8,700)	(0)
	44,000	0	86,500	78,700
Property business income	9,400	6,600	6,500	0
Chargeable gains (11,700 – 2,000)	5,100	0	0	9,700
Total profits	58,500	6,600	93,000	88,400
Less current period loss relief	(0)	(6,600)	(0)	(0)
Less carry back loss relief	(58,500)		(23,250)	(88,400)
	0	0	69,750	0
Less qualifying charitable donations	(0)	(0)	(1,200)	(0)
Taxable total profits	0	0	68,550	0

Loss memorandum

	£
Loss in y/e 31.12.13	73,800
Less used y/e 31.12.13	(6,600)
Less used p/e 31.12.12	(58,500)
Less used y/e 31.12.14	(8,700)
Loss remaining unrelieved	0

	£
Loss in y/e 30.9.16	186,800
Less used p/e 30.9.15	(88,400)
Less: used y/e 31.12.14	
3 months to 31.12.14	
£93,000 × 3/12	(23,250)
Loss remaining unrelieved	75,150

The loss of y/e 30.9.16 can be carried back against total profits of the previous 12 months ie against the 9 month period ending 30.9.15 and 3 months of the y/e 31.12.14.

181 Acebook Ltd

> **Text references.** Capital losses are included in Chapter 21. Chargeable gains for companies are covered in Chapter 20.
>
> **Top tips.** Use the three column pro forma for the company's share pool and take care to add the indexation allowance to the cost in the pool to obtain the indexed cost.
>
> **Easy marks.** Part (a) was a straightforward statement of the use of capital losses for companies.

(a) When a limited company has a capital loss, it is first set off against any chargeable gains arising in the same accounting period.

Any remaining capital loss is then carried forward and set off against the first available chargeable gains of future accounting periods.

(b) **Acebook Ltd – Chargeable gain on disposal on 10 March 2017**

	No of shares	Cost £	Indexed cost £
Purchase June 2003	8,000	25,200	25,200
Bonus issue October 2006 2:1	16,000		
	24,000		
Indexed rise to February 2008 0.166 × £25,200			4,183
Rights issue February 2008 1:5 @ £4.30	4,800	20,640	20,640
	28,800	45,840	50,023
Indexed rise to March 2017 0.248 × £50,023			12,406
			62,429
Disposal	(28,800)	(45,840)	(62,429)

The gain is computed as follows:

	£
Proceeds 28,800 × £3.20	92,160
Less indexed cost	(62,429)
Indexed gain	29,731

182 Black Ltd and Gastron Ltd

Marking scheme

			Marks
(a)	**Maximum potential claim by Black Ltd**		
	After losses brought forward used	1	
	Qualifying charitable donations	½	
	Maximum claim	½	
	Maximum surrender by White Ltd		
	Trading loss – current period only/maximum claim	1	
	Qualifying charitable donations	1	
	Capital losses	½	
	Maximum group relief claim that can be made	½	
			5
(b) (i)	75% shareholding	1	
	50% effective interest	1	
			2
(ii)	Set off of capital loss		1
(iii)	No gain no loss transfers	1	
	Rollover relief	1	
			2
			10

(a) **Black Ltd – Group relief claim for year ended 31 March 2017**

Maximum potential claim by Black Ltd

Black Ltd uses its own losses brought forward in working out the taxable total profits against which it may claim group relief.

Furthermore, group relief is against taxable total profits after all other reliefs for the current period (for example qualifying charitable donations).

The maximum potential claim by Black Ltd is therefore £(396,800 – 57,900 + 21,100 – 4,400) = £355,600.

Maximum potential surrender by White Ltd

White Ltd may surrender its current period trading losses of £351,300. Only current period losses are available for group relief so White Ltd's loss of £21,800 brought forward cannot be group relieved.

White Ltd may also surrender excess qualifying charitable donations (ie to the extent that they exceed total profits before taking account of any losses). Since the qualifying charitable donations of £5,600 do not exceed the total profits of £26,700, there is no excess.

It is not possible to surrender capital losses as part of a group relief claim.

The maximum potential surrender by White Ltd is therefore £351,300.

Maximum group relief claim

The maximum group relief claim is the lower of the claim that can be made by Black Ltd and the surrender that can be made by White Ltd ie £351,300.

(b) (i) Companies form a chargeable gains group if at each level in the group structure there is a 75% shareholding.

However, the parent company must also have an effective interest of over 50% in each group company.

(ii) The election will enable the capital loss of £66,000 to be set against the capital gain of £74,800 and so save tax in the current year. Otherwise the loss would have to be carried forward by Culinary Ltd and set against future gains.

Tutorial note

Alternatively, an election could have been made to transfer the loss of Culinary Ltd to Gastron Ltd to set against the gain. The overall corporation tax effect for the chargeable gains group would have been the same.

(iii) Companies in a chargeable gains group make intra-group transfers of chargeable assets without a chargeable gain or an allowable loss arising.

If a member of a chargeable gains group disposes of an asset eligible for chargeable gains rollover relief it may treat all of the group companies as a single unit for the purpose of claiming such relief.

183 Jogger Ltd (A)

Text references. Capital allowances are dealt with in Chapter 8. Corporation tax computation is dealt with in Chapter 19.

Top tips. Make sure you use the capital allowances proforma in part (a).

Easy marks. There were easy marks in part (b) for the corporation tax computation.

Marking scheme

			Marks
(a)	Operating loss	½	
	Depreciation	½	
	P&M – AIA set against machinery in priority to SLA	1½	
	– FYA	1	
	– Main pool	1½	
	– Special rate pool	1½	
	– Short life asset	1½	
			8
(b)	Bank interest	½	
	Loan interest	1	
	Property business profit	2	
	Chargeable gain	2	
	Loss relief	1	
	Corporation tax	½	
			7
			15

(a) **Jogger Ltd – trading loss y/e 31 March 2017**

	£
Operating profit	156,482
Add depreciation	58,840
	215,322
Less capital allowances (W)	(271,182)
Adjusted trading loss	(55,860)

Working

Plant and machinery

	AIA	FYA	Main pool	Special rate pool	SLA	Allowances
	£	£	£	£	£	£
TWDV b/f			26,600	18,800		
Addition qualifying for AIA						
30.9.16 Machinery	500,000					
AIA	(200,000)		300,000			200,000
Addition qualifying for AIA but not claimed						
15.12.16 Computer					12,500	
Addition qualifying for FYA						
15.8.16 Car		9,000				
FYA		(9,000)				9,000
Addition not qualifying for AIA nor FYA						
31.7.16 Car			11,800			
Disposal						
20.7.16 Car				(11,700)		
				7,100		
14.3.17 Lorry			(8,600)			
			329,800			
WDA @ 18%			(59,364)		(2,250)	61,614
WDA @ 8%				(568)		568
TWDV c/f			270,436	6,532	10,250	
Allowances						271,182

(b) **Jogger Ltd – corporation tax liability y/e 31 March 2017**

	£
Interest income (W1)	33,060
Property income (W2)	126,000
Chargeable gain (W3)	86,980
Total profits	246,040
Less loss relief	(55,860)
Taxable total profits	190,180
£190,180 × 20%	38,036

Workings

1   *Interest income*

		£
Bank interest receivable		8,460
Loan interest	– received 31.12.16	16,400
	– accrued 31.3.17	8,200
		33,060

2   *Property income*

	£
Premium received	100,000
Less 2% × (10 – 1) × £100,000	(18,000)
Taxable as property income	82,000
Add rental income accrued	44,000
	126,000

3   *Chargeable gain*

	£
Disposal proceeds	150,000
Less cost	(47,660)
	102,340
Less indexation allowance £47,660 × $\dfrac{263.4 - 199.2}{199.2}$	(15,360)
Gain	86,980

184 Mice Ltd

Text references. Property business income is dealt with in Chapters 6 and 19. Losses for companies are in Chapter 21.

Top tips. You should use the loss relief pro-forma in part (b).

Easy marks. The calculation of property business profit in part (a) was straightforward and should have been easy marks.

			Marks
(a)	Lease premium received		1½
	Rent receivable	– Property 1	1
		– Property 2	½
		– Property 3	½
	Business rates		½
	Repairs		1
	Advertising		½
	Insurance		1½
	Loan interest		1
			8

BPP
LEARNING MEDIA

(b) **Year ended 31 March 2017**

Property business profit	½
Loan interest	1½
Chargeable gain	1½
Loss relief	1
Other periods	
Trading profit	½
Property business profit	½
Loss relief	1
Qualifying charitable donations	½
	7
	15

(a) **Mice Ltd – property business profit y/e 31 March 2017**

	£	£
Premium received for lease	18,000	
Less £18,000 × 2% × (8 – 1)	(2,520)	
Amount taxable as property business income		15,480
Property 1 rent accrued £3,200 × 4		12,800
Property 2 rent accrued		6,000
Property 3 rent accrued		0
Gross income accrued		34,280
Less: expenses accrued		
business rates	2,200	
repairs (N1)	1,060	
advertising	680	
insurance £(460 + 310 + (480 × 3/12))	890	
loan interest (N2)	0	
		(4,830)
Property business profit		29,450

Notes

1 The enlargement of the car park is capital expenditure which cannot be deducted when calculating the property business profit.

2 Interest paid in respect of a loan to purchase property is set off under the loan relationship rules.

(b) **Mice Ltd – taxable total profits y/e 31 March 2017**

	£	£
Property business profit		29,450
Loan interest		
Received 31 December 2016	6,400	
Accrued 31 March 2017	3,200	
Paid on property 3 loan –		
1 January 2017 to 31 March 2017	(1,800)	
		7,800
Chargeable gain (W)		2,750
Total profits		40,000
Less current period loss relief		(40,000)
Taxable total profits		0

Working

	£
Net disposal proceeds 95% × £34,844	33,102
Less cost	(28,000)
	5,102
Less indexation allowance £28,000 × $\frac{263.4 - 243.0}{243.0}$ (= 0.084)	(2,352)
Gain	2,750

Mice Ltd – taxable total profits for periods ending 31 March 2014, 2015 and 2016

	p/e 31.3.14 £	y/e 31.3.15 £	y/e 31.3.16 £
Trading profit	83,200	24,700	51,200
Property business profit	2,800	7,100	12,200
Total profits	86,000	31,800	63,400
Less carry back loss relief	(0)	(0)	(63,400)
	86,000	31,800	0
Less qualifying charitable donation	(1,000)	(1,500)	(0)
Taxable total profits	85,000	30,300	0

There is no loss relief in the period to 31 March 2014 or the year ended 31 March 2015 because loss relief for a continuing business is restricted to 12 months before the loss making period.

185 Molten-Metal plc

Text references. Computing taxable total profits and the corporation tax liability is covered in Chapter 19. Capital allowances are covered in Chapter 8.

Top tips. This question has a lot to information for you to deal with. Study the layout of the suggested solution, in particular note how detailed calculations are contained in Workings. Try to adopt this layout in your answers.

Easy marks. Working out the corporation tax liability was an easy half mark.

Molten-Metal plc – Corporation tax computation for the year ended 31 March 2017

	£	£
Trading profit		2,170,144
Less: Loan stock interest payable £(22,500 + 3,700 – 4,200)	22,000	
Capital allowances P&M (W1)	240,638	
		(262,638)
		1,907,506
Interest income (W2)		8,700
Taxable total profits		1,916,206
Corporation tax £1,916,206 @ 20%		383,241

Tutorial note

Interest paid in respect of a loan used for trading purposes is deductible in calculating the trading profit.

Workings

1   Capital allowances

	AIA	Main pool	Special rate pool	Short life asset	Allowances
	£	£	£	£	£
TWDVs c/f		87,800			
AIA additions					
Office building	0				
Ventilation system	31,000				
Lift	42,000				
	73,000				
AIA – 100%	(73,000)				73,000
Transfer balance to special rate pool	0		0		
Machinery	186,600				
Building alterations	7,700				
Wall	0				
Partition walls	22,900				
	217,200				
AIA	(127,000)				127,000
Transfer balance to main pool	90,200	90,200			
Other additions					
Computer				2,500	
Motor car			24,000		
Motor cars					
£17,300 × 2		34,600			
		212,600			
WDA @ 18%		(38,268)		(450)	38,718
WDA @ 8%			(1,920)		1,920
TWDVs c/f		174,332	22,080	2,050	
Allowances					240,638

Tutorial notes

1   The ventilation system and lift are both integral to a building and so are special rate pool expenditure. It is beneficial to claim the annual investment allowance of £200,000 initially against this expenditure, as it would otherwise only qualify for writing down allowance at the rate of 8%.

2   The building alterations were necessary for the installation of the machinery, and therefore qualify for capital allowances. Walls are specifically excluded, with the exception of partition walls which are movable and intended to be so moved.

3   The computer will be depooled by making the election and treated as a short life asset. The annual investment allowance should not be claimed against this asset as this will effectively disapply the depooling election.

4   The motor car acquired in November 2016 has CO_2 emissions over 130 grams per kilometre, and therefore qualifies for writing down allowances at the rate of 8% as part of the special rate pool.

5   The motor cars acquired in March 2017 have CO_2 emissions between 76 and 130 grams per kilometre, and therefore qualify for writing down allowances at the rate of 18% as part of the main pool. The private use of a motor car is irrelevant, since such usage will be assessed on the employee as a benefit.

2   *Interest income*

	£
Loan interest receivable £(9,800 + 3,100)	12,900
Bank interest receivable	2,600
	15,500
Less interest payable	(6,800)
Net interest income	8,700

186 Starfish Ltd (A)

Text references. Computing taxable total profits is covered in Chapter 19. Corporation tax losses are dealt with in Chapter 21.

Top tips. Make sure that you set out the computation of taxable total profits in part (b) using the standard layout, leaving space for losses carried forward against trading profits and losses carried back against total profits.

Easy marks. The adjustment of profit computation in part (a) was reasonably straightforward.

Marking scheme

			Marks
(a)	Depreciation		½
	Donations		1
	Impairment loss		½
	Legal fees		1
	Entertaining customers		½
	Counselling services		½
	Plant and machinery	– WDV brought forward	1
		– Addition	1½
		– Main pool proceeds	2
		– Motor car proceeds	1
		– Balancing adjustments	½
			10
(b)	Trading profit		½
	Relief for 2013 loss	– Period ended 31 March 2013	½
		– Carry forward	½
	Bank interest		½
	Relief for 2017 loss	– Year ended 31 March 2014	1
		– Other periods	1
	Qualifying charitable donations		1
			5
			15

(a) **Starfish Ltd – Trading loss for the period ended 31 March 2017**

	£	£
Loss before taxation		(190,000)
Add: Depreciation	25,030	
Donation to political party	900	
Donation paid (qualifying charitable donation)	750	
Impairment loss	0	
Legal fees – Misleading advertisement	2,020	
– Issue of loan notes	0	
Entertaining customers	3,600	
Counselling services	0	
		32,300
		(157,700)
Less capital allowances (W1)		(2,300)
Adjusted trading loss		(160,000)

Workings

1 *Capital allowances*

	Main pool	Special rate pool	Allowances
	£	£	£
TWDVs b/f	23,600	13,200	
Addition – computer (W2)	2,600		
	26,200		
Disposals (W3)	(27,500)	(9,600)	
Balancing charge	(1,300)		(1,300)
Balancing allowance		3,600	3,600
Total allowances			2,300

2 *Computer*

The input VAT on the computer is recoverable and so only the cost net of VAT is eligible expenditure which is £3,120 × 100/120 = £2,600.

3 *Disposal proceeds*

The output VAT charged on the disposals is not part of the proceeds for capital allowance purposes. The main pool proceeds are therefore £([31,200 + 1,800] × 100/120) = £27,500. There is no VAT charged on the sale of the car, as none was recovered on purchase (owing to private usage).

Tutorial notes

1 The cost of obtaining loan finance, even if abortive, is allowable as a trading loan relationship debit.

2 The costs of counselling services for redundant employees are deductible if they qualify for exemption from the employment income charge on employees.

3 The annual investment allowance and writing down allowances are not given for the period in which a trade ceases. Therefore the addition is simply added into the main pool.

(b)   **Starfish Ltd – Taxable total profits**

	P/e 31.3.13	Y/e 31.3.14	Y/e 31.3.15	Y/e 31.3.16	P/e 31.12.16
	£	£	£	£	£
Trading profit	0	64,200	53,900	14,700	49,900
Less c/f loss relief (N1)	0	(12,600)	0	0	0
	0	51,600	53,900	14,700	49,900
Bank interest	600	1,400	1,700	0	0
	600	53,000	55,600	14,700	49,900
Less c/b loss relief (N2)	(0)	(13,250)	(55,600)	(14,700)	(49,900)
	600	39,750	0	0	0
Less: qualifying charitable donations (N3)	(600)	(1,000)	(0)	(0)	(0)
Taxable total profits	0	38,750	0	0	0

Tutorial notes

1   Starfish Ltd would not have made a loss relief claim against total profits for the period ended 31 March 2013 as this would have wasted the £600 of relieved qualifying charitable donations for that period.

2   The trading loss for the period ended 31 March 2017 can be relieved against total profits for the 3 years immediately preceding the start of the loss making period since it is a terminal loss. The 3 year period is between 1 January 2014 and 31 December 2016. Relief is as follows:

	£
Loss of 3 month p/e 31.3.17	160,000
Less used in p/e 31.12.16	(49,900)
	110,100
Less used in y/e 31.3.16	(14,700)
	95,400
Less used in y/e 31.3.15	(55,600)
	39,800
Less used in y/e 31.3.14	
(restricted to 3/12 × £53,000)	(13,250)
Balance unrelieved	26,550

3   The qualifying charitable donations in the period ending 31 March 2017, and earlier years, are also unrelieved.

187 Softapp Ltd

> **Text references.** The computation of taxable total profits and the corporation tax liability is covered in Chapter 19.
>
> **Top tips.** Watch out for the accruals basis in the computation of interest and property business income.
>
> **Easy marks.** There were some easy marks for the calculation of capital allowances and property business income.

Marking scheme

		Marks
Operating profit		½
Depreciation		½
Amortisation		½
Deduction for lease premium:	premium received	½
	amount not assessed on landlord	1
	deduction for trader	1½
Loan stock interest		1
Capital allowances:	building costs	½
	heating system	½
	ventilation system	½
	AIA on special rate pool expenditure	1
	computer equipment	½
	furniture and furnishings	½
	fridge and cooker	½
	AIA on main rate pool expenditure	½
	WDA	½
Chargeable gain:	proceeds	½
	cost	½
	indexation allowance	1
Property business income		1
Interest income		1
Corporation tax		½
		15

Softapp Ltd – Corporation tax computation for the year ended 31 March 2017

		£
Operating profit		711,475
Add:	depreciation	10,170
	amortisation	2,500
		724,145
Less:	deduction for lease premium (W1)	(2,050)
	loan stock interest payable (trading loan relationship)	(67,200)
	capital allowances (W2)	(202,520)
Trading profit		452,375
Property business income (W3)		27,500
Chargeable gain (W4)		61,525
Interest income (non-trading loan relationships) £(5,600 + 2,500)		8,100
Taxable total profits		549,500

Corporation tax liability

£549,500 × 20%		109,900

Workings

1   *Deduction for lease premium*

The amount assessed on the landlord is £82,000, calculated as follows:

	£
Premium	100,000
Less £100,000 × 2% × (10 – 1)	(18,000)
Assessable as property business income on landlord	82,000

This is deductible by a business tenant over the life of the lease so the deduction for Softapp Ltd for the year ended 31 March 2017 is £(82,000/10 × 3/12) = £2,050.

2   *Capital allowances*

	AIA	Main pool	Special rate pool	Allowances
	£	£	£	£
Additions qualifying for AIA				
Building costs	0			
Heating system	3,600			
Ventilation system	4,600			
	8,200			
AIA (part)	(8,200)			8,200
Transfer to SR pool	0		0	
Computer equipment	175,000			
Furniture and furnishings	29,400			
Fridge and cooker	1,400			
	205,800			
AIA (balance)	(191,800)			191,800
Transfer to main pool	14,000	14,000		
WDA @ 18%		(2,520)		2,520
TWDVs c/f		11,480	0	
Allowances				202,520

Tutorial notes

1   The expenditure which is integral to the building is special rate pool expenditure.

2   It is beneficial to claim the annual investment allowance of £200,000 against this expenditure in priority to main pool expenditure, as it would otherwise only qualify for writing down allowance at the rate of 8% in the special rate pool.

3   *Property business income*

	£
Rental income receivable	30,000
Less irrecoverable rent £5,000 × 1/2	(2,500)
Property business income	27,500

4   *Chargeable gain*

	£
Proceeds	93,219
Less cost	(30,000)
Unindexed gain	63,219
Less indexation allowance	
$\dfrac{(263.8 - 249.7)}{249.7} \times £30,000$	(1,694)
Indexed gain	61,525

188 Long Ltd group (A)

Text references. The computation of taxable total profits and the corporation tax liability are covered in Chapter 19. Groups of companies are covered in Chapter 22.

Top tips. A capital loss transferred between group companies can only be set against a capital gain, whereas a trading loss transferred between group companies is deducted in computing taxable total profits.

Easy marks. There were some easy marks for computing the corporation tax.

Marking scheme

		Marks
(a)	**Long Ltd**	
	Depreciation	½
	Capital allowances	
	TWDV b/f	½
	Lorry	½
	AIA	½
	Motor car	½
	WDA	½
	Group relief	1½
	Wind Ltd	½
	Amortisation	½
	Capital allowances	½
	Chargeable gain after loss relief	1½
	Corporation tax	½
	Road Ltd	
	Trading loss	½
	Donations	½
	Capital allowances	½
	Corporation tax computation	
	Interest income	½
	Qualifying charitable donations	½
	Corporation tax	½
		11
(b)	Definition of large company	1
	Application to Long Ltd group	1
	Profit threshold adjusted	½
	Taxable total profits	½
	Dividends from non-group companies	1
		4
		15

(a) **Long Ltd – Corporation tax computation for the year ended 31 March 2017**

	£
Operating profit	817,820
Add depreciation	10,170
	827,990
Less capital allowances (W)	(47,690)
Trading profit	780,300
Less group relief from Road Ltd	(34,900)
Taxable total profits	745,400

Corporation tax	
£745,400 × 20%	149,080

Tutorial note

Group relief is not restricted as the amount claimed is clearly less than 3/12ths of Long Ltd's taxable total profits.

Working

Capital allowances

	AIA £	Main pool £	Allowances £
TWDV b/f		44,800	
Addition qualifying for AIA			
Lorry	36,800		
AIA	(36,800)		36,800
Transfer to pool	0	0	
Addition not qualifying for AIA			
Motor car		15,700	
		60,500	
WDA @ 18%		(10,890)	10,890
TWDV c/f		49,610	
Allowances			47,690

Wind Ltd – Corporation tax computation for the year ended 31 March 2017

	£
Operating profit	59,490
Add depreciation	5,000
	64,490
Less capital allowances: WDA £900 × 100%	(900)
Trading profit	63,590
Chargeable gain £(29,800 – 21,300)	8,500
Taxable total profits	72,090

Corporation tax	
£72,090 × 20%	14,418

Tutorial notes

1 The balance on the main pool is less than £1,000, so a writing down allowance equal to the unrelieved expenditure can be claimed.

2 A joint election can be made to transfer Long Ltd's capital loss since this will give loss relief earlier than if the loss is carried forward against future gains made by Long Ltd.

Road Ltd – Trading loss for the three month period ended 31 March 2017

	£
Operating loss	(26,100)
Add donations	2,800
	(23,300)
Less capital allowances: FYA £11,600 × 100%	(11,600)
Trading loss (surrendered as group relief)	(34,900)

Tutorial notes

1   Political donations are not allowable. The qualifying charitable donations are not allowable in the calculation of the trading loss but will be deducted from total profits (see below).

2   The motor car purchased on 3 October 2016 is pre-trading expenditure and is treated as incurred on 1 January 2017. The motor car has CO_2 emissions up to 75 grams per kilometre and therefore qualifies for the 100% first year allowance.

3   Road Ltd's loss can be surrendered under group relief to either Long Ltd or Wind Ltd but if surrendered to Wind Ltd group relief would be restricted as 3/12ths of Wind Ltd's taxable total profits is less than Road Ltd's loss.

Road Ltd – Corporation tax computation for the three month period ended 31 March 2017

	£
Interest income/Total profits	4,300
Less qualifying charitable donations	(2,400)
Taxable total profits	1,900
Corporation tax	
£1,900 × 20%	380

Tutorial note

The qualifying charitable donations cannot be surrendered as group relief as they are fully relieved against Road Ltd's interest income: only *excess* qualifying charitable donations can be group relieved.

(b)   A large company is one whose profits exceed the profit threshold. Profits are the taxable total profits of the company plus the dividends received from other companies, other than those from 51% subsidiaries (group dividends). The threshold must also be divided by the number of related 51% group companies.

For Long Ltd for the year ended 31 March 2017, it is necessary to look at the situation at 31 March 2016 in respect of related 51% group companies. Wind Ltd was a related 51% group company at that date but Road Ltd was not since it only started trading on 1 January 2017.

The profit threshold is therefore £1,500,000/2 = £750,000.

Long Ltd's profits for the year ended 31 March 2017 are:

	£
Taxable total profits	745,400
Add dividends from non-group companies	32,000
Profits	777,400

Long Ltd is therefore a large company in the year ended 31 March 2017. Long Ltd would have to pay instalments for the year ended 31 March 2017 if it had also been large in the year ended 31 March 2016.

189 Lucky Ltd

Marking scheme

			Marks
(a)	After end of previous period	1	
	Other situations	1	
			2
(b)	Trading profit		
	Advertising	½	
	Depreciation	½	
	Amortisation	½	
	Lease premium deduction	1½	
	Capital allowances		
	Integral feature addition	½	
	Annual investment allowance	½	
	Computer addition	½	
	Office equipment addition	½	
	Annual investment allowance	1	
	WDA	1	
	Car addition	½	
	FYA	½	
	Interest income	½	
	Corporation tax	½	
			9
(c)	Date for retention	1	
	Penalty	1	
			2
(d)	Capital allowances	1	
	National insurance contributions	1	
			2
			15

(a) An accounting period will normally start immediately after the end of the preceding accounting period.

An accounting period will also start when a company commences to trade, or otherwise becomes liable to corporation tax.

(b) **Lucky Ltd – Corporation tax computation for the four-month period ended 31 March 2017**

	£
Operating profit	432,600
Advertising	0
Depreciation	14,700
Amortisation	9,000
Deduction for lease premium £46,800/12 × 4/12	(1,300)
Capital allowances (W1)	(80,291)
Trading profit	374,709
Interest income	700
Taxable total profits	375,409
Corporation tax £375,409 @ 20%	75,082

Tutorial note

The advertising expenditure incurred during September 2016 is pre-trading, and is treated as incurred on 1 December 2016. It is therefore deductible and no adjustment is required.

Workings

1   Capital allowances

	£	Main pool £	Special rate pool £	Allowances £
Additions qualifying for AIA				
Integral features	41,200			
AIA	(41,200)			41,200
Transfer balance to special rate pool			0	
Computer	6,300			
Office equipment	32,900			
	39,200			
AIA (W2)	(25,467)			25,467
Transfer balance to main pool		13,733		
WDA 18% × 4/12		(824)		824
Addition qualifying for FYA				
Motor car	12,800			
FYA 100%	(12,800)			12,800
Transfer balance to main pool		0		
WDV carried forward		12,909	0	
Total allowances				80,291

2   Annual investment allowances

The annual investment allowance is reduced to £66,667 (£200,000 × 4/12) because Lucky Ltd's accounting period is four months long.

Tutorial notes

1   The expenditure which is integral to the building is included in the special rate pool.

2   It is beneficial to claim the annual investment allowance of £66,667 initially against this integral features expenditure, as it would otherwise only qualify for writing down allowance at the rate of 8%.

3   The computer purchased on 19 August 2016 is pre-trading and is treated as incurred on 1 December 2016.

4 The motor car has CO_2 emissions up to 75 grams per kilometre and therefore qualifies for the 100% first year allowance.

(c) Lucky Ltd must retain the records used in preparing its self-assessment corporation tax return until six years after the end of the accounting period, which is 31 March 2023.

A failure to retain records could result in a penalty of up to £3,000 per accounting period. However, the maximum penalty will only be charged in serious cases.

(d) The cost of the car will be included in Lucky Ltd's capital allowance computation and written down at the appropriate rate each year depending on the car's CO_2 emissions.

Lucky Ltd will also have to pay Class 1A national insurance contributions on the company car. Class 1A is deductible from taxable trading profits.

190 Jump Ltd

Text references. The computation of taxable total profits and the corporation tax liability are covered in Chapter 19. Groups of companies are covered in Chapter 22.

Top tips. In part (a), remember to include a zero when an item needs no adjustment, otherwise, you will not be credited for this knowledge.

Easy marks. Most of the adjustments to profit appear regularly in corporation tax questions.

Marking scheme

				Marks
(a)	*Trading loss*			
	Depreciation		½	
	Employee training courses		½	
	Employee pension contributions		½	
	Staff party		½	
	Car lease		1	
	Accountancy		½	
	Legal fees – share capital		½	
	Legal fees – renewal of short lease		½	
	Entertaining UK customers		½	
	Entertaining overseas customers		½	
	Political donations		½	
	Balancing charge adjustment		½	
	Capital allowances			
	Tax written down values b/f		½	
	Motor car 1		1	
	Motor car 2		½	
	Balancing charge		½	
	Writing down allowance		1	
				10
(b)	(i)	Choice of relief		1
	(ii)	Maximum relief claim – 7 m/e 31 Dec 2016	½	
		Maximum relief claim – y/e 31 May 2016	1½	
				2
	(iii)	Maximum surrender	1½	
		Skip Ltd	½	
				2
				15

BPP
LEARNING MEDIA

(a) **Jump Ltd – Trading loss for the three-month period ended 31 March 2017**

	£
Operating loss	(144,700)
Depreciation	8,100
Employee training courses	0
Employee pension contributions	0
Staff party	0
Lease of motor car £1,200 × 15%	180
Accountancy	0
Legal fees – Issue of share capital	3,800
– Renewal of short lease	0
Entertaining UK customers	1,700
Entertaining overseas customers	790
Political donations	800
Balancing charge (W)	3,330
Trading loss	(126,000)

Working – Capital allowances

	Main pool £	Special rate pool £	Allowances £
WDV brought forward	12,100	5,700	
Proceeds – Motor car [1]		(9,300)	
– Motor car [2]	(6,100)		
Balancing charge		3,600	(3,600)
	6,000		
WDA – 18% × 3/12	(270)		270
WDV carried forward	5,730		
Net balancing charge			(3,330)

Tutorial note

The proceeds for motor car [1] are restricted to the original cost figure of £9,300.

(b) (i) The main factor which will influence Jump Ltd's choice of loss relief or group relief claims is the timing of the relief obtained, with an earlier claim generally being preferable.

       Tutorial note:

       The other possible factor is the extent to which relief for qualifying charitable donations will be lost. However, this is not relevant given that Jump Ltd has not made any charitable donations.

   (ii) The maximum loss relief claim for the seven-month period to 31 December 2016 is £42,400, being the total profits for this period.

       The loss relief claim for the year ended 31 May 2016 is restricted to £33,250 ((78,600 + 1,200) × 5/12).

  (iii) The maximum amount of trading loss which can be surrendered to Hop Ltd is £23,625, being the lower of £23,625 (63,000 × 3/8) and £126,000.

       Skip Ltd is not a 75% subsidiary of Jump Ltd, so no group relief claim is possible.

MCQ bank – Value added tax 1

191 C Deposit 18 August 2016, Balancing payment 2 September 2016.

The basic tax point is the date the goods were supplied (26 August 2016). Where payment is received before the basic tax point, then this date becomes the actual tax point. The tax point for the 10% deposit is therefore the date that it is received (18 August 2016). The actual tax point for the balancing payment is the date the invoice was issued (2 September 2016) as this was within 14 days of the basic tax point.

192 C Barry and Chris

Input tax related to zero rated (children's clothing) and standard rated (adult clothing) supplies is recoverable but input tax related to exempt supplies (financial services) is not.

193 C £65

	£
Output VAT: £361 × 1/6	60
Less input VAT: £625 × 20%	(125)
VAT due	(65)

Input VAT on the motor car is not recoverable because there is private use.

194 B Return 7 July 2016, payment 7 July 2016

The time limit for submission of the return and payment is one month plus seven days after the end of the VAT period.

195 C VAT quarter ended 30 June 2017

The value added tax (VAT) on an impaired debt may only be reclaimed once the debt has been outstanding for six months from the due date. The due date in this instance is 10 October 2016; therefore the VAT can be reclaimed in the quarter ended 30 June 2017.

CBE style OTQ bank – Value added tax 2

196 £1,600

The VAT will be calculated on the actual amount received so is £8,000 × 20% = £1,600.

197 £333

Input VAT on the motor car is not recoverable because there is private use. However, since there is some use of car for business purposes, then any VAT charged on repairs and maintenance costs can be treated as input tax without apportionment for private use. The input VAT recoverable is therefore £2,000 × 1/6 = £333.

198 £2,320

	£
New car for salesman	0
New motor van £10,320 × 1/6	1,720
Entertaining UK customers	0
Entertaining overseas customers £3,600 × 1/6	600
Total input VAT recoverable	2,320

199 £270

The following rules apply to pre-registration input tax:

Goods: if acquired within 4 years prior to registration and still held on registration date (so the VAT on the inventory of spare parts is recoverable).

Services: if supplied within 6 months prior to registration (so the VAT on the accountancy fees is recoverable but not that on the legal fees).

200 1 August 2016

Scott is required to notify HMRC within 30 days of exceeding £83,000 registration threshold ie 30 July 2016 (30 days after the year to 30 June 2016). He will then be registered from 1 August 2016.

201 £4,925

	£
Output VAT: £35,250 × 1/6	5,875
Less input VAT: £5,700 × 1/6	
(UK customer entertaining not recoverable)	(950)
VAT due	4,925

202 0%

Charlie will charge VAT at zero rate because this is an EU transaction to a customer who is VAT registered.

203 Date of payment or receipt determines the VAT period in which the transaction is dealt with. Gives automatic impairment loss relief (bad debt relief).

204 £11,400

£120,000 × 9.5% = £11,400. The flat rate percentage is applied to the full tax inclusive turnover including all standard, zero and exempt supplies.

205 Join scheme tax exclusive annual taxable turnover of up to £150,000, leave scheme tax inclusive annual taxable turnover over £230,000.

CBE style OT case – Anne

Text references. Value added tax liability is covered in Chapter 24. Special schemes are dealt with in Chapter 25.

Top tips. Make sure that you read all the information given in the question – you are given this information by the examination team for a reason so you must make use of it when answering the question.

Easy marks. The output tax on cash sales in question 206 should have been easy to deal with.

206 £5,600

Cash sales £28,000 (adult clothes standard rated) × 20%	£5,600

207 £2,292

	£
Credit sales with discount £12,000 × 95% × 90% × 20%	2,052
Credit sales without discount £12,000 × 10% × 20%	240
	2,292

The calculation of output VAT on the credit sales only takes into account the discount for prompt payment for the 90% of customers that took it.

208 £2,400

	£
Purchases and expenses £11,200 × 20%	2,240
Impairment loss £800 × 20%	160
	2,400

Relief for an impairment loss is not given until six months from the time that payment is due. Therefore relief can only be claimed in respect of the invoice due for payment on 10 April 2016. Obviously the customer did not take up the discount for prompt payment.

209   1 and 4

   Anne will be permitted to join the scheme if her expected taxable turnover for the next 12 months does not exceed £1,350,000. If the value of Anne's taxable supplies exceeds £1,600,000 in the 12 months to the end of a VAT period she must leave the scheme immediately.

   Anne will be permitted to join the scheme if she is up-to-date with both her VAT payments and with her VAT returns. Payment in nine monthly instalments is a feature of the annual accounting scheme.

210   2 and 4

   Automatic impairment loss relief (bad debt relief) and output VAT on the 10% of credit sales which are not settled within one month will be accounted for up to one month later than at present.

   The output VAT payable will remain the same and accounting for VAT will also remain the same.

Auy and Bim

> **Text references.** The tax point and VAT liability are covered in Chapter 24. Special schemes are dealt with in Chapter 25.
>
> **Top tips.** Learn the rules about the tax point – they are often examined! For the basic tax point you need to distinguish between supplies of goods (date goods are removed or made available to the customer) and services (date on which services are completed).
>
> **Easy marks.** There were easy marks in questions 212 and 215 for the computation of the VAT paid or payable by the partnership.

211   B   2 and 3

   If the VAT invoice is issued within 14 days after the basic tax point and payment has not been received before the basic tax point, the invoice date becomes the tax point. The tax point determines the VAT period in which output tax must be accounted for and credit for input tax will be allowed.

   The basic tax point for services is the date that services are completed. If VAT invoice is issued and payment is received before the basic tax point, the actual tax point is the earlier of those two dates.

212   C   £25,280

   The partnership's output VAT for the year ended 5 April 2017 is £25,600 and its total input VAT for the year is £(180 + 140) = £320.

   Therefore VAT of £25,280 (25,600 – 320) will have been paid to HM Revenue & Customs for the year ended 5 April 2017.

213   D   1 and 3

   Businesses using the scheme must still issue VAT invoices to their VAT registered customers. Businesses using the scheme cannot reclaim any input tax suffered.

   Under the scheme, businesses calculate VAT by applying a fixed percentage to all their income (ie including reduced rate, zero-rated and exempt income). A 1% reduction off the flat rate percentage can be made by businesses in the first year that they use the flat rate scheme only if it is also the first year of registration.

214   B   Join: expected taxable turnover (excluding VAT) for the next 12 months does not exceed £150,000, Continue to use: until its total turnover (including VAT) for the previous year exceeds £230,000.

215   A   £23,291

   If the partnership had used the flat rate scheme throughout the year ended 5 April 2017 then it would have paid VAT of £(140,762 + 25,600) = £166,362 @ 14% = £23,291.

Aston

216   B   Liable for registration: 31 January 2017, Date of registration: 1 March 2017

Aston would have been liable to compulsory value added tax (VAT) registration when his taxable supplies during any 12-month period (or the period from commencement of trade, if less) exceeded £83,000.

This happened on 31 January 2017 when taxable supplies amounted to £83,200 (6,300 + 6,400 + 21,900 + 4,800 + 11,700 + 17,100 + 13,800 + 1,200).

Registration is required from the end of the month following the month in which the limit is exceeded, so Aston will have been registered from 1 March 2017 or from an agreed earlier date.

217   C   Return: one month and seven days after the end of the VAT period. Payment: one month and seven days after the end of the VAT period.

218   B   2 and 4

Aston's VAT registration number and an identifying number (invoice number).

219   C   1 and 4

The transaction is entered on Aston's VAT return as an output and an input. The service is treated as being supplied in the UK since this is where Aston is situated.

The tax point for a supply of such services is the earlier of the time the service is completed and the time the service is paid for. Supplies of services from VAT registered businesses situated elsewhere within the European Union are categorised in the same way as UK supplies and so are not necessarily zero-rated.

220   D   Maximum penalty 30% of the VAT underpaid, Minimum penalty 0% of the VAT underpaid

HM Revenue and Customs (HMRC) will not charge a penalty if Aston has taken reasonable care, provided he informs them of any errors upon subsequent discovery.

However, applying the incorrect rate of VAT is more likely to be treated as careless, since Aston would be expected to check the VAT classification of his supplies.

The maximum amount of penalty will therefore be 30% of the VAT underpaid, but this penalty could be reduced to 0% as a result of a subsequent unprompted disclosure to HMRC.

Starfish Ltd (B)

			£
221	C	£390	
		Credit sales revenue discount taken up	
		£2,000 × (100 − 4)% × 60% × 20%	230
		Credit sales revenue discount not taken up	
		£2,000 × 40% × 20%	160
			390

			£
222	A	£16,420	
		Cash sales revenue £38,520 × 20/120	6,420
		Sale of inventory on cessation £28,800 × 20/120	4,800
		Sale of non-current assets £31,200 × 20/120	5,200
			16,420

There is no VAT charged on the sale of the car, as none was recovered on purchase (owing to private usage).

			£
223	B	£11,324	
		Expenses £([69,960 − 4,320] = £65,640) × 20/120	10,940
		Impairment loss	384
			11,324

Input VAT on business entertainment for UK customers is not recoverable.

Relief for the impairment loss is available because the claim is made more than six months from the time that payment was due, and the debt has been written off in the company's books.

224 B 7 May 2017

Default interest will be payable from the reckonable date (7 May 2017) to the date of payment.

225 D No output VAT would have been due on the sale of the inventory or the sale of the non-current assets.

A sale of a business as a going concern is outside the scope of VAT, and therefore output VAT would not have been due on the either the sale of the inventory or the sale of the non-current assets.

CBE style OT case – Long Ltd group (B)

Text references. Value added tax calculation and group registration will be found in Chapter 24.

Top tips. It is vital to understand the difference between making exempt supplies and zero-rated supplies – think about whether input VAT can be recovered in either case.

Easy marks. There were some easy marks for dealing with input VAT in questions 227 and 229.

226   £53,780

	£
Sales £(52,640 – 1,760)	50,880
Group sales £(1,940 + 960)	2,900
	53,780

The tax point for the deposit is the date of payment, so this will have been included in output VAT for the quarter ended 31 December 2016.

227   £15,638

	£
Expenses	14,720
Hire of photocopier	
£18 × [(4 years × 12 = 48 months) + 3 months]	918
	15,638

Refunds of VAT are subject to a four-year time limit, so in addition to the input VAT for the hire of the photocopier incurred during the quarter ended 31 March 2017, Long Ltd can also claim for the input VAT incurred during the period 1 January 2013 to 31 December 2016.

228   £0

Wind Ltd's sales are exempt from VAT, so the company cannot be registered for VAT and thus cannot recover input tax.

229   £3,500

	£
Expenses	3,120
Advertising	380
	3,500

Input VAT on services incurred prior to registration is subject to a six-month time limit, so the input VAT of £640 in respect of the advertising expenditure incurred during April 2016 cannot be recovered.

230   2 and 4

Supplies of goods or services to Road Ltd from outside the group will be treated as a supply to Long Ltd. The supplies by Long Ltd to Wind Ltd and Road Ltd would be disregarded for VAT purposes.

Two or more companies are eligible to be treated as members of a group if one of them controls each of the others, or one person (which could be an individual or a holding company) controls all of them, or two or more persons carrying on a business in partnership control all of them. The controlling entity therefore does not need to be a company. It is not necessary for each company, which meets the requirements, to join a particular VAT group.

CBE style OT case – Smart Ltd

231

Register	1 November 2016

Notification	30 November 2016

Smart Ltd was liable to register for VAT from 1 November 2016 because this is the date when it signed the contract valued at £86,000. The company would therefore have known that its taxable supplies for the following 30-day period would have exceeded £83,000. Registration is required from the start of the 30-day period.

Smart Ltd would have had to notify HM Revenue and Customs by 30 November 2016, being the end of the 30-day period.

232

Smart Ltd must file its VAT returns online and pay the VAT which is due electronically	**TRUE**	
Smart Ltd can choose whether to pay the VAT which is due electronically or by cheque		**FALSE**
The deadline for paying any VAT which is due is one month after the end of each quarter		**FALSE**
The deadline for filing the VAT return is one month and seven days after the end of each quarter	**TRUE**	

Smart Ltd must pay the VAT which is due electronically. The deadline for paying any VAT which is due is one month and seven days after the end of each quarter.

233   2 and 3

The basic tax point is the date on which services are completed. If a customer pays for services before the basic tax point, the payment date will be the tax point.

234   1 and 4

The scheme will provide automatic relief for an impairment loss should a customer default on the payment of a debt. Output VAT will be accounted for 60 days later than at present, because the scheme will result in the tax point becoming the date when payment is received from customers.

235   Maximum penalty: 30% of the VAT underpaid. Minimum penalty for prompted disclosure: 15% of the VAT underpaid.

236 Jogger Ltd (B)

> **Text references.** Value added tax default surcharges and special schemes are covered in Chapter 25.
>
> **Top tips.** In part (b) make sure that you make four points to get the available marks.
>
> **Easy marks.** The conditions for Jogger Ltd to join the annual accounting scheme in part (b) should have been easy marks.

Marking scheme

			Marks
(a)	Quarter ended 30 September 2015	2	
	Quarter ended 31 March 2016	2	
	Quarter ended 31 March 2017	2	
			6
(b)	One VAT return	1	
	Payments on account	1	
	Limit	1	
	VAT payments up to date	1	
			4
			10

(a) The late submission of the VAT return for the quarter ended 30 September 2015 will have resulted in HM Revenue and Customs (HMRC) issuing a surcharge liability notice specifying a surcharge period running to 30 September 2016.

The late payment of VAT for the quarter ended 31 March 2016 will have resulted in a surcharge of £778 (£38,900 × 2%) because this is the first default in the surcharge period. The surcharge period will also have been extended to 31 March 2017.

The late payment of VAT for the quarter ended 31 March 2017 will therefore have resulted in a surcharge of £4,455 (£89,100 × 5%) because this is the second default in the surcharge period. The surcharge period will also have been extended to 31 March 2018.

(b) The reduced administration from only having to submit one VAT return each year should mean that default surcharges are avoided in respect of the late submission of VAT returns.

In addition, making payments on account based on the previous year's VAT liability will improve both budgeting and possibly cash flow if Jogger Ltd's business is expanding.

Jogger Ltd can apply to use the annual accounting scheme if its expected taxable turnover for the next 12 months does not exceed £1,350,000 exclusive of VAT.

However, the company must be up to date with its VAT payments before it is allowed to use the scheme.

237 Flick (B)

Marking scheme

			Marks
(a)	Flat rate scheme	1	
	Normal basis	1	
	Conclusion	1	
			3
(b)	No recovery of VAT by customers	1	
	Possible need to absorb VAT	1	
	Conclusion	1	
			3
(c)	VAT period	1	
	Basic tax point	1	
	Deposit	1	
	Balance	1	
			4
			10

(a) Using the flat rate scheme to calculate its VAT liability the partnership will have paid VAT of £(59,700 × 12%) = £7,164 for the quarter ended 31 March 2017.

If the partnership had used the normal basis it would have paid VAT of £(59,700 – 27,300 = 32,400 × 20/120) = £5,400.

It was therefore not beneficial to use the flat rate scheme as the additional cost of £(7,164 – 5,400) = £1,764 for the quarter would appear to outweigh the advantage of simplified VAT administration.

(b) The partnership's sales are all to members of the general public, who cannot recover the input VAT.

It may not therefore be possible to pass the output VAT on to customers in the prices charged. To the extent this is not possible the partnership would have had to absorb all or some of this amount itself as a cost.

It was therefore not beneficial for the partnership to have voluntarily registered for VAT from 1 January 2017. For the quarter ended 31 March 2017 voluntary registration reduced the partnership's profits by a maximum of £7,164 (£5,400 if the normal basis had been used).

(c) Output VAT must be accounted for according to the VAT period in which the supply is treated as being made. This is determined by the tax point.

The basic tax point is the date when the service is completed, which will be the date that a film is screened.

Where payment is received before the basic tax point, then this date becomes the actual tax point. The tax point for each 25% deposit is therefore the date that it is received.

Invoices are issued on the same day as the basic tax point, so this is the tax point for the balance of 75%.

238 Richard (B)

Text references. Registration for VAT is covered in Chapter 24 as is VAT administration. VAT invoices are dealt with in Chapter 25. Ethical considerations are covered in Chapter 1.

Top tips. Ethical considerations are an important part of the F6 (UK) syllabus and you might be asked about them in relation to any tax.

Easy marks. The calculation of the date for registration for VAT in part (a) was straightforward.

Marking scheme

		Marks	
(a)	Compulsory registration limit	½	
	Date registration required	1½	
	Date registration effective	1	
	Consequences of non-registration	1	
			4
(b)	Honest and integrity	½	
	Cease to act and inform HMRC	1	
	Money laundering notification	½	
			2
(c)	Simplified invoice	1	
	Request for invoice	½	
	Details on invoice: ½ mark per item to maximum	2½	
			4
			10

(a) Richard would have been liable to compulsory VAT registration when his taxable supplies during any 12-month period (or from the commencement of trade, if less) exceeded £83,000.

This happened on 31 October 2016 when taxable supplies were £([10,500 × 4]+ [14,000 × 3]) = £84,000.

Registration is required from the end of the month following the month in which the limit is exceeded, so Richard should have been registered from 1 December 2016.

If Richard continued to trade after 1 December 2016 without registering for VAT, he would still have to pay the VAT due from the time he should have been registered.

(b) The matter is one of professional judgement and a trainee Chartered Certified Accountant would be expected to act honestly and with integrity.

If Richard refuses to register for VAT, you should cease to act for him. You must notify HM Revenue and Customs (HMRC) that you no longer act for Richard although you should not provide any reason for this.

You would also be obliged to make a report under the money laundering regulations.

(c) A simplified (or less detailed) VAT invoice can be issued by a trader where the VAT inclusive total of the invoice is less than £250.

Such an invoice should be issued when a customer requests a VAT invoice.

A simplified VAT invoice must show the following information:

- The supplier's name and address
- The supplier's registration number
- The date of the supply
- A description of the goods or services supplied
- The rate of VAT chargeable
- The total amount chargeable including VAT

239 Clueless Ltd (A)

Text references. Special schemes for VAT and overseas aspects of VAT are in Chapter 25.

Top tips. The question stated that the company incurred considerable overtime costs due to its employees working late in order to meet tax return filing deadlines which should have alerted you to one of the advantages of the annual accounting scheme.

Easy marks. There were some easy marks in part (a) for the conditions for the cash accounting and annual accounting schemes.

(a) Clueless Ltd can use both schemes because its expected taxable turnover for the next 12 months does not exceed £1,350,000 exclusive of VAT.

In addition, for both schemes the company is up to date with its VAT payments, and for the cash accounting scheme it is up to date with its VAT returns.

With the cash accounting scheme, output VAT will be accounted for two months later than at present as the date of the cash receipt determines the return in which the transaction is dealt with rather than the invoice date.

The recovery of input VAT on expenses will not be affected as these are dealt with on a cash basis.

With the annual accounting scheme, the reduced administration in only having to file one VAT return each year should save on overtime costs.

(b) (i) **Supplier situated outside the European Union**

Clueless Ltd will have to pay VAT of £22,000 @ 20% = £4,400 to HM Revenue and Customs at the time of importation.

This will then be reclaimed as input VAT on the VAT return for the period during which the machinery is imported.

(ii) **Supplier situated elsewhere within the European Union**

VAT will have to be accounted for according to the date of acquisition. This will be the earlier of the date that a VAT invoice is issued or the 15th day of the month following the month in which the machinery comes into the UK.

The VAT charged of £4,400 will be declared on Clueless Ltd's VAT return as output VAT, but will then be reclaimed as input VAT on the same VAT return.

240 Garfield

> **Text references.** Computation of value added tax, including deduction of input tax and relief for impairment losses is dealt with in Chapter 14. Trade within the European Union and special schemes for VAT are covered in Chapter 25.
>
> **Top tips.** Remember the input VAT on entertaining UK customers is not recoverable but that suffered on entertaining overseas customers is recoverable.
>
> **Easy marks.** Most of the content of this question has appeared a number of times in previous questions and so there were easy marks in part (a) for computing VAT payable.

Marking scheme

			Marks
(a)	*Output VAT*		
	Discounted sale	1	
	Equipment	1	
	Input VAT		
	Equipment	½	
	Impairment losses	1	
	Entertaining	1	
	Motor expenses	1½	
	VAT payable (including figures provided in question)	1	
			7
(b)	Possible schemes	1	
	Identify cash accounting scheme as beneficial	½	
	Benefits of cash accounting scheme (½ mark each)	1½	
			3
			10

(a) **Garfield – Value added tax (VAT) return for the quarter ended 31 March 2017**

	£
Output VAT	
Sales	22,500*
Discounted sale £4,300 × 90% × 20%	774
Equipment £12,400 × 20%	2,480
Fuel scale charge	60*
Input VAT	
Purchases	(11,200)*
Motor car	0*
Equipment	(2,480)
Impairment losses £1,400 × 20%	(280)
Entertaining – UK customers	0*
– Overseas customers £960 × 20/120	(160)
Motor expenses £1,668 (1,008 + 660) × 20/120	(278)
VAT payable	11,416

*Figures provided in question

Tutorial notes

1   Relief for an impairment loss is only available if the claim is made more than six months from the time when payment was due. Therefore, relief can only be claimed in respect of the invoice due for payment on 29 August 2016.

2   Input VAT on business entertainment is recoverable if it relates to the cost of entertaining overseas customers.

(b)   Given Garfield's current annual turnover of £450,000, he can use the cash accounting scheme and the annual accounting scheme, but not the flat rate scheme.

The cash accounting scheme would appear to be the most beneficial scheme for Garfield to use.

The scheme will provide automatic VAT relief for the impairment losses which he is incurring.

Where credit is given to customers, output VAT could be accounted for later than at present.

The recovery of input VAT on most purchases and expenses will not be affected as Garfield pays for these on a cash basis.

Tutorial notes

1   The annual turnover limit for both the annual accounting scheme and the cash accounting scheme is £1,350,000, but for the flat rate scheme it is £150,000.

2   Although the annual accounting scheme would mean only having to submit one VAT return each year (reducing the risk of late return penalties), payments on account are based on the VAT payable for the previous year. From a cash flow viewpoint, this is not beneficial where turnover is decreasing.

Mock exams

ACCA

Paper F6

Taxation (United Kingdom)

Mock Examination 1

Question Paper	
Time allowed	**3 hours 15 minutes**
This paper is divided into two sections:	
Section A – ALL 15 questions are compulsory and MUST be attempted.	
Section B – ALL 15 questions are compulsory and MUST be attempted.	
Section C – ALL THREE questions are compulsory and MUST be attempted.	

DO NOT OPEN THIS PAPER UNTIL YOU ARE READY TO START UNDER EXAMINATION CONDITIONS

SECTION A – ALL 15 questions are compulsory and MUST be attempted

1   On 10 January 2017, a freehold property owned by Winifred was damaged by a fire. The property had been purchased on 29 May 2003 for £73,000. Winifred received insurance proceeds of £37,200 on 23 February 2017, and she spent a total of £41,700 during March 2017 restoring the property. Winifred has elected to disregard the part disposal.

What is the base cost of the restored freehold property for capital gains tax purposes?

A   £68,500
B   £77,500
C   £114,700
D   £35,800

(2 marks)

2   Which **TWO** of the following items of expenditure by an individual are deductible in the calculation of the individual's taxable income?

(1)   A contribution into a personal pension scheme

(2)   A charitable gift aid donation

(3)   A contribution into an employer's HM Revenue and Customs' registered occupational pension scheme

(4)   A charitable donation made under the payroll deduction scheme

A   3 and 4
B   1 and 2
C   2 and 3
D   1 and 4

(2 marks)

3   Benjamin died on 30 November 2016 leaving an estate valued at £890,000. Inheritance tax of £276,000 was paid in respect of the estate. Under the terms of his will, Benjamin left £260,000 to his wife, a specific legacy of £120,000 (free of tax) to his brother, and the residue of the estate to his grandchildren.

What is the amount of inheritance received by Benjamin's grandchildren?

A   £614,000
B   £510,000
C   £354,000
D   £234,000

(2 marks)

4   Yui commenced trading on 1 April 2016, and registered for value added tax (VAT) from 1 January 2017. Her first VAT return is for the quarter ended 31 March 2017. During the period 1 April 2016 to 31 March 2017, Yui incurred input VAT of £110 per month in respect of the hire of office equipment.

How much input VAT in respect of the office equipment can Yui reclaim on her VAT return for the quarter ended 31 March 2017?

A   £660
B   £990
C   £330
D   £1,320

(2 marks)

5   Since 6 April 2016, Nicolas has let out an unfurnished freehold office building. On that date, the tenant paid Nicolas a premium of £82,000 for the grant of a 15-year lease.

How much of the premium of £82,000 will Nicolas include when calculating his property business profit for the tax year 2016/17?

    A   £59,040
    B   £22,960
    C   £82,000
    D   £5,467   **(2 marks)**

---

6   Wan ceased trading on 31 December 2016, having been self-employed since 1 January 2003. On 1 January 2016, the tax written down value of her plant and machinery main pool was £6,200. On 10 November 2016, Wan purchased a computer for £1,600. All of the items included in the main pool were sold for £9,800 on 31 December 2016.

What is the balancing charge which will arise upon the cessation of Wan's trade?

    A   £4,716
    B   £3,404
    C   £2,000
    D   £3,600   **(2 marks)**

---

7   For the year ended 30 June 2016, Forgetful Ltd had a corporation tax liability of £166,250, which it did not pay until 31 July 2017. Forgetful Ltd is not a large company.

How much interest will Forgetful Ltd be charged by HM Revenue and Customs (HMRC) in respect of the late payment of its corporation tax liability for the year ended 30 June 2016?

    A   £1,801
    B   £2,909
    C   £5,403
    D   £1,662   **(2 marks)**

---

8   Mammoth Ltd commenced trading on 1 January 2017. The company's profits have been as follows:

Period	£
Year ended 31 December 2017	524,000
Year ended 31 December 2018	867,000
Year ended 31 December 2019	912,000

Throughout all of these periods, Mammoth Ltd had one related 51% group company.

What is the first year for which Mammoth Ltd will be required to pay its corporation tax liability by quarterly instalments?

    A   Year ended 31 December 2018
    B   None of the years ended 31 December 2017, 2018 or 2019
    C   Year ended 31 December 2019
    D   Year ended 31 December 2017   **(2 marks)**

---

9   On 31 March 2017, Jessica sold a copyright for £28,800. The copyright had been purchased on 1 April 2011 for £21,000 when it had an unexpired life of 15 years.

What is Jessica's chargeable gain in respect of the disposal of the copyright?

    A   Nil
    B   £20,400
    C   £16,200
    D   £7,800   **(2 marks)**

10   Lorna is employed with a gross annual salary for the tax year 2016/17 of £36,000. Sarah is self-employed with trading profit for the year ended 5 April 2017 of £36,000.

How much more national insurance contributions will Lorna suffer for the tax year 2016/17 compared to Sarah?

A   £838
B   £831
C   £692
D   £1,195   **(2 marks)**

---

11   Heng is a wealthy 45 year old who would like to reduce the potential inheritance tax liability on her estate when she dies.

Which of the following actions will NOT achieve Heng's aim of reducing the potential inheritance tax liability on her estate when she dies?

A   Changing the terms of her will so that the residue of her estate goes to her grandchildren rather than her children

B   Making lifetime gifts to trusts up to the value of the nil rate band every seven years

C   Changing the terms of her will so that the residue of her estate goes to her husband rather than her children

D   Making lifetime gifts to her grandchildren early in life   **(2 marks)**

---

12   Which of the following companies will be treated as resident in the UK for corporation tax purposes?

(1)   A Ltd, a company incorporated in the UK, with its central management and control exercised in the UK

(2)   B Ltd, a company incorporated overseas, with its central management and control exercised in the UK

(3)   C Ltd, a company incorporated in the UK, with its central management and control exercised overseas

(4)   D Ltd, a company incorporated overseas, with its central management and control exercised overseas

A   1 only
B   1, 2, 3 and 4
C   2 and 3 only
D   1, 2 and 3 only   **(2 marks)**

---

13   Taxes can be either capital taxes or revenue taxes, although some taxes are neither type of tax.

Which is the correct classification for the following three taxes?

	Value added tax	Inheritance tax	National insurance contributions
A	Neither type	Revenue tax	Capital tax
B	Revenue tax	Capital tax	Neither type
C	Capital tax	Neither type	Revenue tax
D	Neither type	Capital tax	Revenue tax

(2 marks)

14 In the year ended 31 March 2017, Luck Ltd had taxable total profits of £400,000 and received the following dividends:

	£
From unconnected companies	5,200
From a company in which Luck Ltd has an 80% shareholding	4,300
From a company in which Luck Ltd has a 45% shareholding	1,400

What is the value of Luck Ltd's profits for the year ended 31 March 2017 for the purposes of determining whether it should pay corporation tax in instalments?

A £406,600
B £410,900
C £405,700
D £405,200

(2 marks)

15 For the tax year 2016/17, what are the latest dates by which a taxpayer, who does not wish to incur a penalty, should file a self-assessment tax return on paper or online?

	Paper tax return	Online tax return
A	31 October 2017	31 January 2019
B	31 October 2017	31 January 2018
C	31 October 2018	31 January 2018
D	31 October 2018	31 January 2019

(2 marks)

(Total = 30 marks)

SECTION B – ALL 15 questions are compulsory and MUST be attempted

Ginger, Innocent and Nigel (06/13) (amended)

The following scenario relates to questions 16-20.

You should assume that today's date is 1 March 2017.

Ginger

Ginger has a holding of 10,000 £1 ordinary shares in Nutmeg Ltd, an unquoted trading company, which she had purchased on 13 February 2005 for £2.40 per share. The current market value of the shares is £6.40 per share, but Ginger intends to sell some of the holding to her daughter at £4.00 per share during March 2017. Ginger and her daughter will elect to hold over any gain as a gift of a business asset.

For the tax year 2016/17, Ginger will not make any other disposals, and has therefore not utilised her annual exempt amount. She has a loss brought forward from 2015/16 of £(2,000).

Innocent and Nigel

Innocent and Nigel, a married couple, both have shareholdings in Cinnamon Ltd, an unquoted trading company with a share capital of 100,000 £1 ordinary shares.

Innocent has been the managing director of Cinnamon Ltd since the company's incorporation on 1 July 2007, and she currently holds 20,000 shares (with matching voting rights) in the company. These shares were subscribed for on 1 July 2007 at their par value.

Nigel has never been an employee or a director of Cinnamon Ltd, and he currently holds 3,000 shares (with matching voting rights) in the company. These shares were purchased on 23 April 2011 for £46,200.

Either Innocent or Nigel will sell 2,000 of their shares in Cinnamon Ltd during March 2017 for £65,000, but are not sure which of them should make the disposal. For the tax year 2016/17, both Innocent and Nigel have already made disposals which will fully utilise their annual exempt amounts, and they will each have taxable income of £80,000.

16 What is the chargeable gain per share that Ginger will make on her disposal of shares in Nutmeg Ltd to her daughter?

    A   £4.00
    B   £1.60
    C   £2.40
    D   £nil   **(2 marks)**

17 If the chargeable gain per share on Ginger's disposal of shares in Nutmeg Ltd had been £1.54 per share, what would be the maximum number of shares that Ginger could have sold to her daughter without incurring a charge to capital gains tax?

    A   2,046
    B   7,207
    C   8,506
    D   3,275   **(2 marks)**

18   Which **TWO** of the following statements about entrepreneurs' relief are correct?

(1)   Entrepreneurs' relief is only available on shareholdings owned by a director

(2)   There is a lifetime limit of £10,000,000 for entrepreneurs' relief

(3)   Entrepreneurs' relief is only available on shareholdings if they are held in a trading company

(4)   The conditions for entrepreneurs' relief in relation to a shareholding must be satisfied for five years before the disposal

A   1 and 3
B   2 and 4
C   2 and 3
D   1 and 4

(2 marks)

19   What would Innocent's capital gains tax liability be if she sold her shares in Cinnamon Ltd during March 2017?

A   £6,300
B   £5,190
C   £12,600
D   £6,500

(2 marks)

20   What would Nigel's capital gains tax liability be if he sold his shares in Cinnamon Ltd during March 2017?

A   £3,760
B   £6,840
C   £4,620
D   £3,420

(2 marks)

(Total = 10 marks)

Greenzone Ltd (A) (06/13) (amended)

The following scenario relates to questions 21-25.

Greenzone Ltd owns 60% of Are Ltd, 40% of Be Ltd, 90% of Can Ltd and 70% of Doer Inc. All the companies are UK resident except for Doer Inc which also does not have a fixed establishment in the UK.

The following information is available in respect of Greenzone Ltd's value added tax (VAT) for the quarter ended 31 March 2017:

(1)   Output VAT of £38,210 was charged in respect of sales. This figure includes output VAT of £400 on a deposit received on 29 March 2017, which is in respect of a contract that is due to commence on 20 April 2017.

(2)   In addition to the above, Greenzone Ltd also charged output VAT of £4,330 on sales to Can Ltd. Greenzone Ltd does not have group registration.

(3)   The managing director of Greenzone Ltd is provided with free fuel for his company motor car. The total cost of fuel for the motor car for the quarter is £500 and 60% of the total mileage is private mileage. Greenzone Ltd wishes to use the fuel scale charge. The relevant quarterly scale charge is £320. Both these figures are inclusive of VAT.

(4) Input VAT of £12,770 was incurred in respect of expenses (excluding the fuel in (3)). This figure includes the following input VAT:

	£
Entertaining UK customers	210
Entertaining overseas customers	139
Repainting the exterior of the company's office building	1,678
Extending the office building in order to create a new reception area	3,300

21 What is the amount of output VAT charged on the sales in (1) and (2) for the quarter to 31 March 2017?

    A   £42,540
    B   £38,210
    C   £42,140
    D   £37,810   **(2 marks)**

22 What is the net amount of VAT payable or recoverable for the provision of the fuel for the managing director's company motor car in (3)?

    A   £20 payable
    B   £36 recoverable
    C   £53 payable
    D   £30 recoverable   **(2 marks)**

23 What is the amount of input VAT that can be recovered on the expenses in (4)?

    A   £9,260
    B   £7,582
    C   £12,560
    D   £12,421   **(2 marks)**

24 Apart from Can Ltd, which of the following companies could be registered in a VAT group with Greenzone Ltd?

    A   Are Ltd, Be Ltd and Doer Inc
    B   Are Ltd
    C   Doer Inc
    D   Are Ltd and Doer Inc   **(2 marks)**

25 Which **TWO** of the following statements about VAT group registration are correct?

(1) Each VAT group must appoint a representative member which accounts for the group's output tax and input tax

(2) Each VAT group must appoint a representative member which is solely liable for paying the group VAT liability

(3) All eligible companies must be part of the group registration

(4) Any supply of goods or services by a member of the group to another member of the group is disregarded for VAT purposes

    A   1 and 4
    B   3 and 4
    C   2 and 3
    D   1 and 2

    (2 marks)

(Total = 10 marks)

Rosie and Sam (12/12) (amended)

The following scenario relates to questions 26-30.

You should assume that today's date is 15 February 2017.

Rosie

Rosie is the managing director of Hornburg plc. During the tax year 2016/17 Rosie was paid gross director's remuneration of £220,000 and she received dividend income of £500,000. She has made the following gross personal pension contributions:

Tax year	Pension contribution
	£
2013/14	Nil
2014/15	26,000
2015/16	Nil

Rosie was a member of a pension scheme for the tax year 2015/16 but not in the tax year 2013/14.

Sam

In September 2015 Sam invested £7,000 in a cash ISA. In May 2016 he invested a further £6,000 in that cash ISA. He withdrew £5,000 from the cash ISA in October 2016. Sam is now considering investing more cash into the cash ISA before 5 April 2017. He also invested £4,000 in premium bonds and government securities ('gilts') in the tax year 2016/17.

26   What is total amount of pension scheme annual allowances that Rosie has available for the tax year 2016/17?

    A   £114,000

    B   £64,000

    C   £94,000

    D   £54,000

(2 marks)

27   What are the tax implications if Rosie makes pension contributions in excess of her available annual allowances?

    A   Charge at 25% on excess contributions

    B   Charge at 55% on excess contributions

    C   Charge at 20% on excess contributions

    D   Charge at 45% on excess contributions

(2 marks)

28   What are the tax consequences for Rosie if she takes pension benefits under flexible access drawdown?

	Lump sum	Rest of pension fund
A	Up to 10% of fund can be taken tax-free	Taxable as pension income when received
B	Up to 10% of fund can be taken as tax-free lump sum	5% of fund taxable as pension income each year whether or not received
C	Up to 25% of fund can be taken as tax-free lump sum	Taxable as pension income when received
D	Up to 25% of fund can be taken as tax-free lump sum	5% of fund taxable as pension income each year whether or not received

(2 marks)

29   What is the maximum amount that Sam can invest into the cash ISA for the tax year 2016/17 in addition to his investments already made?

A   £9,240
B   £14,240
C   £7,240
D   £10,240   (2 marks)

30   What are the income tax and capital gains tax treatments of Sam's investments in premium bonds and government securities?

	Premium bonds	Government securities
A	Exempt from income tax, chargeable to capital gains tax	Chargeable to income tax and capital gains tax
B	Exempt from both income tax and capital gains tax	Chargeable to income tax, exempt from capital gains tax
C	Chargeable to income tax and capital gains tax	Exempt from both income tax and capital gains tax
D	Chargeable to income tax, exempt from capital gains tax	Exempt from income tax, chargeable to capital gains tax

(2 marks)

(Total = 10 marks)

SECTION C – ALL THREE questions are compulsory and MUST be attempted

31 Pere and Phil (06/13) (amended)

On 23 August 2010, Pere made a gift of a house valued at £420,000 to his son, Phil. This was a wedding gift when Phil got married. The nil rate band for the tax year 2010/11 is £325,000.

Pere

Pere died on 20 March 2017 at which time his estate was valued at £880,000. Under the terms of his will, Pere divided his estate equally, before inheritance tax, between his wife and his son, Phil. Pere had not made any gifts during his lifetime except for the gift of the house to Phil.

Phil

Phil sold the house which he received as a wedding gift from Pere, his father, on 5 April 2017. The following information relates to the property:

	£
Net sale proceeds after costs of disposal	495,500
Cost of new boundary wall around the property (there was previously no boundary wall)	(5,200)
Cost of replacing the property's chimney	(2,800)

Phil has taxable income (after deduction of the personal allowance) of £8,450 in 2016/17. The house was never occupied by Phil.

Required

(a)	Calculate the inheritance tax that will be payable as a result of Pere's death.	**(6 marks)**
(b)	Calculate Phil's capital gains tax liability for the tax year 2016/17.	**(4 marks)**

(Total = 10 marks)

32 Josie (12/12) (amended)

On 30 June 2016 Josie ceased self-employment. On 1 August 2016 she commenced employment with Typo plc. The following information is available for the tax year 2016/17:

Self-employment

(1) Josie's trading profits for the final two periods of trading were as follows:

	£
Year ended 30 April 2016	95,260
Two-month period ended 30 June 2016	10,440

There were no capital allowances.

(2) Josie has unused overlap profits brought forward of £41,700.

Employment

(1) Josie is paid a salary of £15,100 per month by Typo plc. The salary is paid on the last day of each calendar month.

(2) During August 2016 Typo plc paid £11,649 towards Josie's removal expenses when she permanently moved to take up her new employment with the company as she did not live within a reasonable commuting distance. The £11,649 covered both her removal expenses and the legal costs of acquiring a new main residence.

(3) On 1 September 2016 Typo plc provided Josie with an interest free loan of £33,000 that she used to renovate her new main residence. This loan was still outstanding at 5 April 2017.

(4) During the period from 1 August 2016 to 5 April 2017, Josie was provided with free meals in Typo plc's staff canteen. The total cost of these meals to the company was £1,340. The canteen is available to all of the company's employees.

(5) During the period from 1 October 2016 to 5 April 2017, Typo plc provided Josie with a diesel powered motor car with an official CO_2 emission rate of 114 grams per kilometre. The motor car, which has a list price of £14,400, cost Typo plc £13,900. Typo plc does not provide Josie with any fuel for private journeys.

Other information

(1) During the tax year 2016/17 Josie received interest of £1,200 from a holding of £24,000 5% Treasury Stock 2025 and dividends of £7,200.

(2) During the tax year 2016/17 Josie made gift aid donations totalling £4,400 (net) to national charities.

Required

Calculate Josie's income tax liability for the tax year 2016/17.

Note. You should indicate by the use of zero any items that are non-taxable/exempt from tax. **(15 marks)**

(Total = 15 marks)

33 Greenzone Ltd (B) (06/13) (amended)

(a)   Greenzone Ltd is a trading company. The company's summarised statement of profit or loss for the year ended 31 March 2017 is as follows:

	Note	£	£
Gross profit			404,550
Operating expenses			
Depreciation		28,859	
Repairs and renewals	1	28,190	
Other expenses	2	107,801	
			(164,850)
Operating profit			239,700

Notes

1   *Repairs and renewals*

Repairs and renewals are as follows:

	£
Repainting the exterior of the company's office building	8,390
Extending the office building in order to create a new reception area	19,800
	28,190

2   *Other expenses*

Other expenses are as follows:

	£
Entertaining UK customers	3,600
Entertaining overseas customers	1,840
Political donations	740
Donation to a charity where Greenzone Ltd received free advertising in the charity's newsletter. This was not a qualifying charitable donation.	430
Gifts to customers (pens costing £30 each, not displaying Greenzone Ltd's name)	660
Gifts to customers (clocks costing £65 each and displaying Greenzone Ltd's name)	910
Balance of expenditure (all allowable)	99,621
	107,801

3   *Plant and machinery*

On 1 April 2016 the tax written down values of Greenzone Ltd's plant and machinery were as follows:

	£
Main pool	48,150
Special rate pool	9,200

The following motor cars were purchased new during the year ended 31 March 2017:

	Date of purchase	Cost £	CO$_2$ emission rate
Motor car [1]	10 April 2016	10,800	72 grams per kilometre
Motor car [2]	10 June 2016	20,400	110 grams per kilometre

The following motor cars were sold during the year ended 31 March 2017:

	Date of sale	Proceeds £	Original cost £
Motor car [3]	8 March 2017	9,100	8,500
Motor car [4]	8 March 2017	12,400	18,900

The original cost of motor car [3] has previously been added to the main pool, and the original cost of motor car [4] has previously been added to the special rate pool.

Required

Calculate Greenzone Ltd's tax adjusted trading profit for the year ended 31 March 2017.

Note. Your computation should commence with the operating profit figure of £239,700, and should also list all of the items referred to in notes (1) and (2), indicating by the use of zero (0) any items that do not require adjustment. **(10 marks)**

(b) Greenzone Ltd has held shares in four trading companies for many years. All four companies prepare accounts to 31 March. The following information is available for the year ended 31 March 2017:

	Are Ltd	Be Ltd	Can Ltd	Doer Co
Residence	UK	UK	UK	Overseas
Percentage ordinary shareholding	60%	40%	90%	70%
Trading profit/(loss)	£(74,800)	£68,900	£(64,700)	£22,600
Dividends paid to Greenzone Ltd	£36,180	£35,100	£29,400	£16,650

Required

(i) State, giving reasons, which of the four trading companies are treated as related 51% group companies with Greenzone Ltd and how this affects how Greenzone Ltd pays its corporation tax liability for the year ended 31 March 2017. **(3 marks)**

(ii) Calculate the maximum amount of group relief that Greenzone Ltd can claim for the year ended 31 March 2017. **(2 marks)**

(Total = 15 marks)

Answers

Answers

A plan of attack

If this were the real Taxation (UK) exam and you had been told to turn over and begin, what would be going through your mind?

Perhaps you're having a panic. You've spent most of your study time on income tax and corporation tax computations (because that's what your tutor/BPP study Text told you to do), plus a selection of other topics, and you're really not sure that you know enough. So calm down. Spend the first few moments or so **looking at the paper,** and develop a **plan of attack.**

Looking through the paper:

Section A contains **15 Objective Test (OT) questions** each worth **2 marks**. These will cover all sections of the syllabus. Some you may find easy and some more difficult. Don't spend a lot of time on anything you really don't know. For multiple choice questions you are not penalised for wrong answers, so you should answer all of them. If all else fails – guess!

Section B also contains **three OT Case** questions. These have **five subparts** each worth **2 marks**. Make sure you read the scenario carefully before you start to answer the OTs.

In **Section C** you have **three constructed response (long) questions:**

- **Question 31** for **10 marks** concerns a father and son and involves inheritance tax and capital gains tax. It is important to deal with each tax separately.

- **Question 32** for **15 marks** is an income tax question. There are plenty of easy marks available in this question but there is a lot of information to deal with so make sure you mark off each item as you include it in your answer.

- **Question 33** for **15 marks** is a corporation tax question which is divided into two parts. It is important to attempt each part to ensure you gain reasonable marks.

All of these questions are compulsory.

This means that you do not have to waste time wondering which questions to answer.

Allocating your time

BPP's advice is always allocate your time **according to the marks for the question** in total and for the parts of the question. But **use common sense**. If you're confronted by an OTQ on a topic of which you know nothing, pick an answer and move on. Use the time to pick up marks elsewhere.

After the exam…**Forget about it!**

And don't worry if you found the paper difficult. More than likely other candidates will too. If this were the real thing you would need to **forget** the exam the minute you left the exam hall and **think about the next one**. Or, if it's the last one, **celebrate**!

Section A

1   B   £77,500

	£
Cost	73,000
Enhancement expenditure	41,700
Less insurance proceeds	(37,200)
Cost of restored property	77,500

2   A   3 and 4

A contribution into an employer's HM Revenue and Customs' registered occupational pension scheme and a charitable donation made under the payroll deduction scheme are deductible in the calculation of an individual's taxable income. Tax relief is given on personal pensions and gift aid donations at basic rate by the taxpayer making a net payment and higher rate and additional rate relief is given by increasing the basic rate and higher rate limits.

3   D   £234,000

		£
Estate		890,000
Less	IHT	(276,000)
	legacy to wife	(260,000)
	legacy to brother	(120,000)
Residue to grandchildren		234,000

4   B   £990

	£
Pre-registration VAT on services (max six months)	
1.7.16 to 31.12.16 £110 × 6	660
Quarter to 31.3.17	
£110 × 3	330
	990

5   A   £59,040

	£
Premium	82,000
Less £82,000 × (15 − 1) × 2%	(22,960)
Property business income	59,040

6   C   £2,000

	£
TWDV b/f	6,200
Addition	1,600
	7,800
Disposal	(9,800)
Balancing charge	2,000

There is no annual investment allowance nor writing down allowance in the period of cessation.

7   D   £1,662

Due date 1 April 2017, paid 31 July 2017 so four months late. Interest is

4/12 × 3% × £166,250   £1,662

8   C   **Year ended 31 December 2019**

The profit threshold for being a large company is £1,500,000/2 = £750,000 since there is one related 51% group company. This threshold is first exceeded in the year ended 31 December 2018 but a company is not required to pay its corporation tax by instalments in the first year that it is large unless its profits exceed £10,000,000, as reduced by related 51% group companies. Mammoth Ltd is also a large company in the year ended 31 December 2019 and so must pay its corporation tax liability by quarterly instalments for that year.

9   C   **£16,200**

	£
Proceeds	28,800
Less cost £21,000 × 9/15	(12,600)
Chargeable gain	16,200

A copyright is a wasting asset and so the cost is written down over its life on a straight-line basis.

10   C   **£692**

	£
Employee Class 1 £(36,000 – 8,060) = 27,940 @ 12%	3,353
Self employed Class 4 £(36,000 – 8,060) = 27,940 @ 9%	(2,515)
Self employed Class 2 £2.80 × 52	(146)
Extra NIC for Lorna	692

11   A   **Changing the terms of her will so that the residue of her estate goes to her grandchildren rather than her children.**

There will be the same amount of inheritance tax on the residue of the estate if it is left to Heng's children or grandchildren. However, if the estate is left to her husband the spouse exemption will apply. Heng could reduce the potential inheritance tax liability on her estate when she dies by making lifetime gifts to trusts up to the value of the nil rate band every seven years as these will reduce her assets and will not be cumulated if she survives seven years. She could also make lifetime gifts to her grandchildren early in life as these would be potentially exempt transfers and she is more likely to survive seven years the earlier in life she makes the gifts.

12   D   **1, 2, and 3 only**

A company will be treated as resident in the UK for corporation tax purposes if either (or both) it is incorporated in the UK or its central management and control is exercised in the UK.

13   D   Value added tax neither type, Inheritance tax capital tax, National insurance contributions revenue tax

14   A   **£406,600**

	£
Unconnected company	5,200
Group dividend	0
Non-51% group dividend	1,400
Taxable total profits	400,000
Profits	406,600

15   B   Paper return 31 October 2017, Online tax return 31 January 2018

Section B

Ginger, Innocent and Nigel

Text references. Chapter 13 covers the basics of computing chargeable gains. Chapter 15 deals with business reliefs.

Top tips. In questions 19 and 20 think why the disposals by Innocent and Nigel would give rise to different capital gains tax liabilities. Are there different rates of capital gains tax? When do those rates apply?

Easy marks. There were easy marks in question 17 for working out the number of shares that could be sold without incurring a charge to CGT.

---

16   B   £1.60

The disposal is at an undervalue, so only the gift element of the gain can be deferred under gift relief. The consideration paid for each share will be immediately chargeable to capital gains tax to the extent that it exceeds the allowable cost. The chargeable amount is therefore £(4.00 – 2.40) = £1.60 per share.

17   C   8,506

Ginger's annual exempt amount for 2016/17 is £11,100 and she has a loss of £(2,000) brought forward from 2015/16. She can therefore sell (13,100/1.54) = 8,506 shares to her daughter without this resulting in any capital gains tax liability for 2016/17.

18   C   2, 3

There is a lifetime limit of £10,000,000 for entrepreneurs' relief and entrepreneurs' relief is only available on shareholdings if they are held in a trading company.

The individual can be an officer (eg a director) or an employee of the company in which the shares are held. The conditions for entrepreneurs' relief must be satisfied for one year before the disposal.

19   A   £6,300

Innocent makes disposal

	£
Disposal proceeds	65,000
Less cost	(2,000)
Gain	63,000
CGT on £63,000 @ 10%	6,300

20   B   £6,840

Nigel makes disposal

	£
Disposal proceeds	65,000
Less cost (£46,200 × 2,000/3,000)	(30,800)
Gain	34,200
CGT on £34,200 @ 20%	6,840

Greenzone Ltd (A)

21   A   £42,540

	£
Output VAT	
Sales	38,210
Group sales	4,330
Output VAT	42,540

The tax point for the deposit is the date of payment, so no adjustment is required to the output VAT figure of £38,210.

22   D   £30 recoverable

	£
Output VAT	
Fuel scale charge £320 × 20/120	53
Input VAT	
Fuel purchased £500 × 20/120	(83)
VAT recoverable	(30)

23   C   £12,560

	£
Total input VAT	12,770
Entertaining UK customers	(210)
Entertaining overseas customers	0
Repainting office building	0
New reception area	0
	12,560

Input VAT on business entertaining is not recoverable unless it relates to the cost of entertaining overseas customers. There is no distinction between capital and revenue expenditure for VAT so both input tax is recoverable both on the repainting of the office building (revenue) and the building of the new reception area (capital).

24   B   Are Ltd

Are Ltd can register with Greenzone Ltd as a group for VAT purposes as it is UK resident and controlled by Greenzone Ltd. Be Ltd is not controlled by Greenzone Ltd and Doer Inc is not UK resident and does not have a fixed establishment in the UK.

25   A   1, 4

Each VAT group must appoint a representative member which must account for the group's output tax and input tax. Any supply of goods or services by a member of the group to another member of the group is disregarded for VAT purposes

All members of the group are jointly and severally liable for any VAT due from the representative member. It is not necessary for each company, which is eligible for group registration, to join a particular VAT group.

Rosie and Sam

26   B   £64,000

Rosie was a member of a pension scheme for 2015/16, so the full annual allowance for that year is available but the annual allowance is not available for carry forward from 2013/14. Her adjusted income for the tax year 2016/17 is greater than £210,000 so her annual allowance for that tax year is tapered to £10,000.

She has unused allowances of £(40,000 – 26,000) = £14,000 from 2014/15, and £40,000 from 2015/16, so the available annual allowances for 2016/17 are therefore £(10,000 (2016/17) + 14,000 + 40,000) = £64,000.

27   D   Charge at 45% on excess contributions.

28   C   Lump sum: up to 25% of fund can be taken as tax-free lump sum, Rest of fund: taxable as pension income when received.

29   B   £14,240

The ISA amount 2016/17 is £15,240. Sam has already invested £6,000 in the tax year 2016/17, so can invest a further £(15,240 – 6,000) = £9,240. He can also replace the £5,000 withdrawn in October 2016 so the total amount he can now invest is £(9,240 + 5,000) = £14,240.

30   B   Premium bonds: exempt from both income tax and capital gains tax, Government securities chargeable to income tax, exempt from capital gains tax.

Section C

31 Pere and Phil

Text references. Inheritance tax is dealt with in Chapter 18. Chargeable gains and the computation of capital gains tax are in Chapter 13. The points on distinguishing between revenue and capital expenditure are covered in Chapter 7.

Top tips. You don't need to know names of tax cases in the F6 exam, but you are expected to know, and be able to apply, the principles decided, as in part (b) here.

Easy marks. There were some easy marks in part (a) for using the exemptions.

Marking scheme

			Marks
(a)	Lifetime gift		
	Marriage exemption	1	
	Annual exemption – current year	½	
	Annual exemption – brought forward	½	
	Potentially exempt transfer	½	
	IHT @ 0%	½	
	IHT @ 40%	½	
	Taper relief	1	
	Death estate		
	Spouse exemption	1	
	IHT @ 40%	½	
			6
(b)	Disposal proceeds	½	
	Cost	1	
	Enhancement	1	
	Annual exempt amount	½	
	Capital gains tax @ 18%	½	
	Capital gains tax @ 28%	½	
			4
			10

(a) Pere – Inheritance tax (IHT) arising on death

Lifetime transfer 23 August 2010

		£
Gift		420,000
Less:	marriage exemption	(5,000)
	annual exemption 2010/11	(3,000)
	annual exemption 2009/10 b/f	(3,000)
Potentially exempt transfer		409,000
IHT		
£325,000 @ 0%		0
£84,000 @ 40%		33,600
£409,000		
Less taper relief (6 to 7 years @ 80%)		(26,880)
IHT payable		6,720

Tutorial note

The potentially exempt transfer becomes chargeable as a result of Pere dying within seven years of making it.

Death estate

	£
Value of estate	880,000
Less spouse exemption £880,000/2	(440,000)
Chargeable estate	440,000
IHT on £440,000 @ 40%	176,000

(b) **Phil**

Capital gains tax computation 2016/17

	£
Net disposal proceeds	495,500
Less: cost	(420,000)
enhancement expenditure	(5,200)
Gain	70,300
Less annual exempt amount	(11,100)
Taxable gain	59,200

	£
CGT on £23,550 (32,000 – 8,450) @ 18%	4,239
CGT on £35,650 (59,200 – 23,550) @ 28%	9,982
	14,221

Tutorial notes

1   The cost of replacing the property's chimney is revenue expenditure because the chimney is a subsidiary part of the house (see *Samuel Jones & Co v CIR 1951*). The cost of the new boundary wall is capital expenditure as the wall is a separate, distinct, entity (see *Brown v Burnley Football and Athletic Club 1980*).

2   Because the house is residential property, the gain is taxed at 18% and 28% rather than 10% and 20%.

32 Josie

Marking scheme

	Marks
Trading income	
Profit for year ended 30 April 2016	½
Profit for period ended 30 June 2016	½
Overlap profits	1
Employment income	
Salary	1
Removal expenses	1
Beneficial loan	1½
Staff canteen	½
Car benefit – Percentage	1½
– Benefit	1
Investment income	
Gilt interest	1
Dividends	½
Taxable income	
Personal allowance not available	1
Tax payable	
Increase in limits for gift aid donations	1
Tax liability	3
	15

Josie – Income tax computation 2016/17

	Non-savings income £	Savings income £	Dividend income £	Total £
Trading income (W1)	64,000			
Employment income (W2)	126,610			
Gilt interest		1,200		
Dividends			7,200	
Net income	190,610	1,200	7,200	199,010
Less personal allowance (N)	(0)			(0)
Taxable income	190,610	1,200	7,200	199,010

Tax

	£
On non-savings income	
£37,500 (W4) @ 20%	7,500
£118,000 @ 40%	47,200
£155,500 (W6)	
£35,110 @ 45%	15,799
£190,610	
On savings income	
£1,200 @ 45% (no nil rate band for additional rate taxpayer)	540
On dividend income	
£5,000 @ 0%	0
£2,200 (7,200 – 5,000) @ 38.1%	838
Income tax liability	71,877

Tutorial notes

1   Only £8,000 of the relocation costs is exempt.

2   No personal allowance is available as Josie's adjusted net income of £(199,010 – 5,500) = £193,510 exceeds £122,000.

Workings

1   *Trading income*

	£
Year ended 30 April 2016	
Trading profit	95,260
Period ended 30 June 2016	
Trading profit	10,440
Less overlap profits	(41,700)
Trading income	64,000

2   *Employment income*

	£
Salary £15,100 × 8	120,800
Removal expenses £(11,649 – 8,000)	3,649
Loan £33,000 @ 3% × 7/12	577
Staff canteen (exempt)	0
Car benefit (W3)	1,584
Employment income	126,610

3   *Car benefit*

Amount by which CO_2 emissions exceed base level: (110 (rounded down) – 95) = 15 ÷ 5 = 3. Car benefit percentage is 3 + 16 + 3 (diesel supplement) = 22%.

Car available from 1 October 2016 to 5 April 2017 = 6 months.

Car benefit is £14,400 (list price) × 22% × 6/12 = £1,584.

4   *Tax rate limits*

Josie's basic and higher rate tax limits are increased by (£4,400 × 100/80) = £5,500 to £(32,000 + 5,500) = £37,500 and £(150,000 + 5,500) = £155,500.

33 Greenzone Ltd (B)

Marking scheme

			Marks
(a)	Depreciation	½	
	Repainting	½	
	Reception area	½	
	Entertaining UK customers	½	
	Entertaining overseas customers	½	
	Political donations	½	
	Non-qualifying charitable donation	½	
	Pens	½	
	Clocks	½	
	Capital allowances deducted	½	
	Capital allowances		
	TWDVs b/f	1	
	Addition – motor car [2]	½	
	Disposal – motor car [3]	1	
	Disposal – motor car [4]	½	
	Balancing charge on special rate pool	½	
	WDA on main pool	½	
	Addition – motor car [1]	½	
	FYA	½	
			10
(b) (i)	Related 51% group company definition	½	
	Are Ltd and Can Ltd	½	
	Doer Co	½	
	Profit threshold	½	
	Group dividends	1	
			3
(ii)	Maximum group relief		2
			15

(a)   **Greenzone Ltd – Trading profit for the year ended 31 March 2017**

		£
Operating profit		239,700
Add:	Depreciation	28,859
	Repainting office building	0
	New reception area	19,800
	Entertaining UK customers	3,600
	Entertaining overseas customers	1,840
	Political donations	740
	Non-qualifying charitable donation	0
	Gifts to customers: pens	660
	clocks	910
		296,109
Less capital allowances (W)		(18,409)
Trading profit		277,700

Tutorial notes

1   The extension of the office building is not deductible as it is capital in nature. The building has been improved rather than repaired.

2   Gifts to customers are only an allowable expense if they cost less than £50 per recipient per year, are not of food, drink, tobacco or vouchers exchangeable for goods, and carry a conspicuous advertisement for the company.

Working

Capital allowances

	FYA £	Main pool £	Special rate pool £	Allowances £
TWDV brought forward		48,150	9,200	
Addition not qualifying for AIA/FYA				
Motor car [2]		20,400		
		68,550		
Disposals				
Motor car [3]		(8,500)		
Motor car [4]			(12,400)	
Balancing charge			3,200	(3,200)
		60,050		
WDA @ 18%		(10,809)		10,809
Addition qualifying for FYA				
Motor car [1]	10,800			
FYA @ 100%	(10,800)			10,800
WDV carried forward		49,241		
Allowances				18,409

Tutorial notes

1   Motor car [1] has CO_2 emissions up to 75 grams per kilometre and is a new car so therefore qualifies for the 100% first year allowance.

2   Motor car [2] has CO_2 emissions between 76 and 130 grams per kilometre and therefore is added to the main pool.

3   The disposal value for motor car [3] is restricted to the original cost figure of £8,500.

(b)   (i)   Greenzone Ltd has related 51% group companies if it directly or indirectly owns more than 50% of the ordinary shares of those companies.

Are Ltd and Can Ltd are therefore related 51% group companies.

For related 51% group companies purposes, it does not matter where a company is resident, so Doer Co is also a related 51% group company despite being resident overseas.

Greenzone Ltd has three related 51% group companies at the end of the previous accounting period, so that the profit threshold for determining whether the company must pay corporation tax by instalments is reduced to £(1,500,000/4) = £375,000.

The dividends from Are Ltd, Can Ltd and Doer Co are group dividends and are therefore not included in profits for this purpose.

(ii)   The maximum amount of group relief that can be claimed is Can Ltd's trading loss of £64,700.

Tutorial note

Greenzone Ltd cannot claim group relief from Are Ltd as this company is not a 75% subsidiary.

The group relief claim is limited to the lower of Can Ltd's loss and Greenzone Ltd's taxable total profits (equal to trading profits of £277,700) ie Can Ltd's loss of £64,700.

ACCA

Paper F6

Taxation (United Kingdom)

Mock Examination 2

Question Paper	
Time allowed	**3 hours 15 minutes**
This paper is divided into two sections:	

This paper is divided into two sections:

Section A – ALL 15 questions are compulsory and MUST be attempted.

Section B – ALL 15 questions are compulsory and MUST be attempted.

Section C – ALL THREE questions are compulsory and MUST be attempted.

DO NOT OPEN THIS PAPER UNTIL YOU ARE READY TO START UNDER EXAMINATION CONDITIONS

SECTION A – ALL 15 questions are compulsory and MUST be attempted

1   Chan died on 8 December 2016, having made a lifetime cash gift of £500,000 to a trust on 16 October 2015. Chan paid the inheritance tax arising from this gift.

Match the due date payment of the additional inheritance tax arising from the gift made to the trustees and the persons who are responsible for paying this tax.

8 June 2017	30 June 2017

The trustees	The personal representatives of Chan's estate

Due date	

Persons responsible	

(2 marks)

2   Violet Ltd provides one of its directors with a company motor car which is used for both business and private mileage. For the quarter ended 31 March 2017, the total cost of petrol for the car was £600, of which 30% was for private use by the director. The relevant quarterly scale charge is £415. Both these figures are inclusive of value added tax (VAT).

What output VAT and input VAT entries will Violet Ltd include on its VAT return for the quarter ended 31 March 2017 in respect of the company motor car?

○ Output VAT of £69 and input VAT of £70

○ Output VAT of Nil and input VAT of £70

○ Output VAT of Nil and input VAT of £100

○ Output VAT of £69 and input VAT of £100

(2 marks)

3   For the tax year 2016/17, Nog has a chargeable gain of £23,800 and a capital loss of £10,400. She has unused capital losses of £6,100 brought forward from the tax year 2015/16.

What amount of capital losses can Nog carry forward to the tax year 2017/18?

£	

(2 marks)

4   Z Ltd prepared accounts for a 16-month period of account from 1 October 2015 to 31 January 2017.

What is the first accounting period in this period of account?

○ 1 October 2015 to 31 March 2016

○ 1 October 2015 to 31 January 2016

○ 1 October 2015 to 30 September 2016

○ 1 October 2015 to 31 December 2016

(2 marks)

5   Which of the following statements correctly explains the difference between tax evasion and tax avoidance?

    ○ Both tax evasion and tax avoidance are illegal, but tax evasion involves providing HM Revenue and Customs with deliberately false information.

    ○ Tax evasion is illegal, whereas tax avoidance involves the minimisation of tax liabilities by the use of any lawful means.

    ○ Both tax evasion and tax avoidance are illegal, but tax evasion involves providing HM Revenue and Customs with deliberately false information.

    ○ Tax avoidance is illegal, whereas tax evasion involves the minimisation of tax liabilities by the use of any lawful means.

(2 marks)

---

6   Quinn will not make the balancing payment in respect of her tax liability for the tax year 2015/16 until 17 October 2017.

    What is the total percentage penalty which Quinn will be charged by HM Revenue and Customs (HMRC) in respect of the late balancing payment for the tax year 2015/16?

Select... ▼
15%
10%
5%
30%

(2 marks)

---

7   Drago Ltd employs 1,000 employees, some of whom receive part of their remuneration in the form of non-cash benefits.

    Which classes of national insurance contribution is Drago Ltd responsible for paying?

    ○ Both class 2 and class 4

    ○ Class 1 only

    ○ Both class 1 and class 1A

    ○ Class 2 only

(2 marks)

---

8   Alice is in business as a sole trader. On 13 May 2016, she sold a freehold warehouse for £184,000, and this resulted in a chargeable gain of £38,600. Alice purchased a replacement freehold warehouse on 20 May 2016 for £143,000. Where possible, Alice always makes a claim to roll over gains against the cost of replacement assets. Both buildings have been, or will be, used for business purposes by Alice.

    What is the base cost of the replacement warehouse for capital gains tax purposes?

£	

(2 marks)

9   For the tax year 2015/16, Willard filed a paper self-assessment tax return on 10 August 2016.

What is the deadline for Willard to make an amendment to his tax return for the tax year 2015/16, and by what date will HM Revenue and Customs (HMRC) have to notify Willard if they intend to carry out a compliance check into this return?

	Amendment	*Compliance check*
◯	10 August 2017	31 January 2018
◯	10 August 2017	10 August 2017
◯	31 January 2018	10 August 2017
◯	31 January 2018	31 January 2018

(2 marks)

10 Celeste bought £25,000 4% Treasury Stock (gilts) on 1 August 2016. The purchase price included accrued interest. The stock pays interest on 31 March and 30 September each year.

What is the amount of interest taxable on Celeste in respect of the Treasury Stock for 2016/17?

£ [   ]

(2 marks)

11 Samuel is planning to leave the UK to live overseas, having always previously been resident in the UK. Neither the automatic overseas residence nor the automatic UK residence test will apply. Samuel has several ties with the UK and will need to visit the UK for 60 days each tax year. However, he wants to be not resident after he leaves the UK.

For the first two tax years after leaving the UK, what is the maximum number of ties which Samuel could keep with the UK without being treated as resident in the UK?

◯ One

◯ Three

◯ Two

◯ Four

(2 marks)

12 Identify, by clicking on the relevant boxes in the table below, which of the following are NOT deducted when calculating the value of a person's chargeable estate for inheritance tax purposes

An outstanding repayment mortgage	Funeral expenses	A verbal promise to pay a friend's debt
An outstanding interest-only mortgage	An outstanding endowment mortgage	Credit card debts

(2 marks)

13   Naomi is self-employed. For the year ended 5 April 2017 she made a trading loss of £110,000, having made a trading profit of £24,000 for the year ended 5 April 2016. Naomi also had employment income of £92,000 for the tax year 2015/16.

What is the maximum loss relief claim which Naomi can make against her total income for the tax year 2015/16?

£ [   ]

(2 marks)

14   Abdul's tax liabilities for the tax years 2015/16 and 2016/17 are as follows:

	2015/16	2016/17
	£	£
Income tax payable	300	2,400
Class 4 national insurance contributions	320	1,260
Capital gains tax liability	240	0
	860	3,660

What payment on account will Abdul have to make on 31 July 2017 in respect of his tax liability for the tax year 2016/17?

○ £310

○ £1,830

○ £430

○ £Nil

(2 marks)

15   Ten Ltd is the parent company for a group of companies. The group structure is as follows:

Ten Ltd
|
90%
|
Twenty Ltd
|
75%
|
Thirty Ltd
|
70%
|
Forty Ltd

Each percentage holding represents a holding of ordinary share capital.

What is the group relationship between Forty Ltd and Ten Ltd?

○ They form a group for both group relief and chargeable gains purposes

○ They form a group for group relief purposes but not for chargeable gains purposes

○ They form a group for chargeable gains purposes but not for group relief purposes

○ They do not form a group for either group relief or chargeable gains purposes

(2 marks)

(Total = 30 marks)

SECTION B – ALL 15 questions are compulsory and MUST be attempted

Zoe and Luke (06/15) (amended)

The following scenario relates to questions 16-20.

Zoe and Luke are brother and sister who died within a few months of each other.

Zoe

Zoe died on 17 February 2017.

She had always used her annual exemption in April each year and had made the following additional gifts during her lifetime:

(1) On 21 March 2010, Zoe made a cash gift of £633,000 to a trust. Zoe paid the inheritance tax (IHT) arising from this gift. The nil rate band for the tax year 2009/10 is £325,000.

(2) On 17 August 2013, Zoe made a further cash gift of £200,000 to the trust. The trustees paid the IHT arising from the gift. The nil rate band for the tax year 2013/14 is £325,000.

Luke

Luke died on 10 October 2016.

On 7 March 2015, Luke had made a cash gift of £270,000 to his daughter as a wedding gift when she got married.

Luke's wife had died on 25 July 2008. In her will she left £240,000 to her daughter and the remainder of her estate to Luke. She made no lifetime transfers. The nil rate band for the tax year 2008/09 was £312,000.

16 Which **TWO** of the following statements about Zoe and Luke's lifetime transfers are correct?

- [ ] Zoe's transfer in 2010 will not be cumulated with her transfer in 2013 when working out the lifetime IHT on the 2013 transfer.

- [ ] Luke's transfer in 2015 became chargeable to IHT because he died within three years of making it.

- [ ] The transfer made by Zoe in 2010 must be grossed up because Zoe paid the IHT arising.

- [ ] Taper relief will be available when computing the additional IHT on Zoe's transfer made in 2013.

(2 marks)

---

17 What the amount of the gross chargeable transfer made by Zoe on 21 March 2010?

- ○ £708,500
- ○ £710,000
- ○ £694,600
- ○ £756,200

(2 marks)

---

18   What is the additional IHT which will be payable, as result of Zoe's death, in respect of the transfer made on 17 August 2013, assuming that the nil rate band has been completely used by the gross chargeable transfer made by Zoe on 21 March 2010?

Select... ▼
£40,000
£80,000
£24,000
£64,000

(2 marks)

19   What is value of the potentially exempt transfer made by Luke on 7 March 2015?

£ [   ]

(2 marks)

20   What is the amount of Luke's wife's nil rate band which could be transferred and used in calculating the IHT on Luke's death?

○ £75,000

○ £72,000

○ £312,000

○ £325,000

(2 marks)

(Total = 10 marks)

Luna Ltd (06/15) (amended)

The following scenario relates to questions 21-25.

Luna Ltd had the following transactions in shares during the year ended 31 March 2017:

(1)   On 29 November 2016, Luna Ltd sold its entire shareholding of £1 ordinary shares in Pluto plc for £53,400. Luna Ltd had originally purchased these shares in Pluto plc on 14 June 2008 for £36,800.

(2)   On 30 November 2016, Luna Ltd sold 10,000 of its shares in Neptune plc for £26,000. Luna Ltd had originally purchased 16,000 shares in Neptune plc on 10 May 2010 for £32,000.

(3)   On 10 December 2016, Luna Ltd acquired shares under a rights issue in Saturn plc. Luna Ltd had originally purchased 5,000 £1 ordinary shares in Saturn plc for £7,500 in August 2011. There was a one for one bonus issue in July 2013 when the shares were worth £1,75 each. The December 2016 rights issue was on a one for four basis and the cost of the rights issue shares was £2.25 per share.

(4)   On 12 February 2017, Luna Ltd's shareholding in Asteroid plc was taken over by Comet plc. Luna Ltd had originally purchased 10,000 £1 ordinary shares in Asteroid plc and their indexed cost on 12 February 2017 was £33,000.

Under the terms of the takeover, for each of its £1 ordinary shares in Asteroid plc, Luna Ltd received £6.50 in cash plus one £1 ordinary share in Comet plc. Immediately after the takeover, Comet plc's £1 ordinary shares were quoted at £4.50.

Retail price indices (RPIs) are as follows:

June 2008	216.8
May 2010	223.6
November 2016	263.0

21 Which of the following statements about indexation allowance are correct?

    (1)   Indexation allowance can increase a loss
    (2)   Indexation allowance cannot create a loss

    ○ 1 and 2

    ○ 1 only

    ○ 2 only

    ○ Neither 1 nor 2

(2 marks)

22 What is Luna Ltd's chargeable gain on the sale of Pluto plc shares on 29 November 2016?

£ _____

(2 marks)

23 What is the indexed cost of Luna Ltd's holding in Neptune Ltd immediately after the sale on 30 November 2016?

    ○ £12,000

    ○ £37,639

    ○ £23,524

    ○ £14,115

(2 marks)

24 What is the unindexed cost of Luna Ltd's holding in Saturn plc immediately after the rights issue on 10 December 2016?

    ○ £13,125

    ○ £11,875

    ○ £10,313

    ○ £21,875

(2 marks)

25 What is the cost that was used to compute Luna Ltd's chargeable gain on the takeover of Asteroid plc on 12 February 2017?

£ _____

(2 marks)

(Total = 10 marks)

Zim (06/15) (amended)

The following scenario relates to questions 26-30.

Zim has been registered for value added tax (VAT) since 1 April 2006. The following information is available for the year ended 31 March 2017:

(1)   Sales invoices totalling £126,000 were issued, of which £115,200 were in respect of standard rated sales and £10,800 were in respect of zero rated sales. Zim's customers are all members of the general public.

(2)   Purchase invoices totalling £49,200 were received, of which £43,200 were in respect of standard rated purchases and £6,000 were in respect of zero rated purchases.

(3)   On 31 March 2017, Zim wrote off two impairment losses which were in respect of standard rated sales. The first impairment loss was for £780, and was in respect of a sales invoice which had been due for payment on 15 August 2016. The second impairment loss was for £660, and was in respect of a sales invoice which had been due for payment on 15 September 2016.

(4)   During the year ended 31 March 2017, Zim spent £2,600 on mobile telephone calls, of which 40% related to private calls.

(5)   During the year ended 31 March 2017, Zim spent £1,560 on entertaining customers, of which £240 was in respect of overseas customers.

All of the above figures are inclusive of VAT where applicable.

Zim does not use either the cash accounting scheme or the flat rate scheme. If he did use the flat rate scheme the relevant percentage for his business is 12%.

26   What is the net amount of VAT payable on the sales in (1) and the purchases in (2)?

£	

(2 marks)

---

27   What is the amount of input VAT which can be recovered on the impairment losses in (3)?

   ○ £Nil

   ○ £110

   ○ £130

   ○ £240

(2 marks)

---

28   What is the amount of input VAT which can be recovered on the expenditure on the mobile phone calls in (4) and entertaining customers in (5)?

Mobile phone	Customers
○ £0	£220
○ £0	£40
○ £260	£220
○ £260	£40

(2 marks)

29   Match the thresholds for Zim to be able to join and to be required to leave the flat rate scheme.

Taxable turnover excluding VAT not more than £150,000 in next 12 months		Taxable turnover including VAT not more than £230,000 in next 12 months
Taxable turnover including VAT not more than £150,000 in next 12 months		Taxable turnover excluding VAT more than £230,000 in previous 12 months

Join	

Leave	

(2 marks)

30   How much VAT would Zim have paid in the year to 31 March 2017 if he had been in the flat rate scheme for the whole of that year?

   ○ £15,120

   ○ £13,860

   ○ £13,824

   ○ £9,216

(2 marks)

(Total = 10 marks)

SECTION C – ALL THREE questions are compulsory and MUST be attempted

31 Bayle (B) (06/11) (amended)

Bayle is self-employed as a lawyer who prepares accounts to 30 September each year. On 1 December 2016 Bayle is planning to bring a newly qualified lawyer, Fyle, into her business. Fyle will either be taken on as an employee, being paid a gross monthly salary of £3,300, or join Bayle as a partner, receiving a 20% share of the new partnership's profits.

Bayle has forecast that her tax adjusted trading profit will be £216,000 for the year ended 30 September 2017, and £240,000 for the year ended 30 September 2018.

Fyle does not have any other income for the tax year 2016/17. He will be the sole employee of Bayle.

Required

(a)   Assuming that Fyle is employed from 1 December 2016, calculate the total amount of national insurance contributions (if any) that will be paid by Bayle and Fyle in respect of his earnings for the tax year 2016/17;

Note. You are not expected to calculate the national insurance contributions that will be paid in respect of Bayle's earnings. **(4 marks)**

(b)   Assuming that Fyle becomes a partner from 1 December 2016:

(i)   Calculate his trading income assessments for the tax years 2016/17 and 2017/18.

Note. You are not expected to calculate any overlap profits. **(4 marks)**

(ii)   Calculate the total amount of national insurance contributions that will be paid by Bayle and Fyle, if any, in respect of Fyle's trading income assessment for the tax year 2016/17.

Note. You are not expected to calculate the national insurance contributions that will be paid in respect of Bayle's trading income assessment. **(2 marks)**

(Total = 10 marks)

32 Retro Ltd (06/15)

Retro Ltd's summarised statement of profit or loss for the year ended 31 March 2017 is as follows:

	Note	£	£
Gross profit			127,100
Operating expenses			
Depreciation		27,240	
Gifts and donations	1	2,300	
Impairment loss	2	1,600	
Leasing costs	3	4,400	
Other expenses	4	205,160	
			(240,700)
Finance costs			
Interest payable	5		(6,400)
Loss before taxation			(120,000)

Notes

1   *Gifts and donations*

Gifts and donations are as follows:

	£
Gifts to employees (food hampers costing £60 each)	720
Gifts to customers (calendars costing £8 each and displaying Retro Ltd's name)	480
Political donations	420
Qualifying charitable donations	680
	2,300

2   *Impairment loss*

On 31 March 2017, Retro Ltd wrote off an impairment loss of £1,600 relating to a trade debt. This was in respect of an invoice which had been due for payment on 10 November 2016.

3   *Leasing costs*

The leasing costs of £4,400 are in respect of a motor car lease which commenced on 1 April 2016. The leased motor car has CO_2 emissions of 145 grams per kilometre.

4   *Other expenses*

The figure of £205,160 for other expenses includes a fine of £5,100 for a breach of health and safety regulations, and legal fees of £4,860 in connection with the defence of Retro Ltd's internet domain name. The remaining expenses are all fully allowable.

5   *Interest payable*

The interest payable is in respect of the company's 5% loan notes which were repaid on 31 July 2016. Interest of £9,600 was paid on 31 July 2016, and an accrual of £3,200 had been provided for at 1 April 2016. The loan notes were issued in order to finance the company's trading activities.

Additional information

Plant and machinery

On 1 April 2016, the tax written down value of the plant and machinery main pool was £39,300.

The following vehicles were purchased during the year ended 31 March 2017:

	Date of purchase	Cost	CO_2 emission rate
		£	
Motor car [1]	8 June 2016	14,700	124 grams per kilometre
Delivery van	3 August 2016	28,300	162 grams per kilometre
Motor car [2]	19 October 2016	12,400	66 grams per kilometre

Previous results

Retro Ltd commenced trading on 1 September 2014. The company's results for its two previous periods of trading are as follows:

	Year ended 31 August 2015	Period ended 31 March 2016
	£	£
Tax adjusted trading profit	56,600	47,900
Bank interest receivable	1,300	0
Qualifying charitable donations paid	(540)	(330)

Future results

Retro Ltd is expected to return to profitability in the year ended 31 March 2018 and to continue to be profitable in subsequent years.

Required:

(a) Calculate Retro Ltd's tax adjusted trading loss for the year ended 31 March 2017.

Note. Your computation should commence with the loss before taxation figure of £120,000, and should also list all of the items referred to in notes (1) to (5), indicating by the use of zero (0) any items which do not require adjustment. **(9 marks)**

(b) Assuming that Retro Ltd claims relief for its trading loss as early as possible, calculate the company's taxable total profits for the year ended 31 August 2015 and for the seven-month period ended 31 March 2016. **(4 marks)**

(c) Identify the amount of unrelieved trading loss which Retro Ltd will have at 31 March 2017, and state how this can be relieved. **(2 marks)**

(Total = 15 marks)

33 Wai (06/15)

Wai is employed as a sales manager by Qaz plc, and the following information is available in respect of the tax year 2016/17:

(1) During the tax year 2016/17, Wai was paid a gross monthly salary of £10,200.

(2) In addition to her salary, Wai has been paid the following bonuses:

Amount	Date of payment	Date of entitlement	In respect of the six-month period ended
£			
4,600	25 April 2016	31 March 2016	31 December 2015
8,100	20 August 2016	3 July 2016	30 June 2016
2,900	3 May 2017	15 April 2017	31 December 2016

(3) During the period 6 April to 31 August 2016, Wai used her private motor car for both private and business journeys. She was reimbursed by Qaz plc at the rate of 55p per mile for the following mileage:

	Miles
Normal daily travel between home and Qaz plc's offices	2,420
Travel between home and the premises of Qaz plc's clients (none of the clients' premises were located near the offices of Qaz plc)	8,580
Travel between home and a temporary workplace (the assignment was for ten weeks)	2,860
Total mileage reimbursed by Qaz plc	13,860

(4) During the period 1 September 2016 to 5 April 2017, Qaz plc provided Wai with a petrol powered motor car which has a list price of £11,590, and an official CO_2 emission rate of 86 grams per kilometre. Qaz plc does not provide Wai with any fuel for private journeys.

(5) During January 2017, Wai spent ten nights overseas on company business. Qaz plc paid Wai a daily allowance of £10 to cover the cost of personal incidental expenses, such as telephone calls to her family.

(6) Throughout the tax year 2016/17, Qaz plc allowed Wai the use of two mobile telephones. The telephones had each cost £400 when purchased by the company in March 2016.

(7) Throughout the tax year 2016/17, Qaz plc provided Wai with living accommodation. The company had purchased the property on 1 June 2013 for £142,000, and it has been provided to Wai since 1 February 2015. Improvements costing £24,200 were made to the property during October 2013, and further improvements costing £9,800 were made during August 2016. The annual value of the property is £4,828.

Required:

(a) Calculate Wai's taxable income for the tax year 2016/17. **(12 marks)**

(b) Briefly outline the information to be included in PAYE forms P60 and P11D, and state the dates by which they should have been provided to Wai for the tax year 2016/17.

Note. Your answer should be confined to the details which are relevant to Wai, although no figures are required. **(3 marks)**

(Total = 15 marks)

Answers

DO NOT TURN THIS PAGE UNTIL YOU HAVE
COMPLETED THE MOCK EXAM

A plan of attack

If this were the real Taxation (UK) exam and you had been told to turn over and begin, what would be going through your mind?

Perhaps you're having a panic. You've spent most of your study time on income tax and corporation tax computations (because that's what your tutor/BPP study Text told you to do), plus a selection of other topics, and you're really not sure that you know enough. So calm down. Spend the first few moments or so **looking at the paper,** and develop a **plan of attack.**

Looking through the paper:

Section A contains **15 Objective Test (OT) questions** each worth **2 marks**. These will cover all sections of the syllabus. Some you may find easy and some more difficult. Don't spend a lot of time on anything you really don't know. For multiple choice questions you are not penalised for wrong answers, so you should answer all of them. If all else fails – guess!

Section B also contains **three OT Case** questions. These have **five subparts** each worth **2 marks**. Make sure you read the scenario carefully before you start to answer the OTs.

In **Section C** you have **three constructed response (long) questions:**

- **Question 31** for **10 marks** covers national insurance contributions and basis periods for a joining partner. You need to be clear who pays what type of NIC as there are employee, employer and self-employed contributions to be calculated.

- **Question 32** for **15 marks** involves an adjustment to profit computation for a company with capital allowances. Make sure you deal with all the adjustments and mark with a zero in your computation any items which do not require adjustment.

- **Question 33** for **15 marks** is an employment income computation.

All of these questions are compulsory.

This means that you do not have to waste time wondering which questions to answer.

Allocating your time

BPP's advice is always allocate your time **according to the marks for the question** in total and for the parts of the question. But **use common sense**. If you're confronted by an OTQ on a topic of which you know nothing, pick an answer and move on. Use the time to pick up marks elsewhere.

After the exam…**Forget about it!**

And don't worry if you found the paper difficult. More than likely other candidates will too. If this were the real thing you would need to **forget** the exam the minute you left the exam hall and **think about the next one**. Or, if it's the last one, **celebrate**!

Section A

1

Due date	30 June 2017

Persons responsible	The trustees

Examiner's comments. This question tested knowledge of when IHT will be payable and by whom. The correct answer was the trustees on 30 June 2017, which is six months following the month of death. More candidates selected this option than any of the others, but 'The personal representatives of Chan's estate on 30 June 2017 and 'The trustees on 8 June 2017 were both popular choices. This is fairly basic knowledge, and it is the type of question which should represent a very easy (and quick) two marks.

2   Output VAT of £69 and input VAT of £100

Output VAT £415 x 20/120   £69

Input VAT 600 x 20/120   £100

3   £3,800

	£
Gain	23,800
Less current year loss	(10,400)
Net current year gain	13,400
Less loss brought forward (balancing amount)	(2,300)
	11,100
Less annual exempt amount	(11,100)
Taxable gain	0
Loss carried forward £(6,100 – 2,300)	3,800

4   1 October 2015 to 30 September 2016

The first accounting period in a long period of account is always 12 months in length. The second accounting period is the remainder of the period of account (here it will be four months from 1 October 2016 to 31 January 2017).

5   Tax evasion is illegal, whereas tax avoidance involves the minimisation of tax liabilities by the use of any lawful means.

6   10%

The due date for payment was 31 January 2017. The penalty date is 30 days after the due date for the tax. There is a penalty of 5% of the unpaid tax for failing to pay by the penalty date plus a further penalty of 5% of the unpaid tax as the payment is more than five months after the penalty date but not more than 11 months after the penalty date.

7   Both class 1 and class 1A

8   £143,000

The proceeds not reinvested in the new asset are £(184,000 – 143,000) = £41,000. Since this is greater than the gain of £38,600, no rollover relief is available. The cost of the replacement warehouse is therefore £143,000.

9   Amendment 31 January 2018, Compliance check 10 August 2017

Willard may amend his return for 2015/16 within twelve months after the filing date which for this purpose is taken to be 31 January 2017 (not the paper filing date of 31 October 2016 even though he has made a paper return). HMRC must give written notice of its intention to start a compliance check by the first anniversary of the actual filing date as the return was delivered on or before the due filing date, so in this case the notice must be given by 10 August 2017.

10   £667

	£
Interest received 30.9.16	
£25,000 × 4% × 6/12	500
Less relief for accrued interest (amount taxable on seller) for 1.4.16 to 31.7.16	
£25,000 × 4% × 4/12	(333)
Interest received 31.3.17	
£25,000 × 4% × 6/12	500
Total taxable 2016/17	667

11   Two ties

Samuel was previously resident in the UK and will be present in the UK for between 46 and 90 days. He will be UK resident on this basis if he has three ties with the UK so two is the maximum number of ties which Samuel could keep with the UK without being treated as resident in the UK.

12

		A verbal promise to pay a friend's debt
	An outstanding endowment mortgage	

An outstanding endowment mortgage is not deducted because the associated life assurance policy will pay off the loan. A verbal promise to pay a friend's debt is not deducted because it is not legally enforceable.

13   £74,000

In 2015/16, the loss relief claim is not capped against the trading profit of £24,000. Relief against other income is capped at £50,000 since this is greater than £((92,000 + 24,000) × 25%) = £29,000. The total loss relief claim is therefore £(24,000 + 50,000) = £74,000.

14   £Nil

Payments on account are not required because the relevant amount for 2015/16 is £(300 + 320) = £620 which does not exceed £1,000.

15   They do not form a group for either group relief or chargeable gains purposes.

There is not a 75% holding between Thirty Ltd and Forty Ltd so there cannot be either a group relief group nor a chargeable gains group with Forty Ltd and Ten Ltd.

Section B

Zoe and Luke

> **Text references.** Inheritance tax is the subject of Chapter 18.
>
> **Top tips.** Be careful to read the question thoroughly. You were told that Zoe always used her annual exemption in April each year so it was not relevant in Question 17.
>
> **Easy marks.** There were some easy marks for working out the additional IHT due in question 18.

16 The transfer made by Zoe in 2010 must be grossed up because Zoe paid the IHT arising. Taper relief will be available when computing the additional IHT on Zoe's transfer made in 2013.

Zoe's transfer in 2010 will be cumulated with her transfer in 2013 when working out the lifetime IHT on the 2013 transfer because the 2010 transfer is a chargeable lifetime transfer.

Luke's transfer in 2015 became chargeable to IHT because he died within seven years of making it.

17 £710,000

	£
Net chargeable transfer (AEs already used)	633,000
IHT	
£325,000 × 0%	0
£308,000 × 20/80	77,000
£633,000	77,000
Gross chargeable transfer £(633,000 + 77,000)	£710,000

18 £24,000

	£
Gross chargeable transfer	200,000
IHT on death (nil rate band already used)	
£200,000 × 40%	80,000
Less taper relief (3 to 4 years) £80,000 × 20%	(16,000)
	64,000
Less lifetime tax £200,000 × 20%	(40,000)
Additional IHT payable	24,000

19 £259,000

	£
Gift	270,000
Less: marriage exemption	(5,000)
annual exemption 2014/15	(3,000)
annual exemption 2013/14 b/f	(3,000)
Potentially exempt transfer	259,000

20 £65,000

	£
Unused nil rate band at wife's death £(312,000 − 240,000)	72,000
Amount to transfer £325,000 × 72,000/312,000	75,000

Luna Ltd

21 2 only

Indexation allowance cannot increase or create a loss although it can reduce a gain to nil.

22 £8,758

	£
Proceeds	53,400
Less cost	(36,800)
	16,600
Less indexation allowance $\dfrac{263.0 - 216.8}{216.8} \times £36,800$	(7,842)
Gain	8,758

23 £14,115

	No. of shares	Indexed cost £
Acquisition	16,000	32,000
Indexed rise $\dfrac{263.0 - 223.6}{223.6} \times £32,000$		5,639
		37,639
Disposal	(10,000)	(23,524)
	6,000	14,115

24 £13,125

	No. of shares	Cost £
Acquisition	5,000	7,500
Bonus 1 for 1	5,000	0
	10,000	7,500
Rights 1 for 4 @ £2.25	2,500	5,625
	12,500	13,125

25 £19,500

$£33,000 \times \dfrac{(£6.50 \times 10,000)}{(£6.50 \times 10,000) + (£4.50 \times 10,000)}$ £19,500

Zim

26 £12,000

		£	£
Sales	– Standard rated £115,200 × 20/120		19,200
	– Zero rated		0
Purchases	– Standard rate £43,200 × 20/120	7,200	
	– Zero rated	0	
			(7,200)
Net VAT payable			12,000

27 £240

Impairment losses £(780 + 660) = 1,440 × 20/120 = £240

Relief for impairment losses is given once six months have expired from the time when payment was due, so relief can be claimed in respect of both impairment losses.

28 Mobile phone £260, Customers £40

Mobile phone £2,600 × 60% (100% – 40%) × 20/120 = £260

An apportionment is made where a service such as the use of a telephone is partly for business purposes and partly for private purposes.

Customers entertainment £240 × 20/120 = £40

Input VAT on business entertainment is not recoverable unless it relates to the cost of entertaining overseas customers.

29

Join	Taxable turnover excluding VAT not more than £150,000 in next 12 months

Leave	Taxable turnover including VAT more than £230,000 in previous 12 months

30 £15,120

Using the flat rate scheme to calculate his VAT liability, Zim would have paid VAT of £126,000 × 12% = £15,120 for the year ended 31 March 2017.

Section C

31 Bayle (B)

Text references. NICs for both employees and the self-employed are covered in Chapter 12. The basis of assessment will be found in Chapter 9 and partnerships are dealt with in Chapter 11.

Top tips. Think carefully about the implication of Fyle being the sole employee of Bayle.

Easy marks. There were some easy marks in part (a) for national insurance computations.

Marking scheme

				Marks
(a)		Monthly thresholds	½	
		Employee Class 1 NIC	1½	
		Employer Class 1 NIC	2	
				4
(b)	(i)	*Trading income assessments*		
		2016/17	1½	
		2017/18	2½	
				4
	(ii)	*NIC*		
		Class 2 NIC	½	
		Class 4 NIC	1	
		Bayle	½	
				2
				10

(a)   The monthly primary threshold is £672 (£8,060/12) and the monthly secondary threshold is £676 (£8,112/12).

Fyle will pay employee Class 1 NIC for 2016/17 of £1,261 (£(3,300 − 672) = £2,628 @ 12% × 4).

Bayle will not pay employer's Class 1 NIC for 2016/17 since the employment allowance will cover the contributions of £1,448 (£(3,300 − 676) = £2,624 @ 13.8% × 4).

Tutorial note

The alternative approach using the annual earnings threshold and then taking 4/12ths of an annual NIC figure is acceptable.

(b)   (i)   **Trading income assessments**

Fyle's trading income assessment for 2016/17 is £14,400 calculated as follows:

	£
Basis period: 1 December 2016 to 5 April 2017	
£216,000 × 4/12	72,000
Profit share £72,000 × 20%	14,400

The assessment for 2017/18 is £44,000 calculated as follows:

	£
Basis period: 1 December 2016 to 30 November 2017	
£216,000 × 10/12	180,000
£240,000 × 2/12	40,000
	220,000
Profit share £220,000 × 20%	44,000

Tutorial notes

1   The commencement rules apply to Fyle for 2016/17 since he will join as a partner on 1 December 2016.

2   The assessment for 2017/18 is for the 12 months from when Fyle joins the partnership.

(ii) **NIC**

Fyle will pay Class 2 NIC for 2016/17 of £(2.80 × 18) = £50.

He will pay Class 4 NIC for 2016/17 of £(14,400 – 8,060) = 6,340 @ 9% = £571.

There are no NIC implications for Bayle.

Tutorial note

Any reasonable estimate of the number of weeks for Class 2 contributions is acceptable.

32 Retro Ltd

Text references. The computation of taxable total profits is covered in Chapter 19. Losses are dealt with in Chapter 21.

Top tips. For part (a) you might want to start this question by computing the capital allowances. You can then just slot this into the adjustment of profit pro forma at the appropriate place.

Easy marks. There were some easy marks for standard adjustments to profit in part (a).

Examiner's comments. Most candidates had little difficulty with part (a). One poor practice was the use of notes and explanations. It was a simple matter, as per the model answer, to just list all the items of expenditure (and show whether or not an adjustment was required), so the use of notes (such as for the gifts and donations) was completely unnecessary and against the guidance given in the note to the requirement. Since the requirement was for a calculation, explanations are not required, and result in wasted time. As regards the capital allowances, many candidates did not appreciate that the delivery van qualified for the 100% annual investment allowance – instead including it in the special rate pool.

There were many perfect answers to part (b), although disappointingly a few candidates tried to time-apportion profits using the opening year rules.

Part (c) caused few problems, although many candidates did not mention that the carry forward would be against the first available profits.

Marking scheme

		Marks
(a)	*Adjustment to profit*	
	Depreciation	½
	Gifts to employees	½
	Gifts to customers	½
	Political donations	½
	Qualifying charitable donations	½
	Impairment loss	½
	Lease of motor car	1
	Health and safety fine	½
	Legal fees	½
	Interest payable	½
	Capital allowances	
	WDV b/f	½
	Delivery van	½
	AIA	½
	Motor car [1]	½
	WDA	½
	Motor car [2]	½
	FYA	½
		9
(b)	Trading profit	½
	Bank interest	½
	Carry back loss relief p/e 31 March 2016	1
	Carry back loss relief in y/e 31 August 2015	1
	Qualifying charitable donations	1
		4
(c)	Unrelieved trading loss amount	1
	Carry forward loss relief	1
		2
		15

(a) **Trading loss for the year ended 31 March 2017**

	£
Loss before taxation	(120,000)
Depreciation	27,240
Gifts to employees	0
Gifts to customers	0
Political donations	420
Qualifying charitable donations	680
Impairment loss	0
Lease of motor car (4,400 × 15%)	660
Health and safety fine	5,100
Legal fees – Internet domain name	0
Interest payable	0
Capital allowances (working)	(50,420)
Trading loss	(136,320)

Tutorial notes

(1) Gifts to customers are an allowable deduction if they cost less than £50 per recipient per year, are not of food, drink, tobacco or vouchers for exchangeable goods and carry a conspicuous advertisement for the company making the gift. Gifts to employees are an allowable deduction because the gifts will potentially be assessed on the employees as benefits.

(2) Interest on a loan used for trading purposes is deductible on an accruals basis.

Working – Capital allowances

	£	Main pool £	Allowances £
WDV brought forward		39,300	
Additions qualifying for AIA			
Delivery van	28,300		
AIA – 100%	(28,300)		28,300
		0	
Addition – Motor car [1]		14,700	
		54,000	
WDA – 18%		(9,720)	9,720
Addition qualifying for FYA			
Motor car [2]	12,400		
FYA – 100%	(12,400)		12,400
		0	
WDV carried forward		44,280	
Total allowances			50,420

Tutorial notes

(1) Motor car [1] has CO_2 emissions between 76 and 130 grams per kilometre, and therefore qualifies for writing down allowances at the rate of 18%.

(2) Motor car [2] has CO_2 emissions up to 75 grams per kilometre, and therefore qualifies for the 100% first year allowance.

(b)

	Year ended 31 August 2015 £	Period ended 31 March 2016 £
Trading profit	56,600	47,900
Bank interest	1,300	0
	57,900	47,900
Loss against total profits (working)	(24,125)	(47,900)
	33,775	0
Qualifying charitable donations	(540)	
Taxable total profits	33,235	0

Working – Trading loss

For the year ended 31 August 2015, loss relief is restricted to £24,125 (57,900 × 5/12).

(c)　(1)　The amount of unrelieved trading loss at 31 March 2017 is £64,295 (136,320 – 47,900 – 24,125).

　　　(2)　The unrelieved trading loss can be carried forward and will be relieved against the first available trading profits of the same trade.

33 Wai

Marking scheme

			Marks
(a)	Salary		½
	Bonus		1
	Mileage allowance		
		Reimbursement	½
		Ordinary commuting	½
		Travel to clients	½
		Temporary workplace	½
		Tax free amount @ 45p	½
		Tax free amount @ 25p	½
	Car benefit		
		Percentage	½
		Benefit	1
	Incidental expenses		½
	Mobile telephone		1
	Living accommodation		
		Annual value	½
		Additional benefit	
		Cost	½
		Improvements	1
		Limit	1
		Benefit	½
	Personal allowance		1
			12
(b)	Form P60 contents		1½
	Date		½
	Form P11D contents		½
	Date		½
			3
			15

(a) **Wai – Taxable income 2016/17**

	£
Employment income	
Salary (10,200 × 12)	122,400
Bonus	8,100
Mileage allowance (W1)	2,763
Car benefit (W2)	1,014
Incidental expenses	0
Mobile telephone (400 × 20%)	80
Living accommodation – Annual value	4,828
– Additional benefit (W3)	2,736
	141,921
Less personal allowance	0
Taxable income	141,921

Tutorial notes

1   The bonus of £4,600 will have been treated as being received during 2015/16 as Wai became entitled to it during that tax year. Similarly, the bonus of £2,900 will be treated as received during 2017/18.

2   The exemption for mobile telephones does not apply to the second telephone.

3   No personal allowance is available as Wai's adjusted net income of £141,921 exceeds £122,000.

Workings

1 – Mileage allowance

	Miles	£
Reimbursement (13,860 at 55p)		7,623
Business mileage		
Ordinary commuting		
Travel to clients' premises	8,580	
Temporary workplace	2,860	
	11,440	
Tax free amount		
10,000 miles at 45p		(4,500)
1,440 miles at 25p		(360)
Taxable benefit		2,763

Tutorial note

Travel to the temporary workplace qualifies as business mileage because the 24-month limit was not exceeded.

2 – Car benefit

The relevant percentage for the car benefit is 15% because the motor car has CO_2 emissions between 76 and 94 grams per kilometre.

The motor car was available during the period 1 September 2016 to 5 April 2017, so the benefit for 2016/17 is £1,014 (11,590 × 15% × 7/12).

3 – Living accommodation additional benefit

The benefit is based on the cost of the property plus subsequent improvements incurred before the start of the tax year.

	£
Cost	142,000
Improvements (prior to 6 April 2016 only)	24,200
	166,200
Limit	(75,000)
	91,200

The additional benefit is therefore £2,736 (91,200 at 3%).

(b)   **Form P60**

Form P60 will show Wai's taxable earnings, income tax deducted, final tax code, national insurance contributions (NIC), and Qaz plc's name and address.

This form should have been provided to Wai by 31 May 2017.

Form P11D

Form P11D will detail the expenses and benefits provided to Wai.

This form should have been provided to Wai by 6 July 2017.

ACCA

Paper F6

Taxation (United Kingdom)

Mock Examination 3

Specimen Exam

Question Paper	
Time allowed	**3 hours 15 minutes**
This paper is divided into three sections:	

This paper is divided into three sections:

Section A – ALL 15 questions are compulsory and MUST be attempted.

Section B – ALL 15 questions are compulsory and MUST be attempted.

Section C – ALL THREE questions are compulsory and MUST be attempted.

DO NOT OPEN THIS PAPER UNTIL YOU ARE READY TO START UNDER EXAMINATION CONDITIONS

ACCA

Paper F6

Taxation (United Kingdom)

Mock Examination 3

Specimen Exam

Question Paper	
Time allowed	3 hours 15 minutes

The exam is divided into three sections:

Section A – ALL 15 questions are compulsory and MUST be attempted.

Section B – ALL 15 questions are compulsory and MUST be attempted.

Section C – ALL THREE questions are compulsory and MUST be attempted.

DO NOT OPEN THIS PAPER UNTIL YOU ARE READY TO START UNDER EXAMINATION CONDITIONS

SECTION A: ALL 15 questions are compulsory and MUST be attempted

1   William is self-employed, and his tax adjusted trading profit for the year ended 5 April 2017 was £82,700. During the tax year 2016/17, William contributed £5,400 (gross) into a personal pension scheme.

What amount of class 4 national insurance contributions (NIC) will William pay for the tax year 2016/17?

A   £4,987
B   £4,664
C   £3,939
D   £3,831   **(2 marks)**

2   You are a trainee Chartered Certified Accountant and your firm has a client who has refused to disclose a chargeable gain to HM Revenue and Customs (HMRC).

From an ethical viewpoint, which of the following actions could be expected of your firm?

(1)   Reporting under the money laundering regulations
(2)   Advising the client to make disclosure
(3)   Informing HMRC of the non-disclosure
(4)   Warning the client that your firm will be reporting the non-disclosure

A   2 and 4 only
B   1 and 2 only
C   1 and 3 only
D   1, 2, 3, and 4   **(2 marks)**

3   Martin is self-employed and for the year ended 5 April 2017 his trading profit was £109,400. During the tax year 2016/17, Martin made a gift aid donation of £800 (gross) to a national charity.

What amount of personal allowance will Martin be entitled to for the tax year 2016/17?

A   £11,000
B   £6,700
C   £6,300
D   £2,400   **(2 marks)**

4   For the year ended 31 March 2017, Halo Ltd made a trading loss of £180,000.

Halo Ltd has owned 100% of the ordinary share capital of Shallow Ltd since it began trading on 1 July 2016. For the year ended 30 June 2017, Shallow Ltd will make a trading profit of £224,000.

Neither company has any other taxable profits or allowable losses.

What is the maximum amount of group relief which Shallow Ltd can claim from Halo Ltd in respect of the trading loss of £180,000 for the year ended 31 March 2017?

A   £180,000
B   £168,000
C   £45,000
D   £135,000   **(2 marks)**

5   For the year ended 31 March 2016, Sizeable Ltd had taxable total profits of £820,000, and for the year ended 31 March 2017 had taxable total profits of £970,000. The profits accrue evenly throughout the year.

Sizeable Ltd has had one 51% group company for many years.

How will Sizeable Ltd pay its corporation tax liability for the year ended 31 March 2017?

A   Nine instalments of £16,400 and a balancing payment of £46,400
B   Four instalments of £48,500
C   Four instalments of £41,000 and a balancing payment of £30,000
D   One payment of £194,000   **(2 marks)**

6   For the year ended 31 December 2016, Lateness Ltd had a corporation tax liability of £60,000, which it did not pay until 31 March 2018. Lateness Ltd is not a large company.

How much interest will Lateness Ltd be charged by HM Revenue and Customs (HMRC) in respect of the late payment of its corporation tax liability for the year ended 31 December 2016?

A   £900
B   £2,250
C   £300
D   £450   **(2 marks)**

7   On 26 November 2016 Alice sold an antique table for £8,700. The antique table had been purchased on 16 May 2013 for £3,800.

What is Alice's chargeable gain in respect of the disposal of the antique table?

A   £4,500
B   £1,620
C   £4,900
D   £0   **(2 marks)**

8   On 14 November 2016, Jane made a cash gift to a trust of £800,000 (after deducting all available exemptions). Jane paid the inheritance tax arising from this gift. Jane has not made any other lifetime gifts.

What amount of lifetime inheritance tax would have been payable in respect of Jane's gift to the trust?

A   £95,000
B   £190,000
C   £118,750
D   £200,000   **(2 marks)**

9   During the tax year 2016/17, Mildred made the following cash gifts to her grandchildren:

(1)   £400 to Alfred
(2)   £140 to Minnie
(3)   A further £280 to Minnie
(4)   £175 to Winifred

Which of the gifts will be exempt from inheritance tax under the small gifts exemption?

A   1, 2, 3 and 4
B   2, 3 and 4 only
C   2 only
D   4 only   **(2 marks)**

10   For the quarter ended 31 March 2017, Faro had standard rated sales of £49,750 and standard rated expenses of £22,750. Both figures are exclusive of value added tax (VAT).

Faro uses the flat rate scheme to calculate the amount of VAT payable, with the relevant scheme percentage for her trade being 12%. The percentage reduction for the first year of VAT registration is not available.

How much VAT will Faro have to pay to HM Revenue and Customs (HMRC) for the quarter ended 31 March 2017?

A   £5,970
B   £3,888
C   £5,400
D   £7,164

(2 marks)

11   Which of the following assets will ALWAYS be exempt from capital gains tax?

(1)   A motor car suitable for private use
(2)   A chattel
(3)   A UK Government security (gilt)
(4)   A house

A   1 and 3
B   2 and 3
C   2 and 4
D   1 and 4

(2 marks)

12   Winston invested £8,000 into a cash individual savings account (ISA) on 6 April 2016. He withdrew £3,000 from the cash ISA on 30 June 2016. He now wants to invest more funds into the cash ISA over the remainder of the tax year 2016/17.

What is the maximum possible amount which Winston can invest into his cash ISA for the remainder of the tax year 2016/17?

A   £15,240
B   £10,240
C   £3,000
D   £10,620

(2 marks)

13   Ming is self-employed.

How long must she retain the business and non-business records used in preparing her self-assessment tax return for the tax year 2016/17?

	Business records	Non-business records
A	31 January 2019	31 January 2019
B	31 January 2019	31 January 2023
C	31 January 2023	31 January 2023
D	31 January 2023	31 January 2019

(2 marks)

14   Moon Ltd has had the following results:

Period	Profit/(loss)
	£
Year ended 31 December 2016	(105,000)
Four-month period ended 31 December 2015	43,000
Year ended 31 August 2015	96,000

The company does not have any other income.

How much of Moon Ltd's trading loss for the year ended 31 December 2016 can be relieved against its total profits of £96,000 for the year ended 31 August 2015?

A   £64,000
B   £96,000
C   £70,000
D   £62,000

(2 marks)

15   Nigel has not previously been resident in the UK, being in the UK for less than 20 days each tax year. For the tax year 2016/17, he has three ties with the UK.

What is the maximum number of days which Nigel could spend in the UK during the tax year 2016/17 without being treated as resident in the UK for that year?

A   90 days
B   182 days
C   45 days
D   120 days

(2 marks)

(Total = 30 marks)

SECTION B – ALL 15 questions are compulsory and MUST be attempted

Delroy and Marlon

The following scenario relates to questions 16-20.

Delroy and Grant

On 10 January 2017, Delroy made a gift of 25,000 £1 ordinary shares in Dub Ltd, an unquoted trading company, to his son, Grant. The market value of the shares on that date was £240,000. Delroy had subscribed for the 25,000 shares in Dub Ltd at par on 1 July 2006. Delroy and Grant have elected to hold over the gain as a gift of a business asset.

Grant sold the 25,000 shares in Dub Ltd on 18 March 2017 for £240,000.

Dub Ltd has a share capital of 100,000 £1 ordinary shares. Delroy was the sales director of the company from its incorporation on 1 July 2006 until 10 January 2017. Grant has never been an employee or a director of Dub Ltd.

For the tax year 2016/17 Delroy and Grant are both higher rate taxpayers. They have each made other disposals of assets during the tax year 2016/17, and therefore they have both already utilised their annual exempt amount for this year.

Marlon and Alvita

On 28 March 2017, Marlon sold a house for £497,000, which he had owned individually. The house had been purchased on 22 October 2001 for £152,600.

 Throughout the period of ownership the house was occupied by Marlon and his wife, Alvita, as their main residence. One-third of the house was always used exclusively for business purposes by the couple. Entrepreneurs' relief is not available in respect of this disposal.

For the tax year 2016/17, Marlon is a higher rate taxpayer, but Alvita did not have any taxable income. This will remain the case for the tax year 2017/18. Neither of them has made any other disposals of assets during the year.

16   What is Grant's capital gains tax (CGT) liability for the tax year 2016/17 in respect of the disposal of the shares in Dub Ltd?

    A   £43,000

    B   £21,500

    C   £0

    D   £40,780   **(2 marks)**

17   What would the CGT implications have been if Delroy had instead sold the 25,000 shares in Dub Ltd himself for £240,000 on 10 January 2017, and then gifted the cash proceeds to Grant?

    (1)   Entrepreneurs' relief would have been available

    (2)   The CGT liability would have been paid later

    (3)   The cash gift would not have been a chargeable disposal

    (4)   The cash gift would have qualified for holdover relief

    A   1 and 3

    B   2 and 3

    C   2 and 4

    D   1 and 4   **(2 marks)**

18   What is Marlon's chargeable gain for the tax year 2016/17?

      A   £229,600
      B   £0
      C   £114,800
      D   £344,400   (2 marks)

19   What is the amount of CGT which could have been saved if Marlon had transferred 50% ownership of the
      house to Alvita prior to its disposal?

      A   £3,108
      B   £6,308
      C   £3,200
      D   £5,420   (2 marks)

20   Why would it have been beneficial if Marlon had delayed the sale of the house until 6 April 2017?

      A   A lower rate of CGT would have been applicable
      B   Two annual exempt amounts would have been available
      C   Principal private residence relief would have been greater
      D   The CGT liability would have been paid later   (2 marks)

                                                                                          (Total = 10 marks)

Opal

The following scenario relates to questions 21-25.

You should assume that today's date is 15 March 2017.

Opal is aged 71 and has a chargeable estate for inheritance tax (IHT) purposes valued at £950,000.

She owns two properties respectively valued at £374,000 and £442,000. The first property has an outstanding
repayment mortgage of £160,000, and the second property has an outstanding endowment mortgage of £92,000.

Opal owes £22,400 in respect of a personal loan from a bank, and she has also verbally promised to pay legal fees
of £4,600 incurred by her nephew. Opal expects the cost of her funeral to be £5,200, and this cost will be covered
by the £6,000 she has invested in an individual savings account (ISA).

Under the terms of her will, Opal has left all of her estate to her children. Opal's husband is still alive.

On 14 August 2007, Opal had made a gift of £100,000 to her daughter, and on 7 November 2016, she made a gift of
£220,000 to her son. Both these figures are after deducting all available exemptions.

The nil rate band for the tax year 2007/08 is £300,000.

You should assume that both the value of Opal's estate and the nil rate band will remain unchanged for future years.

21   What is the net value for the two properties, and related mortgages, which will have been included in the
      calculation of Opal's chargeable estate of £950,000?

      A   £816,000
      B   £564,000
      C   £656,000
      D   £724,000   (2 marks)

22   What is the total amount of deductions (ignoring mortgage debts) which will have been permitted in calculating Opal's chargeable estate of £950,000?

     A   £28,400
     B   £22,400
     C   £32,200
     D   £27,600   **(2 marks)**

23   What amount of IHT will be payable in respect of Opal's chargeable estate valued at £950,000 were she to die on 20 March 2017?

     A   £250,000
     B   £338,000
     C   £378,000
     D   £335,600   **(2 marks)**

24   By how much would the IHT payable on Opal's death by reduced if she were to live for another seven years until 20 March 2024, compared to if she were to die on 20 March 2017?

     A   £88,000
     B   £40,000
     C   £128,000
     D   £0   **(2 marks)**

25   Which of the following conditions must be met if Opal wants to make gifts out of her income, so that these gifts are exempt from IHT?

     (1)   The gifts cannot exceed 10% of income
     (2)   The gifts must be habitual
     (3)   Opal must have enough remaining income to maintain her normal standard of living
     (4)   Opal must make the gifts monthly or quarterly

     A   3 and 4
     B   1 and 4
     C   2 and 3
     D   1 and 2   **(2 marks)**

                                                                        (Total = 10 marks)

Glacier Ltd

The following scenario relates to questions 26-30.

The following information is available in respect of Glacier Ltd's value added tax (VAT) for the quarter ended 31 March 2017:

(1)   Invoices were issued for sales of £44,600 to VAT registered customers. Of this figure, £35,200 was in respect of exempt sales and the balance in respect of standard rated sales. The standard rated sales figure is exclusive of VAT.

(2)   In addition to the above, on 1 March 2017 Glacier Ltd issued a VAT invoice for £8,000 plus VAT of £1,600 to a VAT registered customer in respect of a contract which will be completed on 15 April 2017. The customer paid for the contract in two instalments of £4,800 on 31 March 2017 and 30 April 2017.

(3)   The managing director of Glacier Ltd is provided with free fuel for private mileage driven in her company motor car. During the quarter ended 31 March 2017, the total cost of fuel for business and private mileage was £720, of which £270 was for private mileage. The relevant quarterly scale charge is £415. All of these figures are inclusive of VAT.

For the quarters ended 30 September 2015 and 30 June 2016, Glacier Ltd was one month late in submitting its VAT returns and in paying the related VAT liabilities. All of the company's other VAT returns have been submitted on time.

26   What is the amount of output VAT payable by Glacier Ltd in respect of its sales for the quarter ended 31 March 2017?

    A   £2,680
    B   £3,480
    C   £10,520
    D   £1,880   **(2 marks)**

27   What output VAT and input VAT entries will Glacier Ltd include on its VAT return for the quarter ended 31 March 2017 in respect of the managing director's company motor car?

    A   Output VAT of £69 and input VAT of £75
    B   Output VAT of £0 and input VAT of £75
    C   Output VAT of £0 and input VAT of £120
    D   Output VAT of £69 and input VAT of £120   **(2 marks)**

28   What surcharge penalty could Glacier Ltd be charged if the company is one month late in paying its VAT liability for the quarter ended 31 March 2017?

    A   5% of the VAT liability
    B   2% of the VAT liability
    C   There will be no penalty
    D   10% of the VAT liability   **(2 marks)**

29   What is the minimum requirement which Glacier Ltd needs to meet in order to revert to a clean default surcharge record?

    A   Submit four consecutive VAT returns on time
    B   Submit any four VAT returns on time and also pay the related VAT liabilities on time
    C   Pay four consecutive VAT liabilities on time
    D   Submit four consecutive VAT returns on time and also pay the related VAT liabilities on time
                                                                                                          (2 marks)

30   In which circumstances will Glacier Ltd be required to issue a VAT invoice?

    A   When a standard rated supply is made to any customer
    B   When any type of supply is made to any customer
    C   When a standard rated supply is made to a VAT registered customer
    D   When any type of supply is made to a VAT registered customer   **(2 marks)**

(Total = 10 marks)

SECTION C – ALL three questions are compulsory and MUST be attempted

31 Sarah

You should assume that today's date is 1 March 2016.

Sarah is currently self employed. If she continues to trade on a self-employed basis, her total income tax liability and national insurance contributions (NIC) for the tax year 2016/17 will be £12,631.

Sarah does not have any employees and therefore cannot currently make use of the £3,000 employment allowance.

However, Sarah is considering incorporating her business on 6 April 2016. The forecast taxable total profits of the new limited company for the year ended 5 April 2017 will be £50,000 (before taking account of any director's remuneration). Sarah will pay herself gross director's remuneration of £30,000 and dividends of £10,000. The balance of the profits will remain undrawn within the new company.

Required

Determine whether or not there will be an overall saving of tax and national insurance contributions (NIC) for the year ended 5 April 2017 if Sarah incorporates her business on 6 April 2016. **(10 marks)**

Notes

1   You are expected to calculate the income tax payable by Sarah, the class 1 NIC payable by Sarah and the new limited company, and the corporation tax liability of the new limited company for the year ended 5 April 2017.

2   You should assume that the rates of corporation tax remain unchanged.

(Total = 10 marks)

32 Simon

On 6 April 2016, Simon commenced employment with Echo Ltd. On 1 January 2017, he commenced in partnership with Art running a small music venue, preparing accounts to 30 April. The following information is available for the tax year 2016/17:

Employment

(1)   During the tax year 2016/17, Simon was paid a gross annual salary of £23,700.

(2)   Throughout the tax year 2016/17, Echo Ltd provided Simon with living accommodation. The company had purchased the property in 2006 for £89,000, and it was valued at £143,000 on 6 April 2016. The annual value of the property is £4,600. The property was furnished by Echo Ltd during March 2016 at a cost of £9,400. The living accommodation is not job related.

(3)   On 1 December 2016, Echo Ltd provided Simon with an interest-free loan of £84,000, which he used to purchase a holiday cottage.

Partnership

(1)   The partnership's tax adjusted trading profit for the four-month period ended 30 April 2017 is £29,700. This figure is before taking account of capital allowances.

(2)   The only item of plant and machinery owned by the partnership is a motor car which cost £18,750 on 1 February 2017. The motor car has a CO_2 emission rate of 155 grams per kilometre. It is used by Art, and 40% of the mileage is for private journeys.

(3)   Profits are shared 40% to Simon and 60% to Art. This is after paying an annual salary of £6,000 to Art.

Property income

(1) Simon owns a freehold house which is let out furnished. The property was let throughout the tax year 2016/17 at a monthly rent of £810.

(2) During the tax year 2016/17, Simon paid council tax and water rates totalling £1,320 in respect of the property.

(3) Simon spent £2,560 on purchasing a new bed for the house which replaced an old one which was sold for £100. The replacement does not represent an improvement in the furniture in the property.

Required

(a) Calculate Simon's taxable income for the tax year 2016/17. **(13 marks)**

(b) State TWO advantages for the partnership of choosing 30 April as its accounting date rather than 5 April. **(2 marks)**

(Total = 15 marks)

33 Naive Ltd

(a) You are a trainee accountant and your manager has asked you to correct a corporation tax computation which has been prepared by the managing director of Naive Ltd. The corporation tax computation is for the year ended 31 March 2017 and contains a significant number of errors:

Naive Ltd – Corporation tax computation for the year ended 31 March 2017

	£
Trading profit (working 1)	372,900
Loan interest received (working 2)	32,100
	405,000
Corporation tax (405,000 at 20%)	81,000

Working 1 – Trading profit

	£
Operating profit before interest and taxation	274,530
Depreciation	15,740
Donations to political parties	400
Qualifying charitable donations	900
Accountancy	2,300
Legal fees in connection with the issue of loan notes (the loan was used to finance the company's trading activities)	5,700
Entertaining suppliers	3,600
Entertaining employees	1,700
Gifts to customers (pens costing £40 each and displaying Naive Ltd's name)	920
Gifts to customers (food hampers costing £45 each and displaying Naive Ltd's name)	1,650
Capital allowances (working 3)	65,460
Trading profit	372,900

Working 2 – Loan interest received

	£
Loan interest receivable	32,800
Accrued at 1 April 2016	10,600
Accrued at 31 March 2017	(11,300)
Loan interest received	32,100

The loan was made for non-trading purposes.

Working 3 – Capital allowances

	Main pool £	Motor car £	Special rate pool £	Allowances £
Written down value (WDV) brought forward	12,400		13,600	
Additions				
Machinery	42,300			
Motor car [1]	13,800			
Motor car [2]		14,000		
	68,500			
Annual investment allowance (AIA)	(68,500)			68,500
Disposal proceeds			(9,300)	
			4,300	
Balancing allowance			(4,300)	(4,300)
Writing down allowance (WDA) – 18%		(2,520) × 50%		1,260
WDV carried forward	0	11,480		
Total allowances				65,460

(1) Motor car [1] has a CO_2 emission rate of 110 grams per kilometre.

(2) Motor car [2] has a CO_2 emission rate of 155 grams per kilometre. This motor car is used by the sales manager and 50% of the mileage is for private journeys.

(3) All of the items included in the special rate pool at 1 April 2016 were sold for £9,300 during the year ended 31 March 2017. The original cost of these items was £16,200.

Required

Prepare a corrected version of Naive Ltd's corporation tax computation for the year ended 31 March 2017.

Note: Your calculations should commence with the operating profit before interest and taxation figure of £274,530, and you should indicate by the use of zero (0) any items in the computation of the trading profit for which no adjustment is required. **(12 marks)**

(b) The managing director of Naive Ltd understands that the company will have to file its self-assessment corporation tax returns online, and that the supporting accounts and tax computations will have to be filed using the inline eXtensible Business Reporting Language (iXBRL). The managing director is concerned with how the company will be able to produce the documents in this format.

Required

Explain the options available to Naive Ltd regarding the production of accounts and tax computations in the iXBRL format. **(3 marks)**

(Total = 15 marks)

Answers

**DO NOT TURN THIS PAGE UNTIL YOU HAVE
COMPLETED THE MOCK EXAM**

CANDIDATE ANSWER BOOKLET

SAMPLE PAGE ONLY

USE THIS PAGE TO RECORD ANSWERS TO MULTIPLE CHOICE QUESTIONS

- If your question paper has less than 60 questions, fill in the relevant answers only.

- Each multiple choice question has only one correct answer. Fill in one bubble only (A, B, C, or D) to indicate your choice of answer.

- The mark available for each question is indicated on your question paper. There is no penalty for incorrect answers or unanswered questions.

- No marks are awarded if you do not clearly indicate your final choice or if more than one bubble per question is filled in.

- To void a selected answer, place a cross (**X**) over the bubble.

HOW TO SHADE THE BUBBLES

EXAMPLE

Right mark   Wrong mark

To amend your selection place a cross over unwanted bubble

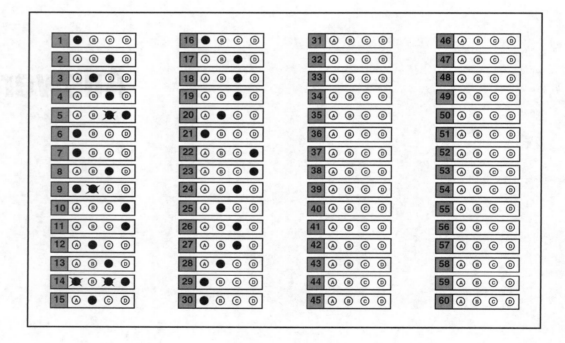

A plan of attack

If this were the real Taxation (UK) exam and you had been told to turn over and begin, what would be going through your mind?

Perhaps you're having a panic. You've spent most of your study time on income tax and corporation tax computations (because that's what your tutor/BPP study Text told you to do), plus a selection of other topics, and you're really not sure that you know enough. So calm down. Spend the first few moments or so **looking at the paper**, and develop a **plan of attack**.

Looking through the paper:

Section A contains **15 Objective Test (OT) questions** each worth **2 marks**. These will cover all sections of the syllabus. Some you may find easy and some more difficult. Don't spend a lot of time on anything you really don't know. For multiple choice questions you are not penalised for wrong answers, so you should answer all of them. If all else fails – guess!

Section B also contains **three OT Case** questions. These have **five subparts** each worth **2 marks**. Make sure you read the scenario carefully before you start to answer the OTs.

In **Section C** you have **three constructed response (long) questions**:

- **Question 31** for **10 marks** is about the potential tax saving by incorporating a sole trader business. You need to work out the individual's income tax, the national insurance contributions for an employee and corporation tax.

- **Question 32** for **15 marks** is an income tax computation and also deals with choice of accounting date.

- **Question 33** for **15 marks** is a corporation tax question and includes capital allowances. Part (b) is about how a company files its corporation tax return and supporting accounts.

All of these questions are compulsory.

This means that you do not have to waste time wondering which questions to answer.

Allocating your time

BPP's advice is always allocate your time **according to the marks for the question** in total and for the parts of the question. But **use common sense**. If you're confronted by an OTQ on a topic of which you know nothing, pick an answer and move on. Use the time to pick up marks elsewhere.

After the exam…**Forget about it!**

And don't worry if you found the paper difficult. More than likely other candidates will too. If this were the real thing you would need to **forget** the exam the minute you left the exam hall and **think about the next one**. Or, if it's the last one, **celebrate**!

Section A

1 C £3,939

	£
£(43,000 − 8,060) = £34,940 × 9%	3,145
£(82,700 − 43,000) = £39,700 × 2%	794
Class 1 primary NICs	3,939

2 B 1 and 2 only

Your firm should advise the client to make disclosure. Your firm should make a report under the money laundering regulations.

You should not inform HMRC of the non-disclosure. Your firm also should not warn the client that it will be reporting the non-disclosure as this might constitute the criminal offence of 'tipping-off'.

3 B £6,700

	£
Personal allowance	11,000
Less restriction £(109,400 − 800 − 100,000) = £8,600/2	(4,300)
Restricted personal allowance	6,700

4 D £135,000

The lower of:

	£
Taxable total profits of Shallow Ltd for the corresponding accounting period (1.7.16 – 31.3.17) £224,000 × 9/12	168,000
Losses of Halo Ltd for the corresponding accounting period £180,000 × 9/12	135,000

5 B Four instalments of £48,500

Profits threshold £1,500,000/2 (related 51% company)	£750,000

Sizeable Ltd was therefore a large company in both years.

Each instalment for the year to 31 March 2017 is £(970,000 @ 20%) = 194,000/4	£48,500

6 A £900

Interest runs from due date (1 October 2017) to the date of payment (31 March 2018) which is six months.

£60,000 × 3% × 6/12	£900

7 A £4,500

	£
Proceeds	8,700
Less cost	(3,800)
Gain	4,900

The maximum gain is 5/3 × £(8,700 − 6,000) = £4,500.

The chargeable gain is the lower of £4,900 and £4,500, so it is £4,500.

8 C £118,750

	£
Net chargeable transfer	800,000
Less nil rate band	(325,000)
	475,000
IHT £475,000 × 20/80 (donor paid tax)	118,750

9   D   4 only

Outright gifts to individuals totalling £250 or less per donee in any one tax year are exempt under the small gifts exemption. The £400 gift to Alfred is therefore not exempt under the small gifts exemption. If gifts total more than £250 the whole amount is chargeable. Therefore neither of the gifts to Minnie which total £(140 + 280) = £420 are exempt under the small gifts exemption. The gift of £175 to Winifred is exempt under the small gifts exemption.

10   D   £7,164

£(49,750 × 120/100) = 59,700 × 12%   £7,164

Under the flat rate scheme, a business calculates VAT by applying a fixed percentage to its tax inclusive turnover. However, the business cannot reclaim any input tax suffered.

11   A   1 and 3

A motor car suitable for private use and a UK Government security (gilt) are always exempt. A wasting chattel is exempt, as is a chattel sold for gross proceeds of £6,000 or less. Other chattels are chargeable assets. A house may be exempt if principal private residence relief applies, but is otherwise a chargeable asset.

12   B   £10,240

£(15,240 – 8,000) + £3,000 (replace funds withdrawn)   £10,240

13   C   Business records 31 January 2023, non-business records 31 January 2023

Records must be retained until five years after the 31 January following the tax year where the taxpayer is in business. This applies to all of the records, not only the business records.

14   D   £62,000

		£
Loss incurred in y/e 31.12.16		105,000
p/e 31.12.15		(43,000)
		62,000
y/e 31.8.15		
Lower of £96,000 × 8/12 = £64,000 and unused loss		(62,000)
C/f		0

Loss relief by deduction from total profits may be given by deduction from current period profits and from the previous 12 months. Therefore relief can be given in the four month period ended 31 December 2015 and for eight months of the year ended 31 August 2015.

15   A   90 days

Nigel was not previously resident in the UK. He will be UK resident for 2016/17 with three UK ties if he spends at least 91 days in the UK during that tax year. Therefore maximum number of days that Nigel could spend in the UK during the tax year 2016/17 without being treated as UK resident for that year is 90 days.

Section B

Delroy and Marlon

16   A   £43,000

		£
Ordinary shares in Dub Ltd		
Proceeds		240,000
Less cost		(25,000)
Gain		215,000
Less annual exempt amount (already used as stated in question)		(0)
Taxable gain		215,000
CGT: £215,000 × 20%		43,000

Tutorial notes

1   The effect of the gift relief election is that Grant effectively took over Delroy's original cost of £25,000.

2   The disposal does not qualify for entrepreneurs' relief as Grant was neither an officer nor an employee of Dub Ltd and, in any case, had only owned the shares for just over two months (the minimum period for the conditions for the relief to be satisfied is one year).

17   A   1 and 3

Delroy's disposal would have qualified for entrepreneurs' relief because for at least one year prior to the disposal:

- Dub Ltd was Delroy's personal company as he owned at least 5% of the ordinary share capital.
- Dub Ltd was a trading company.
- Delroy was an officer or employee of Dub Ltd.

There are no capital gains tax implications of a gift of cash.

18   C   £114,800

	£
House	
Proceeds	497,000
Less cost	(152,600)
Gain before PPR relief	344,400
Less PPR relief (W)	(229,600)
Gain after PPR relief	114,800

Working

One-third of Marlon's house was always used exclusively for business purposes, so the principal private residence relief exemption is restricted to £(344,400 × 2/3) = £229,600.

19   B   £6,308

		£
Annual exempt amount	£11,100 × 28%	3,108
Basic rate band	£32,000 × (28 – 18)%	3,200
Total tax saving		6,308

The 50% ownership of the house would have been transferred from Marlon to Alvita on a no gain, no loss basis. The effect of this is that 50% of the gain on disposal would accrue to Marlon and 50% to Alvita.

Transferring 50% ownership of the house to Alvita prior to its disposal would have enabled her annual exempt amount and basic rate tax band for 2016/17 to be utilised.

20   D   The CGT liability would have been paid later

The disposal on 6 April 2017 would fall into tax year 2017/18 and so the payment date for capital gains tax would be 31 January 2019, rather than 31 January 2018 if the disposal had been made on 28 March 2017 in 2016/17.

Opal

Text references. Inheritance tax is covered in Chapter 18.

Top tips. Try drawing a time line and mark on it the date of Opal's death and the lifetime transfers. Then mark the date which is seven years before Opal's death. It will be clear that the lifetime transfer in 2007 falls more than seven years before Opal's death and is therefore exempt.

Easy marks. There were some easy marks for working out the IHT on the death estate in question 23.

21   C   £656,000

	£	£
Property one	374,000	
Less repayment mortgage	(160,000)	
		214,000
Property two	442,000	
Less endowment mortgage	0	442,000
Net value of two properties		656,000

There is no deduction in respect of the endowment mortgage as this will be repaid upon death by the life assurance element of the mortgage.

22   D   £27,600

	£
Bank loan	22,400
Legal fees	0
Funeral costs	5,200
Total amount of deductions	27,600

The promise to pay the nephew's legal fees is not deductible as it is not legally enforceable.

23   B   £338,000

	£
Chargeable estate	950,000
105,000 (W) × 0%	0
845,000 × 40%	338,000
950,000	
IHT on death estate	338,000

Working

	£
Nil rate band at death	325,000
Less: PET 14 August 2007	(0)
PET 7 November 2016	(220,000)
Available nil rate band	105,000

The potentially exempt transfer on 14 August 2007 is exempt from inheritance tax as it was made more than seven years before 20 March 2017.

24   A   £88,000

If Opal were to live for another seven years, then the potentially exempt transfer on 7 November 2016 would become exempt.

The inheritance tax payable in respect of her estate would therefore decrease by £(220,000 × 40%) = £88,000.

25   C   2 and 3

For the normal expenditure out of income exemption to apply the gifts must be habitual and Opal must have enough remaining income to maintain her usual standard of living.

Glacier Ltd

Text references. Value added tax is covered in Chapters 24 and 25.

Top tips. The tax point is frequently examined and is relevant in question 26. The basic tax point for a supply of services is the date when they are completed, but if a VAT invoice is issued or payment received before the basic tax point, then this becomes the actual tax point.

Easy marks. There were easy marks in questions 28 and 29 concerning the default surcharge penalty.

26   B   £3,480

	£
Sales	
VAT registered customers £(44,600 − 35,200) = £9,400 × 20%	1,880
Additional contract (1 March 2017)	1,600
Output VAT	3,480

The tax point for the contract is when the VAT invoice was issued on 1 March 2017.

27   D   Output VAT of £69 and input VAT of £120

Output VAT £415 × 20/120	£69
Input VAT £720 × 20/120	£120

28   A   5% of the VAT liability

Glacier Ltd was late in submitting VAT returns and paying the related VAT liability for two previous quarters. The late payment of VAT for the quarter ended 31 March 2017 will therefore result in a surcharge of 5% of the VAT liability for that period since this is the second default during the surcharge period.

29   D   Submit four consecutive VAT returns on time and also pay the related VAT liabilities on time

30   C   When a standard rated supply is made to a VAT registered customer

Section C

31 Sarah

> **Text references.** Employment income is covered in Chapter 3. The income tax computation is the subject of Chapter 2. National insurance contributions are dealt with in Chapter 12. Corporation tax is covered in Chapter 19.
>
> **Top tips.** Note 1 outlines the steps that you need to take to complete the question.
>
> **Easy marks.** There were some easy marks for basic income tax and corporation tax computations.

Marking scheme

	Marks
Income tax liability	
Director's remuneration	½
Dividends	1
Personal allowance	½
Basic rate on earnings	½
Basic rate on dividends	½
Tax credit on dividend	½
National insurance contributions	
Class 1 employee	1
Class 1 employer	1
Employment allowance	1
Corporation tax	
Trading profit	½
Director's remuneration	½
Employer's Class 1 NIC	½
Corporation tax	½
Total tax cost if incorporates	1
Overall tax saving	½
	10

Sarah – Income tax liability 2016/17

	Non-savings income £	Dividend income £	Total income £
Director's remuneration	30,000		
Dividends		10,000	
Net income	30,000	10,000	40,000
Less personal allowance	(11,000)		
Taxable income	19,000	10,000	29,000

Tax	
Non-savings income	
£19,000 @ 20%	3,800
Dividend income	
£5,000 @ 0%	0
£5,000 (10,000 – 5,000) @ 7.5%	375
Income tax liability	4,175

Sarah – National insurance contributions 2016/17

	£
Employee class 1 £(30,000 – 8,060) = 21,940 @ 12%	2,633
Employer class 1 £(30,000 – 8,112) = 21,888 @ 13.8%	3,021

The employment allowance is not available to a company director who is the sole employee of their company.

Corporation tax liability of the new limited company for the year ended 5 April 2017

	£
Trading profit	50,000
Less director's remuneration	(30,000)
employer's Class1 NIC	(3,021)
Taxable trading profit	16,979
Corporation tax £16,979 @ 20%	3,396

The total tax and NIC cost if Sarah incorporates her business is £13,225 (4,175 + 2,633 + 3,021 + 3,396).

Therefore, if Sarah incorporated her business there would not be a saving in tax and NIC as there would be an increase of £594 (12,631 – 13,225) compared to continuing on a self-employed basis.

32 Simon

Marking scheme

			Marks
(a)	Employment income		
	Salary		½
	Living accommodation	annual value	½
		additional benefit – market value	1
		additional benefit – limit	½
		additional benefit – benefit	½
		furniture	1
	Loan benefit		1
	Trading income		
	Accounts profit		½
	Capital allowances – addition		½
	Capital allowances – WDA		1½
	Salary paid to Art		1
	Profit share		½
	Trading income 2016/17		1
	Property business income		
	Rent receivable		½
	Council tax		½
	Furniture		1½
	Personal allowance		½
			13
(b)	Payment of tax delayed		1
	Calculation of profits in advance of end of tax year		1
			2
			15

(a)   **Simon – Taxable income 2016/17**

	£
Employment income	
Salary	23,700
Living accommodation – annual value	4,600
Living accommodation – additional benefit (W1)	2,040
Living accommodation – furniture £9,400 × 20%	1,880
Loan benefit £84,000 × 3% × 4/12	840
	33,060
Trading income (W2)	8,220
Property business income (W4)	5,940
Net income	47,220
Less personal allowance	(11,000)
Taxable income	36,220

Workings

1   *Living accommodation – additional benefit*

	£
Market value when first provided to Simon	143,000
Less limit	(75,000)
	68,000
Additional benefit £68,000 × 3%	2,040

Tutorial note

Where the property was acquired by the employer more than six years before first being provided to the employee, the market value when first so is used as the cost of providing the living accommodation.

2   *Trading income*

Simon's share of the partnership's trading profit for the period ended 30 April 2017 is £10,960 calculated as follows:

	£
Trading profit	29,700
Less capital allowances (W3)	(300)
	29,400
Less salary paid to Art £6,000 × 4/12	(2,000)
	27,400
Profit share £27,400 × 40%	10,960
Simon's trading income 2016/17 £10,960 × 3/4	8,220

Tutorial note

Simon's trading income for 2016/17 is for the period 1 January 2017 to 5 April 2017 as this is his first year of trading and the actual basis applies.

3   *Capital allowances*

	Motor car		Allowances
4 month period to 30 April 2017	£		£
Addition	18,750		
WDA @ 8% × 4/12	(500)	× 60%	300
WDA c/f	18,250		

Tutorial note

The partnership's motor car has CO_2 emissions over 130 grams per kilometre and therefore qualifies for writing down allowances at the rate of 8%.

4   *Property business income*

	£	£
Rent receivable £810 × 12		9,720
Council tax and water rates	1,320	
Replacement furniture £(2,560 - 100)	2,460	
		(3,780)
Property business income		5,940

(b)   The interval between earning profits and paying the related tax liability will be 11 months longer. This can be particularly beneficial where profits are rising.

It will be possible to calculate taxable profits well in advance of the end of the tax year, making it much easier to implement tax planning and make pension contributions.

33 Naive Ltd

Text references. The computation of taxable total profits and the computation of the corporation tax liability are covered in Chapter 19. The adjustment to trading profits is dealt with in Chapter 7 and capital allowances in Chapter 8.

Top tips. The best approach to this style of question is to start new computations using the information given in the question, rather than trying to correct the wrong computations.

Easy marks. There were some easy marks for the adjustment to trading profit and computation of corporation tax in part (a).

Marking scheme

		Marks
(a)	Trading profit	
	Depreciation	½
	Donations to political parties	½
	Qualifying charitable donations	½
	Accountancy	½
	Legal fees	½
	Entertaining suppliers	½
	Entertaining employees	½
	Gift to customers – pens	½
	Gift to customers – food hampers	½
	Capital allowances brought from working	½
	Capital allowances	
	WDV brought forward	1
	Annual investment allowance	1
	Addition – motor car [1]	½
	Addition – motor car [2]	½
	Disposal	½
	WDA @ 18%	½
	WDA @ 8%	1
	Loan interest	1
	Qualifying charitable donations	½
	Corporation tax	½
		12
(b)	HMRC software automatically to produce in iXBRL	1
	Other software automatically to produce in iXBRL	1
	Tagging services and software used by Naive Ltd to tag	1
		3
		15

(a) Naïve Ltd – Corporation tax computation for the year ended 31 March 2017

	£
Trading profit (W1)	248,340
Loan interest	32,800
Total profits	281,140
Less qualifying charitable donations	(900)
Taxable total profits	280,240
Corporation tax	
£280,240 × 20%	56,048

Workings

1 *Trading profit for the year ended 31 March 2017*

	£
Operating profit before interest and taxation	274,530
Add: Depreciation	15,740
Donations to political parties	400
Qualifying charitable donations	900
Accountancy	0
Legal fees	0
Entertaining suppliers	3,600
Entertaining employees	0
Gifts to customers – pens	0
Gifts to customers – food hampers	1,650
	296,820
Less capital allowances (W2)	(48,480)
Adjusted trading profit	248,340

2 *Capital allowances*

	AIA £	Main pool £	Special rate pool £	Allowances £
WDV brought forward		12,400	13,600	
AIA additions				
Machinery	42,300			
AIA	(42,300)			42,300
Transfer to pool	0	0		
Non-AIA additions				
Motor car [1]		13,800		
Motor car [2]			14,000	
Disposal				
Special rate pool items			(9,300)	
		26,200	18,300	
WDA @ 18%		(4,716)		4,716
WDA @ 8%			(1,464)	1,464
WDV carried forward		21,484	16,836	
Allowances				48,480

Tutorial notes

1 Motor car [1] has CO_2 emissions between 76 and 130 grams per kilometre and therefore qualifies for writing down allowances at the rate of 18%. Cars do not qualify for the AIA.

2 Motor car [2] has CO_2 emissions over 130 grams per kilometre and therefore qualifies for writing down allowances at the rate of 8%. The private use of the motor car is irrelevant, since such usage will be assessed on the employee as a benefit.

(b) If Naive Ltd has straightforward accounts, it could use the software provided by HM Revenue and Customs. This automatically produces accounts and tax computations in the iXBRL format.

Alternatively, other software which automatically produces iXBRL accounts and computations could be used.

A tagging service could be used to apply the appropriate tags to the accounts and tax computations, or Naive Ltd could use software to tag documents itself.

Tax tables

SUPPLEMENTARY INFORMATION

1. Calculations and workings need only be made to the nearest £.
2. All apportionments may be made to the nearest month.
3. All workings should be shown in Section C.

TAX RATES AND ALLOWANCES

The following tax rates and allowances are to be used in answering the questions.

Income tax

		Normal rates	Dividend rates
Basic rate	£1 – £32,000	20%	7.5%
Higher rate	£32,001 – £150,000	40%	32.5%
Additional rate	£150,001 and over	45%	38.1%

		£
Savings rate nil rate band	– Basic rate taxpayers	£1,000
	– Higher rate taxpayers	£500
Dividend nil rate band		£5,000

A starting rate of 0% applies to savings income where it falls within the first £5,000 of taxable income.

Personal allowance

	£
Personal allowance	11,000
Transferable amount	1,100
Income limit	100,000

Residence status

Days in UK	Previously resident	Not previously resident
Less than 16	Automatically not resident	Automatically not resident
16 to 45	Resident if 4 UK ties (or more)	Automatically not resident
46 to 90	Resident if 3 UK ties (or more)	Resident if 4 UK ties
91 to 120	Resident if 2 UK ties (or more)	Resident if 3 UK ties (or more)
121 to 182	Resident if 1 UK tie (or more)	Resident if 2 UK ties (or more)
183 or more	Automatically resident	Automatically resident

Child benefit income tax charge

Where income is between £50,000 and £60,000, the charge is 1% of the amount of child benefit received for every £100 of income over £50,000.

Car benefit percentage

The base level of CO_2 emissions is 95 grams per kilometre.

The percentage rates applying to petrol cars with CO_2 emissions up to this level are:

50 grams per kilometre or less	7%
51 grams to 75 grams per kilometre	11%
76 grams to 94 grams per kilometre	15%
95 grams per kilometre	16%

Car fuel benefit

The base figure for calculating the car fuel benefit is £22,200.

Individual savings accounts (ISAs)

The overall investment limit is £15,240.

Pension scheme limits

Annual allowance	– 2014/15 to 2016/17	£40,000
	– 2013/14	£50,000
Minimum allowance		£10,000
Income limit		£150,000

The maximum contribution that can qualify for tax relief without any earnings is £3,600.

Authorised mileage allowances: cars

Up to 10,000 miles	45p
Over 10,000 miles	25p

Capital allowances: rates of allowance

Plant and machinery

Main pool	18%
Special rate pool	8%

Motor cars

New cars with CO_2 emissions up to 75 grams per kilometre	100%
CO_2 emissions between 76 and 130 grams per kilometre	18%
CO_2 emissions over 130 grams per kilometre	8%

Annual investment allowance

Rate of allowance	100%
Expenditure limit	£200,000

Cap on income tax reliefs

Unless otherwise restricted, reliefs are capped at the higher of £50,000 or 25% of income.

Corporation tax

Rate of tax	20%
Profit threshold	£1,500,000

Value Added Tax (VAT)

Standard rate	20%
Registration limit	£83,000
Deregistration limit	£81,000

Inheritance tax: tax rates

£1 – £325,000		Nil
Excess	– Death rate	40%
	– Lifetime rate	20%

Inheritance tax: taper relief

Years before death	Percentage reduction
Over 3 but less than 4 years	20%
Over 4 but less than 5 years	40%
Over 5 but less than 6 years	60%
Over 6 but less than 7 years	80%

Capital gains tax

	Normal rates	Residential property
Rates of tax – Lower rate	10%	18%
– Higher rate	20%	28%
Annual exempt amount		£11,100
Entrepreneurs' relief – Lifetime limit		£10,000,000
– Rate of tax		10%

National insurance contributions
(Not contracted-out rates)

Class 1 Employee	£1 – £8,060 per year	Nil
	£8,061 – £43,000 per year	12%
	£43,001 and above per year	2%
Class 1 Employer	£1 – 8,112 per year	Nil
	£8,113 and above per year	13.8%
	Employment allowance	£3,000
Class 1A		13.8%
Class 2	£2.80 per week	
	Small profits threshold	£5,965
Class 4	£1 – £8,060 per year	Nil
	£8,061 – £43,000 per year	9%
	£43,001 and above per year	2%

Rates of Interest (assumed)

Official rate of interest	3%
Rate of interest on underpaid tax	3%
Rate of interest on overpaid tax	0.5%

Review Form – Paper F6 (UK) Taxation (10/16)

Name: _____   Address: _____

_____

_____

How have you used this Kit?
(Tick one box only)

☐ On its own (book only)

☐ On a BPP in-centre course _____

☐ On a BPP online course

☐ On a course with another college

☐ Other _____

Why did you decide to purchase this Kit?
(Tick one box only)

☐ Have used the complimentary Study Text

☐ Have used other BPP products in the past

☐ Recommendation by friend/colleague

☐ Recommendation by a lecturer at college

☐ Saw advertising

☐ Other _____

During the past six months do you recall seeing/receiving any of the following?
(Tick as many boxes as are relevant)

☐ Our advertisement in *Student Accountant*

☐ Our advertisement in *Pass*

☐ Our advertisement in *PQ*

☐ Our brochure with a letter through the post

☐ Our website www.bpp.com

Which (if any) aspects of our advertising do you find useful?
(Tick as many boxes as are relevant)

☐ Prices and publication dates of new editions

☐ Information on product content

☐ Facility to order books

☐ None of the above

Which BPP products have you used?

Study Text	☐	*Passcards*	☐	*Other*	☐
Practice & Revision Kit	☑	*i-Pass*	☐		

Your ratings, comments and suggestions would be appreciated on the following areas.

	Very useful	Useful	Not useful
Passing F6 (UK)	☐	☐	☐
Questions	☐	☐	☐
Top Tips etc in answers	☐	☐	☐
Content and structure of answers	☐	☐	☐
Mock exam answers	☐	☐	☐

Overall opinion of this Practice & Revision Kit   Excellent ☐   Good ☐   Adequate ☐   Poor ☐

Do you intend to continue using BPP products?   Yes ☐   No ☐

The BPP author of this edition can be emailed at: accaqueries@bpp.com

Please return this form to: Head of ACCA & FIA Programmes, BPP Learning Media Ltd, FREEPOST, London, W12 8AA

Review Form (continued)

TELL US WHAT YOU THINK

Please note any further comments and suggestions/errors below.